The Spirit of Modern India

Gandhi, Kasturba, and Tagore
at Shantiniketan, 1940 *(S. Shaha)*

The Spirit of Modern India

Writings in Philosophy,
Religion, & Culture

Edited by
Robert A. McDermott
&
V.S. Naravane

Lindisfarne Books

Lindisfarne Books
an imprint of SteinerBooks/ Anthroposophic Press, Inc.

www.lindisfarne.org
www.steinerbooks.org

Copyright © 1974, 2010 by Robert A. McDermott and V.S. Naravane

Previously published by Thomas Y. Crowell Company, 1974.
This edition published by Lindisfarne Books, 2010.

ISBN 978-1-58420-084-0

Copyright acknowledgments appear on page 301.

Contents

Preface

This volume presents the dominant ideas of the modern Indian thinkers who have dramatically influenced both their own culture and the contemporary West. To a marked degree, the personalities and their ideas are inseparable: as political and moral leaders, philosophers, poets, and yogis, they were all committed to what Gandhi called "experiments with truth." In this sense, the "Spirit" of the title refers not only to the key ideas of modern Indian thought and culture, but equally to the abiding power of the personalities who fashioned and exemplify these ideas. To appreciate the uniqueness of this spirit, one need only envision Jawaharlal Nehru writing the history of India while in prison, and sending installments of his history of civilization in letters to his thirteen-year-old daughter Indira (now prime minister of India); or Mohandas K. Gandhi, the Mahatma, on one of his twenty-one–day fasts against caste oppression while in jail for "sedition"; or Sri Aurobindo Ghose, the radical political leader, experiencing advanced yogic states while meditating on the Bhagavad-Gītā during his year in prison prior to his trial for "conspiracy"; or the scholarly Bhave walking through the villages of India, waging a quietly effective battle for land reform; or Sarvepalli

Radhakrishnan, translating and writing commentaries on the Indian scriptures before beginning each day's work as ambassador to Moscow, chairman of UNESCO, or president of India; or Rabindranath Tagore—poet, painter, musician, dramatist, and educationist—traveling the world in search of a formula for peace and world unity. Thus, by their ideals and historical import, these figures have reaffirmed the significance of Indian spirituality; by demonstrating the practical and historical import of selfless action, modern India offers a viable model for other societies.

Consistent with the achievements of these figures, the writings in this volume are neither technical exercises nor pious exhortations. All the writers reprinted here express timely and largely humanistic values in terms both accessible and lofty. Their accessibility stems in large measure from the press of cultural problems which are still very much with us, their loftiness to the creativity, and capacity for transcendence. Since each transformed the milieu in which he lived, they serve as models as much for our own culture as for theirs. As they drew significantly from the West while retaining and deepening their essentially Indian traits, so their significance transcends India by complementing and correcting some of the inadequacies of Western value systems.

The period designated as "modern" refers to the remarkable century and a half from the 1820s to the present. More broadly, modern, in this context, refers to the period that begins after the prominence of Ram Mohan Roy during the second quarter of the nineteenth century, and with the work of Keshub Chunder Sen, Debendranath Tagore, and Sri Ramakrishna in the mid-nineteenth century. Soon after that the renaissance began: Rabindranath Tagore was born in 1861, Swami Vivekananda in 1862, Gandhi in 1869, and Sri Aurobindo in 1872. The end of that era can probably be fixed in 1947, the culmination of the nationalist movement in independence from Britain. Of the major figures, all but Nehru and Radhakrishnan had completed their life's work by that date: Tagore died in 1941, Gandhi in 1948, and Sri Aurobindo in 1950.

The aspects of modern India presented in this volume are intellectual and cultural—or, as designated in the subtitle, the philosophical, religious, and cultural. Since there are ample publications on the social-scientific (social, political, economic, and historical) aspects of modern India, this volume seeks to fill the need for an introduction to the primary sources of Indian thought on such diverse yet related areas as philosophy, religion, ethics, aesthetics, education, spiritual discipline, and national consciousness. None of the selections have been altered; except for the excerpted selections from Keshub Chunder Sen, S. Dasgupta and Rabindranath Tagore's "An Eastern University," all of the selections are complete.

Although the editors worked closely together from the earliest conception of the volume, a division of responsibility can be assigned as follows: Robert A. McDermott wrote the Preface, Chronology, Glossary, Bibliography, the introductions to the chapters on Indian philosophy, dharma, karmayoga, and spiritual discipline, chose the interstitial passages and prepared the manuscript for publication; V. S. Naravane wrote the introduction to the chapters on the new awakening, aesthetics, education, and national consciousness, and translated one of Tagore's poems from Bengali. Professor McDermott brought a special competence on Indian philosophy, ethics, and spiritual discipline, especially relating to Radhakrishnan and Sri Aurobindo; Professor Naravane contributed a special competence on Rabindranath Tagore, Coomaraswamy, and virtually all aspects of Indian culture.

From the date of its inception in the summer of 1971 at the

home of our mutual friend, Lalit Thapalyal, this volume has been the occasion for the rare blending of our personalities, families, respective cultures, and our common dedication to the riches of modern Indian thought and culture.

Both editors have benefited from the friendship and wise counsel of Ned Arnold, formerly of E. P. Dutton and presently senior editor at Liveright. For expert and patient assistance during the preparation of this publication the editors are grateful to the copy-editing department of T. Y. Crowell.

As ever, Ellen Dineen McDermott and Indu Naravane rendered valuable assistance with characteristic generosity and good sense. Our volume is dedicated to our parents.

Let My Country Awake

Where the mind is without fear and the head is held high,
Where knowledge is free;
Where the world has not been broken up into fragments by
    narrow domestic walls;
Where words come out from the depth of truth;
Where tireless striving stretches its arms towards perfection;
Where the clear stream of reason has not lost its way into
    the dreary desert sand of dead habit;
Where the mind is led forward by thee into ever-widening
    thought and action—
into that heaven of freedom,
my Father,
let my country awake.

—Rabindranath Tagore

The Spirit of Modern India

New Awakening

Introduction

"The East," said Napoleon during his Egyptian campaign, "is like a sleeping giant. When he gets up, he will shake the world."

Even as "the little corporal" was addressing his troops in the shadow of the ageless pyramids, one of the Asian giants was already getting up. And later, while Napoleon's star was setting at Waterloo, Raja Ram Mohan Roy was establishing the Atmiya Sabha (Society of Friends) at Calcutta. A group of earnest-minded scholars, representing diverse religious and philosophical persuasions, had come together to study their spiritual and intellectual heritage with reverence tempered by reason. The following year Ram Mohan Roy published his *Vedānta-sāra*, in which he pleaded for the adoption of Vedantic monotheism in place of the crude, ritual-ridden polytheism then prevalent even among the educated middle classes.

In 1828, the Raja founded the Brahma Samāj (Society of God). India was now awake. This awakening was not destined to "shake the world"—a role that is perhaps more congenial to some other Oriental giant—but to make the world think, reflect, compare, sympathize, and understand. The Manifesto of the Brahma Samāj is remarkable for the maturity of its approach. "No graven image shall be brought into the Samāj. No sermon, discourse, hymn or prayer shall be delivered except such as may have a tendency to promote the contemplation of the Author and Preserver of the Universe, to the furtherance of charity, morality, piety, benevolence, virtue, and the strengthening of the bonds of union between men of all religious persuasions and creeds." But, having thus stated its position clearly, the manifesto continues: "No object, animate or inanimate, that has been or is an object of worship shall be reviled or spoken of slightingly or contemptuously." Here we have humanism, tolerance, and a comprehensive understanding of the inner spirit of religion. It is worth noting that these words were written at a time when most of the theologians the world over were still plunged in dogmatic slumber.

The mantle of Raja Ram Mohan Roy fell on the competent shoulders of Debendranath Tagore. The literature of the Brahma Samāj now acquired a distinct poetic flavor. Debendranath—popularly known as the Maharshi ("great sage")—was less concerned with the absolute monism of the Upanishads than with their profound and vivid insight into the nature of religious experience. Monotheism still remained the cardinal principle of the Samāj. But in his *Brahmadharma Grantha*, which was adopted by the Samāj for the use of its members, Debendranath gave a theistic and somewhat mystical interpretation of the Upanishads. The influence of Islamic bhakti ("devotion"), as expressed by the Sufi poets, can also be easily seen in the Maharshi's ideas. In his later years Debendranath Tagore became increasingly mystical in his outlook, and the leadership of the movement initiated by Ram Mohan Roy passed into the hands of Keshub Chunder Sen.

Of all the leaders of the new Enlightenment—or the Indian Renaissance, as it has been described—Keshub Chunder Sen was the most dynamic. It was largely through his efforts that the movement spread to other parts of India, particularly Maharashtra and Madras. He traveled widely and invited outstanding leaders from other parts of India to visit Bengal. Moreover, Keshub was the first to think in terms of the unity of the Asian tradition. "I am a child of Asia," he declared. "In standing forward as Asia's servant and spokesman I feel as I never did feel—never can feel—as a mere Indian. From one end of Asia to another, I boast of a vast home, a wide nationality and an extended kinship." In one of the selections that follow, the reader can see how deeply Keshub was stirred by this consciousness of Asian unity. "Sinai is mine, saith Asia, and Jordan is mine, and the sacred Ganges is mine. The Vedas and the Bible are mine, the Cross and the Crescent are mine."

While Keshub and his scholarly friends were discussing the intricate questions of philosophy and religion in the drawing rooms of Calcutta, an unlettered yogi was sitting in a temple courtyard in the tiny village of Dakshineshvar on the outskirts of the metropolis. And in his own way this humble man, who combined in himself a child's curiosity and a sage's certainty, was bringing about another revolution every whit as important as the one that Ram Mohan Roy had initiated.

It is characteristic of the Indian tradition that the urban intellectuals were themselves fully aware of the significance of Ramakrishna's teachings. In another country he might have been taken for just one more visionary, not far different from others who have arisen in every age, who have attracted a little attention and have then been quickly forgotten. But Debendranath Tagore and Keshub Chunder Sen instinctively realized that India's soul spoke more directly and powerfully through the lips of Ramakrishna than through the learned journals and books that were being published in Calcutta. In India, wisdom has always been prized far above theoretical scholarship. And Ramakrishna was offering wisdom that came straight from the heart, wisdom that had the sanction of forty centuries behind it. Though formally illiterate, Ramakrishna was thoroughly conversant with all the major philosophical and religious viewpoints that India had evolved. He had not only understood them, but he had also lived them. In the inspired utterances of Ramakrishna, recorded in detail by his ever faithful disciple "M," the most profound questions of metaphysics are explained through parables taken from the daily life of the Indian village. There is humor in these teachings, and sympathy, and such richness of imagery as might excite the envy of many a poet. Whether he is speaking of the Formless Absolute or of God with forms, of worldly attachments or of the power of thoughts over deeds, his grasp is equally sure. Ramakrishna shows how differing viewpoints can be reconciled through tolerance, and how paradoxes dissolve at the magic touch of love. But, though he accepts the partial worth of every important darshana (philosophical viewpoint) and parampara (tradition) his own preference for Advaita Vedanta (Absolute Monism) is never in doubt. On the dizzy heights of mystic realization there is room for only One. "I am He," "I am He"—this is the recurring note.

"The cyclonic monk from India"—that is how delegates to the Parliament of Religions at Chicago in 1894 described Ramakrishna's great disciple, Vivekananda. The master was meek and gentle; the pupil, vigorous and assertive. Romain Rolland, in his admirable biography of this "tamer of souls," refers to Vivekananda's dominating personality in these words: "A great voice is meant to fill the sky. The whole world is its sounding-box. . . . Men like Vivekananda are not meant to whisper. They can only proclaim. The sun cannot moderate its own rays." Vivekananda's own writings are marked by a finality of conviction and a missionary zeal rarely seen in Indian religious literature. He was deeply conscious of his role. To bring Vedanta out of its obscurity and present it in a rationally acceptable manner; to arouse among his countrymen an awareness of their own spiritual heritage and restore their self-confidence; to show that the deepest truths of Vedanta are universally valid, and that India's mission is to communicate these truths to the whole world—these were the goals he set before himself.

Vivekananda was a sannyasin, a man of renunciation. He demanded stern self-control, unyielding struggle against temptations.

> He conquers all who conquers Self. Know this
> And never yield, Sannyasin bold! Say—
> "Om Tat Sat, Om!"

Self-realization is impossible without discipline and self-reliance. "You must not merely learn what the Rishis taught. Those Rishis are gone. . . . You must be Rishis yourself. . . . You must stand on your own feet. . . . The true man is he who is strong as strength itself and yet possesses a woman's heart. You must feel for the millions of beings around you, and yet you must be strong and inflexible, and also possess obedience; though it may seem a little paradoxical you must possess these apparently contradictory virtues." In the light of these remarks it is easy to understand Vivekananda's deep reverence for the Buddha: "I wish I had one infinitesimal part of the Buddha's heart. Buddha may or may not have believed in God; that does not matter to me. He reached the same state of perfection to which others come by bhakti—love of God—yoga, or jnāna. Perfection does not come from belief or faith. Talk does not count for anything. Parrots can do that. Perfection comes through the distinterested performance of action."

Indian culture has, through the ages, shown some persistent characteristics: a spirit of assimilation, a tendency to evolve unity in and through diversity, and a corresponding tendency to make adjustments to changing situations without losing the fundamental continuity. All these distinctive features of Indian thought and culture are reflected in the ideas of the thinkers who represent the "new awakening." One can hardly think of men more dissimilar in outlook and temperament than Ram Mohan Roy, Keshub Chunder Sen, Debendranath Tagore, Ramakrishna, and Vivekananda. Yet they all represent a tradition that is distinctively Indian. All of them were aware of the challenges of the modern age. Even Ramakrishna was in touch with the developments that were taking place in Calcutta. But they also delved deep into India's ancient and medieval heritage. The roots are firmly embedded in Indian soil, even though some of the flowers have acquired a new fragrance because foreign strains have been grafted on some of the branches.

It is particularly noteworthy that all the four major faiths of mankind—Hinduism, Buddhism, Christianity, and Islam—have contributed to the rich treasure house of nineteenth-century Indian thought. Hinduism—itself a veritable "museum of religions"—is, of course, represented in all its forms. Ram Mohan Roy and Debendranath Tagore emphasized two different aspects of the Upanishads; Keshub Chunder Sen was drawn toward the Vaishnava tradition; Ramakrishna went through Vaishnava, Vedantic, and Shakta phases; Vivekananda too, like his master, was as much a bhakta (devotee) as a jnāni (knower). As for Buddhism, Ram Mohan Roy in his early years is said to have studied the Buddhist tradition in Tibet; and Vivekananda's reverence for the Buddha has already been commented upon. The Christian influence is seen most clearly in Keshub Chunder Sen. But it also played an important part in molding Ram Mohan Roy's world view. Islam, particularly the Sufi tradition, had shaped the thought and culture of India for at least five centuries before Ram Mohan Roy's time. But apart from the natural appeal that Sufism has for the mystical Indian temperament, even the uncompromising monotheism of orthodox Islam is clearly reflected in the Brahma Samāj movement, particularly in its earlier phases.

All in all then, the period between the publication of Ram Mohan Roy's first important work, *Gifts for Monotheists* (1803), and the establishment of the Ramakrishna Mission by Vivekananda (1897) constitutes a remarkable chapter in the history of Indian civilization. It is extremely important to remember that the nationalist movement of the twentieth century was preceded by a long period of intellectual and spiritual awakening in the nineteenth. Without the Brahma Samāj and Ramakrishna and Vivekananda, Indian nationalism could not have attained that maturity and many-sided grasp of the Indian tradition that it showed in the hands of Sri Aurobindo, Rabindranath Tagore, and Gandhi. If one compares the nationalist movements in the various countries of Asia and Africa that have resulted in political independence during the last three decades, one can see at once that Indian nationalism is unique in the firmness of its foundations. The thinkers of what we have called the Age of New Awakening saved India from a vacuum and ensured the continuity of its quest. That is why India was not startled when a little man in a loincloth came along and quietly suggested: "Let us fight the world's strongest empire with the power of the spirit."

Keshub Chunder Sen

Asia's Message to Europe

Asia is not the land of history but of introspection, not of logical reflection but of intuitive apperception, not of cold dogmatism but of flaming faith. We have no theology but religion. The Bible as the book of the past has no existence for us; we see in it only living characters and fresh scenes. Do you not know that we Asiatics never read books but converse with them, and that we never study Nature but commune with her? In the East all is full of life, all is full of God. The Goddess of Force, Shakti, meets us at every turn. The beautiful Goddess of Nature, Prakriti, is resplendent everywhere. There is nothing godless in the East, there is nothing profane. All is sacred. I never keep a secular establishment,—says Asia. All my things are sacred, my whole history is ecclesiastical, all my science is scripture, my whole literature is sacred poetry. Behold, says Asia, all my hills and mountains, all my rills and rivers, all my seas and oceans, are effulgent with the light of Heaven. Blessed are the trees that grow on my soil, for they are divine; even the humble blade of grass in the East is holy,

for the great God comes down to dwell in it. Verily there is
nothing secular in Asia. Learned Europe, study nature; we
shall commune with nature. Europe, study botany like a
scholar; we prefer to live as devotees in the garden of Eden.
Europe, rise on the wings of science and study the stars in the
firmament above; we shall indulge in the highest contemplation
in the heavens above. Europe, the Lord has blessed thee with
scholarship and science and philosophy, and with these thou art
great among the nations of the earth. Add to these the faith and
intuition and spirituality of Asia, and thou shalt be far greater
still. Asia honours thy philosophy; do thou honour, O Europe,
Asia's spirituality and communion? Thus shall we rectify each
other's errors and supplement mutual deficiencies. Europe will
correct and purify Eastern communion with the hard logic of
science, and remove all the superstitious and idolatrous rites
and all the mystical delusions which have encrusted around it
in the course of ages. While on the other hand we shall take
the dry facts of Western science, fill them with the flesh and
blood of Eastern sentiment, and spiritualize and vivify them
with a living faith.

The Future Church

The Hindu's notion of God is sublime. In the earliest Hindu
scriptures God is represented as the Infinite Spirit dwelling in
His own glory, and pervading all space, full of peace and joy.
On the other hand, the Mohammedans describe their God as
infinite in power, governing the universe with supreme
authority as the Lord of all. Hence the principal feature of the
religion of the Hindu is quiet contemplation, while that of the

religion of the Mohammedan is constant excitement and active service. The one lives in a state of quiet communion with his God of peace; the other lives as a soldier, ever serving the Almighty Ruler, and crusading against evil. These are the primary and essential elements of the two creeds, and, if blended together, would form a beautiful picture of true theology, which will be realized in the future church of this country. As the two creeds undergo development, their errors and differences will disappear, and they will harmoniously coalesce in their fundamental and vital principles. The future creed of India will be a composite faith, resulting from the union of the true and divine elements of Hinduism and Mohammedanism, and showing the profound devotion of the one and the heroic enthusiasm of the other. The future sons and daughters of this vast country will thus inherit precious legacies from Hinduism and Mohammedanism, and while enjoying the blessings of the highest and sweetest communion with the God of love, will serve Him in the battlefield of life with fidelity to truth and unyielding opposition to untruth and sin. As regards Christianity and its relation to the future church of India, I have no doubt in my mind that it will exercise great influence on the growth and formation of that church. The spirit of Christianity has already pervaded the whole atmosphere of Indian society, and we breathe, think, feel, and move in a Christian atmosphere. Native society is being roused, enlightened, and reformed under the influence of Christian education. If it is true that the future of a nation is determined by all the circumstances and agencies which to-day influence its nascent growth, surely the future church of this country will be the result of the purer elements of the leading creeds of the day, harmonized, developed, and shaped under the influence of Christianity.

But the future church of India must be thoroughly national;

it must be an essentially Indian Church. The future religion of the world I have described will be the common religion of all nations, but in each nation it will have an indigenous growth, and assume a distinctive and peculiar character. All mankind will unite in a universal church; at the same time, it will be adapted to the peculiar circumstances of each nation, and assume a national form. No country will borrow or mechanically imitate the religion of another country; but from the depths of the life of each nation its future church will naturally grow up. And shall not India have its own national church? Dr. Norman McLeod, in expounding last year, in this very hall, his ideas of the future church of this country, said emphatically that it would be a purely Indian Church, and not a reproduction of any of the established churches of the West. Though I differ from that learned and liberal-minded gentleman in regard to the doctrines and tenets of that church as set forth by him, I fully agree with him that that church must have a strictly national growth and a national organization. Neither will Germany adopt the religious life of China, nor will India accept blindly that of England or of any other European country. India has religious traditions and associations, tastes and customs, peculiarly sacred and dear to her, just as every other country has, and it is idle to expect that she will forego these; nay, she cannot do so, as they are interwoven with her very life. In common with all other nations and communities, we shall embrace the Theistic worship, creed, and gospel of the future church—we shall acknowledge and adore the Holy One, accept the love and service of God and man as our creed, and put our firm faith in God's almighty grace as the only means of our redemption. But we shall do all this in a strictly national and Indian style. We shall see that the future church is not thrust upon us, but that we independently and naturally grow into it; that it does not come to us as a foreign plant, but that it strikes its roots deep in the national heart of India, draws its sap from our national resources, and develops itself with all the freshness and vigour of indigenous growth. One religion shall be acknowledged by all men; One God shall be worshipped throughout the length and breadth of the world; the same spirit of faith and love shall pervade all hearts; all nations shall dwell together in the Father's house—yet each shall have its own peculiar and free mode of action. There shall, in short, be unity of spirit, but diversity of forms; one body, but different limbs; one vast community, with members labouring, in different ways and according to their respective resources and peculiar tastes, to advance their common cause.

Sri Ramakrishna

The Knowledge of Brahman

Brahman is beyond vidyā and avidyā, knowledge and ignorance. It is beyond māyā, the illusion of duality. The world
consists of the illusory duality of knowledge and ignorance. It
contains knowledge and devotion, and also attachment of
"woman and gold"; righteousness and unrighteousness, good
and evil. But Brahman is unattached to these. Good and evil
apply to the jiva, the individual soul, as do righteousness and
unrighteousness. But Brahman is not at all affected by them.

One man may read the Bhagavata by the light of a lamp;
another may commit a forgery by that very light. The lamp is
unaffected. The sun sheds its light on the wicked as well as
the virtuous. What Brahman is cannot be described. All things
in the world—the Vedas, the Puranas, the Tantras, the six
systems of philosophy—have been defiled, like food that has
been touched by the tongue, for they have been read or uttered
by the tongue. Only one thing has not been defiled, and that is
Brahman.

Men often think they have understood Brahman fully. Once

an ant went to a hill of sugar. One grain filled its stomach. Taking another grain in its mouth it started homeward. On the way it thought: "Next time I shall carry home the whole hill." That is the way shallow minds think. They don't know that Brahman is beyond words and thought. However great a man may be, how much can he know of Brahman? Sukadeva and sages like him may have been big ants; but even they could carry at the most eight or ten grains of sugar!

In Samadhi one attains the knowledge of Brahman, one realizes Brahman. In that state reasoning stops altogether, and man becomes mute. He has no power to describe the nature of Brahman. Once a salt doll went to measure the depth of the ocean. It wanted to tell others how deep the water was. But this it could never do, for no sooner did it get into the water than it melted. Now who was there to report the ocean's depth? . . . After the vision of Brahman a man becomes silent. He reasons about It only as long as he has not realized it. If you heat butter in a pan on the stove, it makes a sizzling sound as long as the water it contains has not dried up. But when no trace of water is left, the clarified butter makes no sound. If you put an uncooked cake of flour in that butter, it sizzles again. After the cake is cooked all sound stops. . . . The bee buzzes as long as it is not sitting on a flower. It becomes silent when it begins to sip the honey. But sometimes, intoxicated by the honey, it buzzes again. . . . An empty pitcher makes a gurgling sound when it is dipped in water. When it fills up, it becomes silent. But if the water is poured from it into another pitcher, then you will hear the sound again.

Formless Absolute and God with Forms

No one can say with finality that God is only "this" and nothing else. He is formless, and again He has forms. For the bhakta He assumes forms. But He is formless for the jnāni, that is for him who looks upon the world as a mere dream. The bhakta feels that he himself is one entity, and the world is another. Therefore God reveals Himself to him as a Person. But the jnāni always reasons, applying the process of "not this, not this." Through this discrimination he realizes that the ego and the universe are both illusory, like a dream. Then the jnāni realizes Brahman in his own consciousness.

Think of Brahman—Existence-Knowledge-Bliss Absolute —as a shoreless ocean. Through the cooling influence, as it were, of the bhakta's love, the water has frozen at places into blocks of ice. In other words, God now and again assumes various forms for his lovers. But with the rising of the sun of Knowledge, the blocks of ice melt. Then one does not feel any more that God is a person, nor does one see God's forms.

Once a man entered a wood and saw a small animal on a tree. He came back and told another man that he had seen a creature with a beautiful red color. The second man said: "When I went into the wood I also saw that animal. But why do you call it red? It is green." Another man who was present contradicted them both and insisted that it was yellow. Presently others arrived and contended that it was gray, violet, blue, and so on. At last they started quarreling among themselves. To settle the dispute they all went to the tree. They saw a man sitting under it. On being asked, this man replied: "Yes, I live under this tree, and I know the animal very well. All your descriptions are true. Sometimes it appears red, sometimes yellow, and at other times blue, violet or gray. It is a chameleon. Sometimes it has no colour at all. Now it has a colour, now it has none."

In like manner one who constantly thinks of God can know His real nature. He alone knows that God reveals Himself to seekers in various forms and aspects. God has attributes; then again He has none. Only the man who lives under the tree knows. . . . It is the others who suffer the agony of futile argument. Kabir used to say: "The Formless Absolute is my Father, and God with form is my Mother."

Worldly Attachments

Bound creatures, entangled in worldliness, do not come to their senses. They suffer so much misery and agony, they face so many dangers, and yet they will not wake up. The camel loves to eat thorny bushes. The more he eats the thorns, the more the blood gushes from its mouth. Still it must eat thorny plants and will never give them up.

Once a fisherwoman was a guest in the house of a gardener who raised flowers. She came there with her empty basket, after selling fish in the market, and was asked to sleep in a room where flowers were kept. But, because of the fragrance of the flowers, she could not get to sleep for a long time. Her hostess saw her condition and said: "Hello! Why are you tossing from side to side so restlessly?" The fishwife said: "I don't know, friend. Perhaps the smell of the flowers has been disturbing my sleep. Can you give me my fish-basket? Perhaps that will put me to sleep." The basket was brought to her. She sprinkled water on it and set it near her nose. Then she fell sound asleep and snored all night.

There was a sannyāsi whose only possessions were two pairs of loincloths. One day a mouse nibbled at one of these. So the holy man kept a cat to protect his loincloths from the mouse. Then he had to keep a cow to supply milk for the cat. Later he had to engage a servant to look after the cow. Gradually the number of his cows multiplied. He acquired pastures and farmlands. He had to engage a number of servants. Thus he became, in course of time, a sort of landlord. And, last of all, he had to take a wife to look after his big household. One day one of his friends, another monk, happened to visit him and was surprised to see his altered circumstances. When asked the reason, the holy man said: "It is all for the sake of a piece of loincloth."

Thoughts and Deeds

Once two friends were going along the street, when they saw some people listening to a reading of the Bhagavata. "Come, friend," said one of them to the other, "let us hear the sacred book." So saying he went in and sat down. The second man peeped in and went away. He entered a house of ill fame. But very soon he felt disgusted with the place. "Shame on me," he said to himself. "My friend has been listening to the sacred word of Hari, and see where I am!" But the friend who had been listening to the Bhagavata also became disgusted. "What a fool I am," he said. "I have been listening to this fellow's blah-blah, and my friend is having a grand time." In course of time they both died. The messenger of death came for the soul of the one who had listened to the Bhagavata and dragged it off to hell. The messenger of God came for the soul of the one who had been to the house of prostitution, and led it up to heaven.

God's Sport

This world is the līlā of God. It is like a game. In this game there are joy and sorrow, virtue and vice, knowledge and ignorance, good and evil. In the game of hide-and-seek one must touch the "granny" in order to be free. But the "granny" is never pleased if she is touched at the very outset. It is God's wish that the game should continue for some time. Then:

> Out of a hundred thousand kites, one or two break free; And thou dost laugh and clap thy hands, O Mother, watching them.

In other words, after the practice of hard spiritual discipline one or two have the vision of God, through His grace, and are liberated. Then the Divine Mother claps her hands in joy and exclaims: "Bravo! There they go!"

(A disciple: "But this play of God is our death.") Please tell me who *you* are. God alone has become all this—māyā, the universe, living beings and the twenty-four cosmic principles. "As the snake I bite, and as the charmer I cure." It is God himself who has become both vidyā and avidyā.

Swami Vivekananda

The Song of the Sannyāsin[1]

Wake up the note! the song that had its birth
Far off, where worldly taint could never reach;
In mountain caves, and glades of forest deep;
Whose calm no sigh for lust or wealth or fame
Could ever dare to break; where rolled the stream
Of knowledge, truth, and bliss that follows both.
Sing high that note, Sannyāsin bold! Say—
                              "Om Tat Sat, Om!"

Strike off thy fetters! Bonds that bind thee down,
Of shining gold, or darker, baser ore;
Love, hate—good, bad—and all the dual throng.
Know, slave is slave, caressed or whipped, not free;
For fetters, though of gold, are not less strong to bind;
Then, off with them, Sannyāsin bold! Say—
                              "Om Tat Sat, Om!"

[1] Composed at Thousand Island Park, U.S.A. in July 1895

Let darkness go; the will-o'-the-wisp that leads
With blinking light to pile more gloom on gloom,
This thirst for life, for ever quench; it drags
From birth to death, and death to birth, the soul.
He conquers all who conquers self. Know this
And never yield, Sannyāsin bold! Say—
                              "Om Tat Sat, Om!"

"Who sows must reap," they say, "and cause must bring
The sure effect; good, good; bad, bad; and none
Escape the law. But whoso wears a form
Must wear the chain." Too true; but far beyond
Both name and form is Ātman, ever free.
Know thou art That, Sannyāsin bold! Say—
                              "Om Tat Sat, Om!"

They know not truth who dream such vacant dreams
As father, mother, children, wife, and friend.
The sexless Self! Whose father He? whose child?
Whose friend, whose foe is He who is but One?
The Self is all in all, none else exists;
And thou art That, Sannyāsin bold! Say—
                              "Om Tat Sat, Om!"

There is but One—The Free, The Knower, Self!
Without a name, without a form or stain.
In Him is Māyā, dreaming all this dream.
The Witness, He appears as nature, soul.
Know thou art That, Sannyāsin bold! Say—
                              "Om Tat Sat, Om!"

Where seekest thou? That freedom, friend, this world
Nor that can give. In books and temples vain

Thy search. Thine only is the hand that holds
The rope that drags thee on. Then cease lament,
Let go thy hold, Sannyāsin bold! Say—
                    "Om Tat Sat, Om!"

Say, "Peace to all: From me no danger be
To aught that lives. In those that dwell on high,
In those that lowly creep, I am the Self in all!
All life both here and there, do I renounce,
All heavens, and earths and hells, and hopes and fears."
Thus cut thy bonds, Sannyāsin bold! Say—
                    "Om Tat Sat, Om!"

Heed then no more how body lives or goes:
Its task is done. Let Karma float it down;
Let one put garlands on, another kick,
This frame; say naught. No praise or blame can be
Where praiser, praised, and blamer, blamed are one.
Thus be thou calm, Sannyāsin bold! Say—
                    "Om Tat Sat, Om!"

Truth never comes where lust and fame and greed
Of gain reside. No man who thinks of woman
As his wife can ever perfect be;
Nor he who owns the least of things, nor he
Whom anger chains, can ever pass thro' Māyā's gates.
So, give these up, Sannyāsin bold! Say—
                    "Om Tat Sat, Om!"

Have thou no home. What home can hold thee, friend?
The sky thy roof, the grass thy bed; and food,
What chance may bring—well cooked or ill, judge not.
No food or drink can taint that noble Self

Which knows Itself. Like rolling river free
Thou ever be, Sannyāsin bold! Say—
                    "Om Tat Sat, Om!"

Few only know the truth. The rest will hate
And laugh at thee, great one; but pay no heed.
Go thou, the free, from place to place, and help
Them out of darkness, Māyā's veil. Without
The fear of pain or search for pleasure, go
Beyond them both, Sannyāsin bold! Say—
                    "Om Tat Sat, Om!"

Thus, day by day, till Karma's powers spent
Release the soul for ever. No more is birth,
Nor I, nor thou, nor God, nor man. The "I"
Has All become, the All is "I" and Bliss.
Know thou art That, Sannyāsin bold! Say—
                    "Om Tat Sat, Om!"

Lord Buddha

In every religion we find one type of self-devotion particularly developed. The type of working without a motive is most
highly developed in Buddhism. Do not mistake Buddhism and
Brahminism. In this country you are very apt to do so.
Buddhism is one of our sects. It was founded by a great man
called Gautama, who became disgusted with the eternal
metaphysical discussions of his day, and the cumbrous rituals,
and more especially with the caste system. Some people say
that we are born to a certain state, and therefore we are

superior to others who are not thus born. He was against this as also against the tremendous priestcraft. He preached a religion in which there was no motive power, and was perfectly agnostic about metaphysics or theories about God. He was often asked if there was a God, and he answered he did not know. When asked about right conduct, he would reply—Do good and be good. There came five Brahmins who asked him to settle their discussion. One said, "Sir, my Book says that God is such and such, and that this is the way to come to God." Another said, "That is wrong, for my Book says such and such, and this is the way to come to God"; and so did the others. He listened calmly to all of them and then asked them one by one, "Does any one of your Books say that God becomes angry, that He ever injures any one, that He is impure?" "No, sir, they all teach that God is pure and good." "Then, my friends, why do you not become pure and good first, that you may know what God is?"

Of course I do not endorse all his philosophy. I want a good deal of metaphysics for myself. I entirely differ in many respects, but because I differ, is that any reason why I should not see the beauty of the man? He was the only man who was bereft of all motive power. There were other great men who all said they were the Incarnations of God Himself, and that those who would believe in them would go to heaven. But what did Buddha say with his dying breath? "None can help you; help yourself; work out your own salvation." He said about himself, "Buddha is the name of infinite knowledge, infinite as the sky; I, Gautama, have reached that state; you will all reach that too if you struggle for it." Bereft of all motive power, he did not want to go to heaven, did not want money; he gave up his throne and everything else, and went about begging his bread through the streets of India, preaching for the good of men and animals with a heart as wide as the ocean. He was the only man who was ever ready to give up his life for animals, to stop a sacrifice. He once said to a king, "If the sacrifice of a lamb helps you to go to heaven, sacrificing a man will help you better, so sacrifice me." The king was astonished. And yet this man was without any motive. He stands as the perfection of the active type, and the very height to which he attained shows that through the power of work we can also attain to the highest spirituality.

To many the path becomes easier if they believe in God. But the life of Buddha shows that even a man who does not believe in God, has no metaphysics, belongs to no sect, and does not go to any church, or temple, and is a confessed materialist, even he can attain to the highest. We have no right to judge him. I wish I had one infinitesimal part of Buddha's heart. Buddha may or may not have believed in God; that does not matter to me. He reached the same state of perfection to which others come by bhakti—love of God, yoga, or jnāna. Perfection does not come from belief or faith. Talk does not count for anything. Parrots can do that. Perfection comes through the disinterested performance of action.

Sannyāsa: Its Ideal and Practice

This is not the time for a long lecture. But I shall speak to you in brief about a few things which I should like you to carry into practice. First, we have to understand the ideal, and then the methods by which we can make it practical. Those of you who are Sannyāsins must try to do good to others, for Sannyāsa means that. There is no time to deliver a long discourse on "Renunciation," but I shall very briefly characterise it as *"the love of death."* Worldly people love life. The Sannyāsin is to love death. Are we to commit suicide then? Far from it. For suicides are not lovers of death, as it is often seen that when a man trying to commit suicide fails, he never attempts it for a second time. What is the love of death, then? We must die, that is certain; let us die then for a good cause. Let all our actions—eating, drinking, and everything that we do—tend towards the sacrifice of our self. You nourish your body by eating. What good is there in doing that if you do not hold it as a sacrifice to the well-being of others? You nourish your minds by reading books. There is no good in doing that unless you hold it also as a sacrifice to the whole world. . . . It is right for you that you should serve your millions of brothers rather than aggrandise this little self. . . . Thus you must die a gradual death. In such a death is heaven, all good is stored therein—and in its opposite is all that is diabolical and evil.

Then as to the methods of carrying the ideal into practical life. First, we have to understand that we must not have any impossible ideal. An ideal which is too high makes a nation weak and degraded. This happened after the Buddhistic and the Jain reforms. On the other hand, too much practicality is also wrong. If you have not even a little imagination, if you have no ideal to guide you, you are simply a brute. So we must not lower our ideal, neither are we to lose sight of practicality. We must avoid the two extremes. In our country the old idea is to sit in a cave and meditate and die. To go ahead of others in salvation is wrong. One must learn sooner or later that one cannot get salvation if one does not try to seek the salvation of his brothers. You must try to combine in your life immense idealism with immense practicality. You must be prepared to go into deep meditation now, and the next moment you must be ready to go and cultivate these fields. You must be prepared to explain the difficult intricacies of the Shastras now, and the next moment to go and sell the produce of the fields in the market. You must be prepared for all menial services, not only here, but elsewhere also.

The next thing to remember is that the aim of this institution is to make men. You must not merely learn what the Rishis taught. Those Rishis are gone, and their opinions are also gone with them. You must be Rishis yourselves. You are also men as much as the greatest men that were ever born—even our Incarnations. What can mere book-learning do? What can meditation do, even? What can the Mantras and Tantras do? You must stand on your own feet. You must have this new method—the method of man-making. The true *man* is he who is strong as strength itself and yet possesses a woman's heart. You must feel for the millions of beings around you, and yet you must be strong and inflexible, and you must also possess obedience; though it may seem a little paradoxical —you must possess these apparently conflicting virtues. If your superior orders you to throw yourself into a river and catch a crocodile you must first obey and then reason with him. Even if the order be wrong, first obey and then contradict it. The bane of sects, especially in Bengal, is that if any one happens to have a different opinion, he immediately starts a new sect, he has no patience to wait. So you must have a deep regard for your Sangha. There is no place for disobedience here. Crush it out without mercy. No disobedient members here, you must turn them out. There must not be any traitors in the camp. You must be as free as the air, and as obedient as the plant and the dog.

Debendranath Tagore on God and Man

The Universe is like a chandelier, and each living being is a light in it. Man manifests the glory of God. Otherwise, who could know the universe? Without the lights no one can see the chandelier itself.

Philosophy

Introduction

When Sarvepalli Radhakrishnan was studying philosophy at Madras Christian College during the first decade of the twentieth century, he followed the standard philosophy curriculum used in all Indian colleges—British Hegelianism and Christian theology. The "New Awakening" which had transformed the social and religious thought of Bengal's elite had not yet penetrated the British hold on Indian higher education. In 1909, Radhakrishnan wrote his master's thesis defending all that he had learned of Vedanta in response to the critiques leveled against it by his British professors. The young Radhakrishnan's fledgling effort eventually yielded the first of his two-volume study, *Indian Philosophy* (1923 and 1927), which has remained a standard work since it was published fifty years ago. This staying power is the more remarkable in that his work was the first history of Indian philosophy ever written.

Throughout his voluminous writings on Indian philosophy, Radhakrishnan contends that in contrast to Western systems of thought, which are "generally characterized by a greater adherence to critical intelligence," Indian thought is based on creative intuition as a source of knowledge deeper and surer than intellect. As he explains in *An Idealist View of Life* (1932):

> Hindu thinkers as a class hold with great conviction that we possess a power more interior than intellect by which we become aware of the real in its intimate individuality, and not merely in its superficial or discernible aspects. For the Hindus a system of philosophy is an insight, a *darshana*. It is the vision of truth and not a matter for logical argument and proof.[1]

Yet Radhakrishnan's *Indian Philosophy* and, of course, Surendranath Dasgupta's five-volume *History of Indian Philosophy* contain countless logical arguments and proofs. When pressed for clarification on the nature of Indian philosophy, Radhakrishnan explained:

> The material for the philosopher is supplied by empirical research, the inspection of facts, logical investigation, or insight of the soul. The fact of the existence of elaborate discussion and commentaries shows that intuition is not accepted on its own authority.[2]

This point is important for an understanding not only of the selections printed in this section, but for the larger task of understanding the Indian philosophical tradition. Radhakrishnan's "Introduction" to the Bhagavad-Gītā, like virtually all commentaries on Indian scriptures, accepts the veracity of the scripture but at the same time attempts to establish its intellectual content by logical reasoning. He insists: "Any system of thought derives its authority as a philosophy from • its own rational evidence and not from agreement with this or that system of dogma."[3] The writings of Radhakrishnan,

---

[1] S. Radhakrishnan, *An Idealist View of Life*, London: George Allen & Unwin, 1958, p. 127.

[2] S. Radhakrishnan, "Reply to Critics," in Paul Arthur Schilpp, ed., *The Philosophy of Sarvepalli Radhakrishnan*, New York: Tudor Publishing Company, 1952, p. 819.

[3] *Ibid.*

Dasgupta, and Sri Aurobindo confirm this principle.

In the following selections, Dasgupta outlines the development of Indian thought from its origin in Vedic ritual and sacrifice to the blend of philosophical speculation and mystical experience in the Upanishads. Radhakrishnan interprets the concept of Brahman, or Ultimate Reality, as expounded in the Bhagavad-Gītā. Finally the selection by Sri Aurobindo places in a hierarchical scheme the levels of existence from Absolute Being to the lowest form in the physical world. The entire section then falls within the traditional mainstream of Indian philosophical and religious thought: these selections represent the work of philosophers who are not limited by, but whose insights have been largely fashioned by, the Vedas, the Upanishads, and the Bhagavad-Gītā.

Professor Dasgupta, in his outline of "Indian Idealism," shows that the Vedic sacrifices, and the laws of cosmic harmony which they presupposed, led the Vedic seers to the conception of a "Universal Creator, who held the destinies of the universe under His control." But the nature of the highest deity was not fully described until, in the Upanishads, the divine was explained in relation to the inner self of man. This definition was generated by the strong mystical impulse of the Upanishadic seers, but was expressed in the philosophical doctrine of Ātman, or the essence of man which is ultimately identical with the Absolute Brahman.

Radhakrishnan and Dasgupta—as indeed most Indian philosophers—agree that true philosophizing draws its substance from spiritual experience; the descriptions of such experience are philosophically so varied, however, that the result exhibits the same range as a philosophical tradition without a spiritual basis. Radhakrishnan's description of Ultimate Reality in the following selection, for example, refers to the Upanishads and the Bhagavad-Gītā, but finds its counterpart in many other philosophical systems, Western as well as Indian. As this selection shows, Radhakrishnan holds that the Divine has two aspects, the impersonal Absolute as described in the Upanishads and the personal deity Īshvara (or Lord), as described in the Bhagavad-Gītā. Īshvara, in the person of Krishna, the avatar of Vishnu, is ultimately identical with the Absolute Brahman, but this identity remains hidden so long as the world, Īshvara's creation, remains out of phase with the divine order. Krishna's message for reordering the world includes adherence to divinely sanctioned duties and selfless action (or dharma and karma-yoga, as expounded in the next two chapters).

According to Sri Aurobindo, the world has been ordered and reordered by a series of evolutionary steps, the latest of which is the descent of the Supramental into the mental, psychic, vital, and material levels of existence. This vision and expectation, described in his one-thousand-page metaphysical treatise, *The Life Divine*, is based primarily on his spiritual experience, first during his political career, and then during four decades of yoga discipline. When Sri Aurobindo meditated on the Gītā during his year in prison (1908–09), he combined Krishna's teaching on dharma and karma-yoga with his own view of historical and spiritual evolution.

In the following selection, Sri Aurobindo explains the concept of Supermind as the mediating power between two hemispheres of existence, the lower consisting of four evolutionary stages—material, vital, psychic, and mental—and the higher consisting of Sat-Chit-Ananda (Brahman or existence, consciousness or conscious force, and bliss or delight). The term for the higher level is well established in Indian thought, but the terms of the lower levels vary considerably in different systems and in Sri Aurobindo's own writings. He frequently posits three lower terms—matter, life, and mind—and places Supermind between these two triads. So, in "The Sevenfold Chord of Being" he writes:

> This Supermind then is the Truth or Real-Idea, inherent in all cosmic force and existence, which is necessary, itself remaining infinite, to determine and combine and uphold relation and order and the great lines of the manifestation. In the language of the Vedic Rishis, as infinite Existence, Consciousness and Bliss are the three highest and hidden names of the Nameless, so this Supermind is the fourth Name—fourth to That in its descent, fourth to us in our ascension.

Just as the Supermind is concealed, and potentially manifest in each of the levels below it, so it contains concealed and potentially manifest "the triune glory of Satchidananda." The process by which Satchidananda manifests itself in lower levels of existence is called involution (i.e., Satchidānanda, or simply Spirit, involved in the world); the effort of the world, slowed by matter, destructive instincts, and the excesses of the human ego, to realize its spiritual capacity, is called evolution. This dual process of involution and evolution is possible because of the divine unfolding and human effort. On the basis of his historical perspective and spiritual experience, Sri Aurobindo contends that the force of the Supermind is now creating the conditions necessary for the advent of a spiritual age. This possibility, which Sri Aurobindo calls the next evolutionary stage, will be realized when man develops sufficient daring and discipline to move beyond the essential but limited function of reason to "the spiritual order of things" and the great Truth which "is already there within us." Additional selections by Sri Aurobindo on education and spiritual discipline suggest some of the steps which he considers necessary for this personal and historical transformation.

S. Dasgupta

Indian Idealism

The development of Indian life from the Vedic to the
Upanishadic stage marks its transition from a pure unspecula-
tive realism and ritualistic magic for the satisfaction of
mundane interests to a form of mystical idealism which not
only transcended the bonds of corporal life, the attractions of
worldly enjoyments and interests, but also soared beyond the
limits of speculative philosophy and merged itself in a mystical
experience which is beyond life, beyond mind and beyond
thought—unspeakable, unthinkable and unfathomable. The
protest against the sacrificial school of thought, which is
sometimes observed in the abuses that have been heaped on its
followers by such expressions as "It is only the beasts that
follow the sacrificial line," may well be understood when one
notes the departure of the Upanishadic thought from that of
the ritualists. It is important, however, to observe that when
the Vedic thought of a mystical ruler and creator of the
universe oscillated back to the self of man the enquiry
regarding the nature of the self did not reveal to the enquirers a

mere subjectivistic thought, a mere *esse est percipi,* for the perceiver admits the existence of things because he perceives them but had found this immortal self beyond all thought. In order to appreciate the real nature of Indian idealism one has, therefore, to disabuse one's mind of the associations that this word has got in European philosophy. It is, therefore, doubtful whether this Upanishadic philosophy should be called idealism or mysticism. It has also given rise to a discussion, In what sense can this type of thought be called philosophy in any technical sense of the word? To one trained in the European schools of philosophy it becomes difficult to expect any one to go beyond the thought. Yet here we have a philosophy which does not seek to explain the nature of ordinary thought or of life or of physical events or of original knowledge or of any kind of cosmology, but which surrenders itself to the joyous transcendental experience of reality which is beyond all mundane experience—which can be reached only by transcending all thoughts speakable, all thoughts nameable, and all thoughts definable. To the question as to what is the nature of this mystical slef, the answer that has been given again and again is that just as a lump of salt when thrown into water loses its form and retains only its taste, so does one who approaches this reality lose himself in it, and then everything he would call his own and everything that he could define and name vanishes, and what is left behind is some transcendent joy, self-complete, self-sustained, self-illuminating and immortal.

*   *   *

We have made a brief survey of all the central doctrines of the principal Upanishads, and we are satisfied that the dominant spirit of these Upanishads reveals an idealism in which all reality is ascribed to the spirit as the ultimate inner essence of man, which is different from what we ordinarily understand by soul, the five senses, and the vital powers of the mind. We have found that in some of the Upanishads the idea of an external Brahman or lord as controlling the universe and also the inner functions of man, has been introduced; but in others this Brahman is definitely pronounced to be the inner essence of man; until we come to the Brihadāranyaka the nature of this inner essence of man remains very largely a mystery, and though in some of the other Upanishads the idea may lie scattered here and there, it is in the Brihadāranyaka that the view that this inmost self is of the nature of a pure perceiving consciousness is very definitely emphasised. No attempt is made anywhere in the Upanishads to show how from this one reality of a pure perceiving consciousness the diverse experiences which make up our psychological being can be explained; we are however sometimes told that this universe is only Brahman, or that this universe has sprung out of Brahman and would return back to it, or that this universe is a transformation or manifestation of the nature of Brahman, or that this universe has for its inner controller the Brahman who is of the nature of our inmost self, no attempt is made to explain by what operation the inmost self of man can be regarded as the source or cause of this manifold world. In understanding the nature of the self we are gradually pushed to a mystical conception of it, which is so subtle as to transcend the realms of thought; it cannot be grasped by the senses or by the cognitional modes of our experiences, it can only be realised through self-control, the cessation of all desires, and the meditation of the spiritual reality. In some cases the Upanishadic sages anticipated our difficulty of understanding how this subtle mystical essence could be regarded as the cause of this visible, apparently material and ponderable universe. Many illustrations are offered to make us believe that it is so still. It does not seem that the Upanishads actually deny the reality of the visible world, but they urge that the ultimate reality underlying it is Brahman or the mystical self within us. But how the "many" of the world can arise out of one, the self, and in what sense the reality of the world can be regarded as spiritually grounded, remains a question which has never been explained in the Upanishads. The sages of the Upanishads liberated Indian thought from the grasp of the ritualistic thinkers and also from purely deistic or theistic concepts. The whole atmosphere of the Upanishads seems to be ringing with the mystical music, and the sages were almost intoxicated with their discovery of the highest reality or the inmost self of man, that whatever we perceive around us is Brahman, that all our thoughts, all our beings, all our experiences are grounded in it, and that in spite of apparent diversities there is the one ultimate reality in which both the microcosm and the macrocosm are united.

S. Radhakrishnan

Ultimate Reality

The Gītā does not give any arguments in support of its metaphysical position. The reality of the Supreme is not a question to be solved by a dialectic which the vast majority of the human race will be unable to understand. Dialectic in itself and without reference to personal experience cannot give us conviction. Only spiritual experience can provide us with proofs of the existence of Spirit.

The Upanishads affirm the reality of a Supreme Brahman, one without a second, without attributes or determinations, who is identical with the deepest self of man. Spiritual experience centres round a sovereign unity which overcomes the duality between the known and the knowing. The inability to conceptualize the experience leads to such descriptions as identity, pure and simple. Brahman, the subsistent simplicity, is its own object in an intuition which is its very being. It is the pure subject whose existence cannot be ejected into the external or objective world.

Strictly speaking we cannot give any description of Brahman. The austerity of silence is the only way in which we can bring out the inadequacy of our halting descriptions and imperfect standards.[1] The Brihadāranyaka Upanishad says: "Where everything indeed has become the Self itself, whom and by what should one think? By what can we know the universal knower?"[2] The duality between knowing and knowable characteristic of discursive thought is transcended. The Eternal One is so infinitely real that we dare not even give It the name of One since oneness is an idea derived from worldly experience (vyavahara). We can only speak of It as the non-dual, advaita, that which is known when all dualities are resolved in the Supreme Identity. The Upanishads indulge in negative accounts, that the Real is not this, not this (na iti, na iti), "without sinews, without scar, untouched by evil,"[3] "without either shadow or darkness, without a within or a without."[4] The Bhagavad-Gītā supports this view of the

[1] Cf. Lao Tze: "The Tao which can be named is not the true Tao." "The reality of the formless, the unreality of that which has form—is known to all. Those who are on the road to attainment care not for these things, but the people at large discuss them. Attainment implies non-discussion; discussion implies non-attainment. Manifested Tao has no objective value; hence silence is better than argument. It cannot be translated into speech; better, then, say nothing at all. This is called the great attainment." Soothill: *The Three Religions of China*, second edition (1923), pp. 56–7. The Buddha maintained a calm silence when he was questioned about the nature of reality and nirvāna. Jesus maintained a similar silence when Pontius Pilate questioned him as to the nature of truth.

Cf. Plotinus: "If any one were to demand of nature why it produces, it would answer, if it were willing to listen and speak: You should not ask questions, but understand keeping silence as I keep silence, for I am not in the habit of speaking."

[2] II, 4, 12–14.

[3] Isha Upanishad, 8. The Supreme, *tad ekam*, is without qualities and attributes, "neither existent nor non-existent." Rig Veda X, 129. The Madhyamika Buddhists call the Ultimate Reality void or *śunya*, lest by giving it any other name they may be betrayed into limiting it. For them it is that which shall be known when all oppositions are resolved in the Supreme Identity.

[4] Brihadāranyaka Upanishad, III, 8, 8. In the Mahābhārata the Lord who is the teacher tells Nārada that His real form is "invisible, unsmellable, untouchable,

Upanishads in many passages. The Supreme is said to be "unmanifest, unthinkable and unchanging," [5] "neither existent nor nonexistent." [6] Contradictory predicates are attributed to the Supreme to indicate the inapplicability of empirical determinations. "It does not move and yet it moves. It is far away and yet it is near." [7] These predicates bring out the twofold nature of the Supreme as being and as becoming. He is para or transcendent and apara or immanent, both inside and outside the world.

The impersonality of the Absolute is not its whole significance. The Upanishads support Divine activity and participation in nature and give us a God who exceeds the mere infinite and the mere finite. The interest which inspired Plato's instruction to the astronomers of the Academy "to save the appearances," made the seers of the Upanishads look upon the world as meaningful. In the words of the Taittiriya Upanishad, the Supreme is that "from which these beings are born, that by which they live and that into which, when departing, they enter." According to the Veda, "He is the God who is in fire, in water, who pervades the entire universe; He who is in plants, in trees, to Him we make our obeisance again and again." "Who would have exerted, who would have lived, if

---

quality-less, devoid of parts, unborn, eternal, permanent and actionless." See Santiparva, 339, 21–38. It is the "cloud darkness," "the silent desert of the divinity . . . who is properly no being" in the words of Eckhart. Cf. Also Plotinus: "Generative of all, the Unity is none of all, neither thing nor quality, nor intellect nor soul, not in motion, not at rest, not in place, not in time; it is the self-defined, unique in form or, better, formless, existing before Form was or Movement or Rest, all of which are attachments of Being and make Being the manifold it is." (*Enneads*, E.T., by Mackenna, VI, 9)

[5] II, 25.
[6] XIII, 12; XIII, 15–17.
[7] Isha Upanishad, 5: see also Mundaka Upanishad, II, 1, 6–8; Katha Upanishad, II, 14; Brihadāranyaka Upanishad, II, 37; Svetasvatara Upanishad, III, 17.

this supreme bliss had not been in the heavens?" The theistic emphasis becomes prominent in the Svetasvatara Upanishad. "He, who is one and without any colour (visible form), by the manifold wielding of His power, ordains many colours (forms) with a concealed purpose and into whom, in the beginning and the end, the universe dissolves, He is the God. May He endow us with an understanding which leads to good actions." [8] Again "Thou art the woman, thou art the man; thou art the youth and also the maiden; thou as an old man totterest with a stick, being born. Thou art facing all directions." [9] Again, "His form is not capable of being seen; with the eye no one sees Him. They who know Him thus with the heart, with the mind, as abiding in the heart, become immortal." [10] He is a universal God who Himself is the universe which He includes within His own being. He is the light within us, hrdyantar jyotih. He is the Supreme whose shadow is life and death.[11]

In the Upanishads, we have the account of the Supreme as the Immutable and the Unthinkable as also the view that He is the Lord of the universe. Though He is the source of all that is, He is Himself unmoved for ever.[12] The Eternal Reality not only supports existence but is also the active power in the world. God is both transcendent, dwelling in light inaccessible and yet in Augustine's phrase "more intimate to the soul than the soul to itself." The Upanishad speaks of two birds perched on one tree, one of whom eats the fruits and the other eats not but watches, the silent witness withdrawn from enjoyment.[13]

---

[8] IV, 1.

[9] IV, 3.

[10] IV, 20.

[11] Rig Veda, X, 121, 2: see also Katha Upanishad, III, 1. Cp. Deuteronomy: "I kill and make alive," xxxii. 39.

[12] Cf. Rūmi: "Thy light is at once joined to all things and apart from all." *Shams-i-Tabriz* (E.T. by Nicholson), Ode IX.

[13] Mundaka Upanishad, III, 1, 1–3. Cf. Boehme: "And the deep of the darkness is as

Impersonality and personality are not arbitrary constructions or fictions of the mind. They are two ways of looking at the Eternal. The Supreme in its absolute self-existence is Brahman, the Absolute and as the Lord and Creator containing and controlling all, is Ishvara, the God. "Whether the Supreme is regarded as undetermined or determined, this Shiva should be known as eternal; undetermined He is, when viewed as different from the creation and determined, when He is everything." If the world is a cosmos and not an amorphous uncertainty, it is due to the oversight of God. The Bhagavata makes out that the one Reality which is of the nature of undivided consciousness is called Brahman, the Supreme Self or God. He is the ultimate principle, the real self in us as well as the God of worship. The Supreme is at once the transcendental, the cosmic and the individual reality. In Its transcendental aspect, It is the pure self unaffected by any action or experience, detached, unconcerned. In Its dynamic cosmic aspect, It not only supports but governs the whole cosmic action and this very Self which is one in all and above all is present in the individual.[14]

Ishvara is not responsible for evil except in an indirect way. If the universe consists of active choosing individuals who can be influenced but not controlled, for God is not a dictator, conflict is inevitable. To hold that the world consists of free spirits means that evil is possible and probable. The alternative to a mechanical world is a world of risk and adventure. If all tendencies to error, ugliness and evil are to be excluded, there

---

great as the habitation of the light; and they stand not one distant from the other but together in one another and neither of them hath beginning nor end." *Three Principles*, XIV, 76.

[14] Cf. Shankara on Brihadāranyaka Up., III, 8, 12. Roughly we may say that the Self in its transcendental, cosmic and individual aspects answers to the Christian Trinity of Father, Son and Holy Ghost.

can be no seeking of the true, the beautiful and the good. If there is to be an active willing of these ideals of truth, beauty and goodness, then their opposites of error, ugliness and evil are not merely abstract possibilities but positive tendencies which we have to resist. For the Gītā, the world is the scene of an active struggle between good and evil in which God is deeply interested. He pours out His wealth of love in helping man to resist all that makes for error, ugliness and evil. As God is completely good and His love is boundless, He is concerned about the suffering of the world. God is omnipotent because there are no external limits to His power. The social nature of the world is not imposed on God, but is willed by Him. To the question, whether God's omniscience includes a foreknowledge of the way in which men will behave and use or abuse their freedom of choice, we can only say that what God does not know is not a fact. He knows that the tendencies are indeterminate and when they become actualized, He is aware of them. The law of karma does not limit God's omnipotence. The Hindu thinkers even during the period of the composition of the Rig Veda, knew about the reasonableness and lawabidingness of nature. Rita or order embraces all things. The reign of law is the mind and will of God and cannot therefore be regarded as a limitation of His power. The personal Lord of the universe has a side in time, which is subject to change.

The emphasis of the Gītā is on the Supreme as the personal God who creates the perceptible world by His nature (prakriti). He resides in the heart of every being;[15] He is the enjoyer and lord of all sacrifices.[16] He stirs our hearts to devotion and grants our prayers.[17] He is the source and

[15] XVIII, 61.
[16] IX, 24.
[17] VII, 22.

sustainer of values. He enters into personal relations with us in worship and prayer.

The personal Ishvara is responsible for the creation, preservation and dissolution of the universe.[18] The Supreme has two natures, the higher (para) and the lower (apara).[19] The living souls represent the higher and the material medium the lower. God is responsible for both the ideal plan and the concrete medium through which the ideal becomes the actual, the conceptual becomes the cosmic. The concretization of the conceptual plan requires a fullness of existence, an objectification in the medium of potential matter. While God's ideas are seeking for existence, the world of existence is striving for perfection. The Divine pattern and the potential matter, both these are derived from God who is the beginning, the middle and the end, Brahma, Vishnu, and Shiva. God with His creative ideas is Brahma. God who pours out His love and works with a patience which is matched only by His love is Vishnu, who is perpetually at work saving the world. When the conceptual becomes the cosmic, when heaven is established on earth, we have the fulfillment represented by Shiva. God is at the same time wisdom, love and perfection. The three functions cannot be torn apart. Brahma, Vishnu and Shiva are fundamentally one though conceived in a threefold manner. The Gītā is interested in the process of redeeming the world. So the aspect of Vishnu is emphasized. Krishna represents the Vishnu aspect of the Supreme.

Vishnu is a familiar deity in the Rig Veda. He is the great pervader, from vis, to pervade. He is the internal controller who pervades the whole universe. He gathers to Himself in an

---

[18] Cf. Jacob Boehme: "Creation was the act of the Father; the incarnation that of the Son; while the end of the world will be brought about through the operation of the Holy Ghost."

[19] VII, 4–5.

ever increasing measure the position and dignity of the Eternal Supreme. Taittiriya Aranyaka says: "To Narayana we bring worship; to Vasudeva our meditations and in this may Vishnu assist us." [20]

Krishna,[21] the teacher of the Gītā, becomes identified with Vishnu, the ancient Lord of the Sun, and Narayana, an ancient God of cosmic character and the goal or resting place of gods and men.

The Real is the supracosmic, eternal, spaceless, timeless Brahman who supports this cosmic manifestation in space and time. He is the Universal Spirit, Paramātman, who ensouls the cosmic forms and movements. He is the Parameshvara who presides over the individual souls and movements of nature and controls the cosmic becoming. He is also the Purushottama, the Supreme Person, whose dual nature is manifested in the evolution of the cosmos. He fills our being, illumines our understanding and sets in motion its hidden springs.

All things partake of the duality of being and non-being from Purushottama downwards. Even God has the element of negativity or māyā though He controls it. He puts forth His active nature (svam prakritim) and controls the souls who work out their destinies along lines determined by their own natures. While all this is done by the Supreme through His native power exercised in this changing world, He has another aspect untouched by it all. He is the impersonal Absolute as well as the immanent will; He is the uncaused cause, the unmoved mover. While dwelling in man and nature, the Supreme is greater than both. The boundless universe in an endless space and time rests in Him and not He in it. The God

---

[20] X, 1, 6.

[21] He who attracts all or arouses devotion in all is Krishna. Krishna is derived from krish, to scrape, because he scrapes or draws away all sins and other sources of evil from his devotees.

of the Gītā cannot be identified with the cosmic process for He extends beyond it. Even in it He is manifest more in some aspects than in others. The charge of pantheism in the lower sense of the term cannot be urged against the Gītā view. While there is one reality that is ultimately perfect, everything that is concrete and actual is not equally perfect.

Sri Aurobindo

The Sevenfold Chord of Being

> In the ignorance of my mind, I ask of these steps of the
> Gods that are set within. The all-knowing Gods have taken
> the Infant of a year and they have woven about him seven
> threads to make this weft.—*Rig Veda, I, 164, 5.*

We have now, by our scrutiny of the seven great terms of
existence which the ancient seers fixed on as the foundation
and sevenfold mode of all cosmic existence, discerned the
gradations of evolution and involution and arrived at the basis
of knowledge towards which we were striving. We have laid
down that the origin, the continent, the initial and the ultimate
reality of all that is in the cosmos is the triune principle of
transcendent and infinite Existence, Consciousness and Bliss
which is the nature of divine being. Consciousness has two
aspects, illuminating and effective, state and power of self-
awareness and state and power of self-force, by which Being
possesses itself whether in its static condition or in its dynamic
movement; for in its creative action it knows by omnipotent

self-consciousness all that is latent within it and produces and governs the universe of its potentialities by an omniscient self-energy. This creative action of the All-Existent has its nodus in the fourth, the intermediate principle of Supermind or Real-Idea, in which a divine Knowledge one with self-existence and self-awareness and a substantial Will which is in perfect unison with that knowledge, because it is itself in its substance and nature that self-conscious self-existence dynamic in illumined action, develop infallibly the movement and form and law of things in right accordance with their self-existent Truth and in harmony with the significances of its manifestation.

The creation depends on and moves between the biune principle of unity and multiplicity; it is a manifoldness of idea and force and form which is the expression of an original unity, and it is an eternal oneness which is the foundation and reality of the multiple worlds and makes their play possible. Supermind therefore proceeds by a double faculty of comprehensive and apprehensive knowledge; proceeding from the essential oneness to the resultant multiplicity, it comprehends all things in itself as itself the One in its manifold aspects and it apprehends separately all things in itself as objects of its will and knowledge. While to its original self-awareness all things are one being, one consciousness, one will, one self-delight and the whole movement of things a movement one and indivisible, it proceeds in its action from the unity to the multiplicity and from multiplicity to unity, creating an ordered relation between them and an appearance but not a binding reality of division, a subtle unseparating division, or rather a demarcation and determination within the indivisible. The Supermind is the divine Gnosis which creates, governs and upholds the worlds: it is the secret Wisdom which upholds both our Knowledge and our Ignorance.

We have discovered also that Mind, Life and Matter are a triple aspect of these higher principles working, so far as our universe is concerned, in subjection to the principle of Ignorance, to the superficial and apparent self-forgetfulness of the One in its play of division and multiplicity. Really, these three are only subordinate powers of the divine quaternary: Mind is a subordinate power of Supermind which takes its stand in the standpoint of division, actually forgetful here of the oneness behind though able to return to it by reillumination from the supramental; Life is similarly a subordinate power of the energy aspect of Satchidānanda, it is Force working out form and the play of conscious energy from the standpoint of division created by Mind; Matter is the form of substance of being which the existence of Satchidānanda assumes when it subjects itself to this phenomenal action of its own consciousness and force.

In addition, there is a fourth principle which comes into manifestation at the nodus of mind, life and body, that which we call the soul; but this has a double appearance, in front the desire-soul which strives for the possession and delight of things, and, behind and either largely or entirely concealed by the desire-soul, the true psychic entity which is the real repository of the experiences of the spirit. And we have concluded that this fourth human principle is a projection and an action of the third divine principle of infinite Bliss, but an action in the terms of our consciousness and under the conditions of soul-evolution in this world. As the existence of the Divine is in its nature an infinite consciousness and the self-power of that consciousness, so the nature of its infinite consciousness is pure and infinite Bliss; self-possession and self-awareness are the essence of its self-delight. The cosmos also is a play of this divine self-delight and the delight of that play is entirely possessed by the Universal; but in the individual owing to the action of ignorance and division it is held back in the subliminal and the superconscient being; on our surface it lacks and has to be sought for, found and possessed by the development of the individual consciousness towards universality and transcendence.

We may, therefore, if we will, pose eight[1] principles instead of seven, and then we perceive that our existence is a sort of refraction of the divine existence, in inverted order of ascent and descent, thus ranged,—

Existence	Matter
Consciousness-Force	Life
Bliss	Psyche
Supermind	Mind

The Divine descends from pure existence through the play of Consciousness-Force and Bliss and the creative medium of Supermind into cosmic being; we ascend from Matter through a developing life, soul and mind and the illuminating medium of Supermind towards the divine being. The knot of the two, the higher and the lower hemisphere,[2] is where mind and Supermind meet with a veil between them. The rending of the veil is the condition of the divine life in humanity; for by that rending, by the illumining descent of the higher into the nature of the lower being and the forceful ascent of the lower being into the nature of the higher, mind can recover its divine light in the all-comprehending Supermind, the soul realise its divine self in the all-possessing all-blissful Ananda, life re-possess its divine power in the play of omnipotent Conscious-Force and Matter open to its divine liberty as a form of the divine Existence. And if there be any goal to the evolution which finds here its present crown and head in the human

---

[1] The Vedic Seers speak of the seven Rays, but also of eight, nine, ten or twelve.
[2] Parardha and Aparardha.

being, other than an aimless circling and an individual escape from the circling, if the infinite potentiality of this creature, who alone here stands between Spirit and Matter with the power to mediate between them, has any meaning other than an ultimate awakening from the delusion of life by despair and disgust of the cosmic effort and its complete rejection, then even such a luminous and puissant transfiguration and emergence of the Divine in the creature must be that high-uplifted goal and that supreme significance.

But before we can turn to the psychological and practical conditions under which such a transfiguration may be changed from an essential possibility into a dynamic potentiality, we have much to consider; for we must discern not only the essential principles of the descent of Satchidānanda into cosmic existence, which we have already done, but the large plan of its order here and the nature and action of the manifested power of Conscious-Force which reigns over the conditions under which we now exist. At present, what we have first to see is that the seven or the eight principles we have examined are essential to all cosmic creation and are there, manifested or as yet unmanifested, in ourselves, in this "Infant of a year" which we still are,—for we are far yet from being the adults of evolutionary Nature. The higher Trinity is the source and basis of all existence and play of existence, and all cosmos must be an expression and action of its essential reality. No universe can be merely a form of being which has sprung up and outlined itself in an absolute nullity and void and remains standing out against a non-existent emptiness. It must be either a figure of existence within the infinite Existence who is beyond all figure or it must be itself the All-Existence. In fact, when we unify our self with cosmic being, we see that it is really both of these things at once; that is to say, it is the All-Existent figuring Himself out in an infinite series of rhythms in His own conceptive extension of Himself as Time and Space. Moreover we see that this cosmic action or any cosmic action is impossible without the play of an infinite Force of Existence which produces and regulates all these forms and movements; and that Force equally presupposes or is the action of an infinite Consciousness, because it is in its nature a cosmic Will determining all relations and apprehending them by its own mode of awareness, and it could not so determine and apprehend them if there were no comprehensive Consciousness behind that mode of cosmic awareness to originate as well as to hold, fix and reflect through it the relations of Being in the developing formation or becoming of itself which we call a universe.

Finally, Consciousness being thus omniscient and omnipotent, in entire luminous possession of itself, and such entire luminous possession being necessarily and in its very nature Bliss, for it cannot be anything else, a vast universal self-delight must be the cause, essence and object of cosmic existence. "If there were not," says the ancient seer, "this all-encompassing ether of Delight of existence in which we dwell, if that delight were not our ether, then none could breathe, none could live." This self-bliss may become subconscient, seemingly lost on the surface, but not only must it be there at our roots, all existence must be essentially a seeking and reaching out to discover and possess it, and in proportion as the creature in the cosmos finds himself, whether in will and power or in light and knowledge or in being and wideness or in love and joy itself, he must awaken to something of the secret ecstasy. Joy of being, delight of realisation by knowledge, rapture of possession by will and power or creative force, ecstasy of union in love and joy are the highest terms of expanding life because they are the essence of existence itself in its hidden roots as on its yet unseen heights. Wherever, then, cosmic existence manifests itself, these three must be behind and within it.

But infinite Existence, Consciousness and Bliss need not throw themselves out into apparent being at all or, doing so, it would not be cosmic being, but simply an infinity or figures without fixed order or relation, if they did not hold or develop and bring out from themselves this fourth term of Supermind, of the divine Gnosis. There must be in every cosmos a power of Knowledge and Will which out of infinite potentiality fixes determined relations, develops the result out of the seed, rolls out the mighty rhythms of cosmic Law and views and governs the worlds as their immortal and infinite Seer and Ruler.[3] This power indeed is nothing else than Satchidānanda Himself; it creates nothing which is not in its own self-existence, and for that reason all cosmic and real Law is a thing not imposed from outside, but from within, all development is self-development, all seed and result are seed of a Truth of things and result of that seed determined out of its potentialities. For the same reason no Law is absolute, because only the infinite is absolute, and everything contains within itself endless potentialities quite beyond its determined form and course, which are only determined through a self-limitation by Idea proceeding from an infinite liberty within. This power of self-limitation is necessarily inherent in the boundless All-Existent. The Infinite would not be the Infinite if it could not assume a manifold finiteness; the Absolute would not be the Absolute if it were denied in knowledge and power and will and manifestation of being a boundless capacity of self-determination. This Super-mind then is the Truth or Real-Idea, inherent in all cosmic force and existence, which is necessary, itself remaining

[3] The Seer, the Thinker, He who becomes everywhere, the Self-existent.—*Isha Upanishad*, 8.

infinite, to determine and combine and uphold relation and order and the great lines of the manifestation. In the language of the Vedic Rishis, as infinite Existence, Consciousness and Bliss are the three highest and hidden Names of the Nameless, so this Supermind is the fourth Name[4]—fourth to That in its descent, fourth to us in our ascension.

But Mind, Life and Matter, the lower trilogy, are also indispensable to all cosmic being, not necessarily in the form or with the action and conditions which we know upon earth or in this material universe, but in some kind of action, however luminous, however puissant, however subtle. For Mind is essentially that faculty of Supermind which measures and limits, which fixes a particular centre and views from that the cosmic movement and its interactions. Granted that in a particular world, plane or cosmic arrangement, mind need not be limited, or rather that the being who uses mind as a subordinate faculty need not be incapable of seeing things from other centres or standpoints or even from the real Centre of all or in the vastness of a universal self-diffusion, still if he is not capable of fixing himself normally in his own firm standpoint for certain purposes of the divine activity, if there is only the universal self-diffusion or only infinite centres without some determining or freely limiting action for each, then there is no cosmos but only a Being musing within Himself infinitely as a creator or poet may muse freely, not plastically, before he proceeds to the determining work of creation. Such a state must exist somewhere in the infinite scale of existence, but it is not what we understand by a cosmos. Whatever order there may be in it, must be a sort of unfixed, unbinding order such as Supermind might evolve before it had proceeded to the work

---

[4] *Turīyam svid,* "a certain Fourth", also called *turīyam dhāma,* the fourth placing or poise of existence.

of fixed development, measurement and interaction of relations. For that measurement and interaction Mind is necessary,
though it need not be aware of itself as anything but a
subordinate action of Supermind nor develop the interaction of
relations on the basis of a self-imprisoned egoism such as we
see active in terrestrial Nature.

Mind once existent, Life and Form of substance follow; for
life is simply the determination of force and action, of relation
and interaction of energy from many fixed centres of consciousness,—fixed, not necessarily in place or time, but in a
persistent coexistence of beings or soul-forms of the Eternal
supporting a cosmic harmony. That life may be very different
from life as we know or conceive it, but essentially it would be
the same principle at work which we see here figured as
vitality,—the principle to which the ancient Indian thinkers
gave the name of Vayu or Prana, the life-stuff, the substantial
will and energy in the cosmos working out into determined
form and action and conscious dynamis of being. Substance too
might be very different from our view and sense of material
body, much more subtle, much less rigidly binding in its law of
self-division and mutual resistance, and body or form might be
an instrument and not a prison, yet for the cosmic interaction
some determination of form and substance would always be
necessary, even if it be only a mental body or something yet
more luminous, subtle and puissantly and freely responsive
than the freest mental body.

It follows that wherever Cosmos is, there, even if only one
principle be initially apparent, even if at first that seem to be
the sole principle of things and everything else that may appear
afterwards in the world seem to be no more than its forms and
results and not in themselves indispensable to cosmic existence,
such a front presented by being can only be an illusory mask
or appearance of its real truth. Where one principle is manifest

in Cosmos, there all the rest must be not merely present and passively latent, but secretly at work. In any given world its scale and harmony of being may be openly in possession of all seven at a higher or lower degree of activity; in another they may be all involved in one which becomes the initial or fundamental principle of evolution in that world, but evolution of the involved there must be. The evolution of the sevenfold power of being, the realisation of its septuple Name, must be the destiny of any world which starts apparently from the involution of all in one power.[5] Therefore the material universe was bound in the nature of things to evolve from its hidden life apparent life, from its hidden mind apparent mind, and it must in the same nature of things evolve from its hidden Supermind apparent Supermind and from the concealed Spirit within it the triune glory of Satchidānanda. The only question is whether the earth is to be a scene of that emergence or the human creation on this or any other material scene, in this or any other cycle of the large wheelings of Time, its instrument and vehicle. The ancient seers believed in this possibility for man and held it to be his divine destiny; the modern thinker does not even conceive of it or, if he conceived, would deny or doubt. If he sees a vision of the Superman, it is in the figure of increased degrees of mentality or vitality; he admits no other emergence, sees nothing beyond these principles, for these have traced for us up till now our limit and circle. In this progressive world, with this human creature in whom the divine spark has been kindled, real wisdom is likely to dwell with the higher aspiration rather than with the denial of aspiration or with the hope that limits and circumscribes itself

[5] In any given world there need not be an involution but only a subordination of the other principles to one or their inclusion in one; then evolution is not a necessity of that world-order.

S. Radhakrishnan *(Calcutta Studio)*

Sri Aurobindo, 1950 *(Henri Cartier-Bresson)*

within those narrow walls of apparent possibility which are only our intermediate house of training. In the spiritual order of things, the higher we project our view and our aspiration, the greater the Truth that seeks to descend upon us, because it is already there within us and calls for its release from the covering that conceals it in manifested Nature.

Radhakrishnan on the Function of Philosophy

Philosophy has for its function the ordering of life and the guidance of action. It sits at the helm and directs our course through the changes and chances of the world. When philosophy is alive, it cannot be remote from the life of the people. The ideas of thinkers are evolved in the process of their life history. We must learn not only to reverence them, but to acquire their spirit. The names of Vashishtha and Vishvāmitra, Yājnavalkya and Gārgī, Buddha and Mahāvīra, Gautama and Kanāda, Kapila and Patanjali, Bādarāyana and Jaimini, Shankara and Rāmānuja, are not merely themes for the historian but types of personality. With them philosophy is a world-view based on reflection and experience. Thought, when it thinks itself out to the end, becomes religion by being lived and tested by the supreme test of life. The discipline of philosophy is at the same time the fulfilment of a religious vocation.

Radhakrishnan on Indian Philosophy

The dominant character of the Indian mind which has coloured all its culture and moulded all its thoughts is the spiritual tendency. Spiritual experience is the foundation of India's rich cultural history. It is mysticism, not in the sense of involving the exercise of any mysterious power, but only as insisting on a discipline of human nature, leading to a realisation of the spiritual. While the sacred scriptures of the Hebrews and the Christians are more religious and ethical, those of the Hindus are more spiritual and contemplative. The one fact of life in India is the Eternal Being of God.

Dharma

Introduction

When Arjuna explains to his divine charioteer, Krishna, the avatar of Vishnu, that he will not fight in the battle that is about to commence, Krishna reminds him that as a warrior his duty is to fight in a just war. In so advising, Krishna affirms the inviolability of dharma. The simple statement that it is his dharma is sufficient rationale for Arjuna's compliance; there was no question that it was his duty to comply. This is the first level of Krishna's message, and the first level of the Hindu theory of value.

As he learns from Krishna, Arjuna's duties are defined first in functional terms—e.g., his duties as warrior—and later in ultimate terms—liberation from the ego, and selfless union with the Divine and the world. The second duty, however, cannot be undertaken until the more basic duties are under control: when Arjuna is tempted to leave the battle in order to live as a recluse, Krishna explains that this will not lead to moksha (liberation) because he had not yet mastered the duties concerning his time of life, caste, and personal needs. Each level of duty must be considered as though necessary, fixed and eternal; but by recasting the spiritual order, each avatar alters as well as affirms the various dharmas. The following selections help to clarify the types and functions of dharma and their metaphysical basis.

As is emphasized in every treatment of the subject, the term dharma has a variety of meanings on several levels. In a passage in this section, Radhakrishnan explains that dharma "is the norm which sustains the universe, the principle of a thing in virtue of which it is what it is." Sri Aurobindo lists three meanings of dharma: the fundamental law of our being, the law of the divine within us, and the ideal pattern of social relations which enables each being to realize its divine capacity. In Hiriyanna's systematic treatment which follows, dharma is described on three levels: first, as one of the four values or goals of human life, along with artha (wealth), kāma (pleasure) and moksha (liberation); second, as an aid or preparation for moksha (this is the function of dharma in Krishna's advice to Arjuna); third, as an end in itself (i.e., as a self-sufficient ethical and religious ideal). Hiriyanna's third meaning of dharma, which represents an effort to make the ethical an adequate goal of human life (as it is generally in the Western and Chinese traditions), has governed the lives of the Indian masses but has occupied a subordinate position in the traditional Indian scale of values. According to the Upanishads, the Gītā, Indian Buddhism, and virtually every prominent Indian religious thinker, dharma performs an instrumental function for the ultimate goal of liberation.

Although the Indian tradition has held to the ultimacy of moksha over the instrumentality of dharma, or the primacy of the spiritual over the ethical, dharma is nevertheless a necessary stage in that it requires control of all values and activities on and below the ethical level. The proper fulfillment of one's personal duty (swadharma), duty concerning time of life (ashrama-dharma), and caste duty (varna-dharma) spiritualizes all of one's activities. Thus dharma perfects artha (earning one's livelihood) and kāma (pursuit of pleasure) and points to the ultimate value, moksha. The dedicated pursuit of moksha, in turn, transforms and ultimately negates the social and moral duties prescribed by the various dharmas.

Whereas dharma has many meanings, all of which can be articulated, moksha has but one meaning, and resists articulation. For a working definition, it is probably safe to say that moksha refers to the equanimity and delight of mind and spirit, such that knowledge and knower, being and becoming, the divine and the self, are all experienced in perfect fullness and unity. The attainability and transformative power of moksha typifies the spiritual optimism of the Indian tradition. This optimism rests on an elaborate metaphysics and on the influence of remarkable spiritual personalities. The ideals and experiences of great spiritual personalities are revealed in later chapters; the metaphysics is outlined in the previous chapter and in the selection by Radhakrishnan in this chapter.

In his effort to base ethics on mysticism, Radhakrishnan in effect reaffirms the traditional Hindu relationship between dharma and moksha. In this scheme, the concept of religion refers to both dharma and moksha in that it supports the ethical life and leads to the spiritual life. The ideals of dharma and moksha, or religion, are based on a theory of self as "uncreated and deathless and absolutely real."

M. Hiriyanna

Philosophy of Values

Indian thinkers commonly speak of two functions of knowledge—one which is theoretical, viz. revealing the existence of some object (artha-paricchitti), and the other which is practical, viz. affording help in the attainment of some purpose in life (phala-prapti). The results of these two functions of knowledge are respectively what we mean by "fact" and "value." A thirsty traveller, who happens to come upon a sheet of fresh water, discovers a fact; and, when later he quenches his thirst by drinking the water, he realizes a value. These functions are regarded as closely connected with each other, since the knowledge of a fact usually leads to the pursuit of some value. The number of facts that may be known, it is clear, are innumerable; and the values that may be realized through their knowledge are equally so. It is with the latter that we are concerned here. The Sanskrit word used for "value" means "the object of desire" (ishta), and the term may therefore be generally defined as "that which is desired." The opposite of value or "disvalue" may be taken as "that which is shunned or avoided" (dvishta). For the sake of brevity, we shall speak only of values; but what is said of them will, with appropriate changes, apply to disvalues also.

FOUR CLASSES OF VALUES

One of the distinguishing features of Indian philosophy is that, as a consequence of the pragmatic view it takes of knowledge, it has, throughout its history, given the foremost place to values. Indeed, they form its central theme; and questions like those of "being" and of "knowing" come in only as a matter of course. It may, on this account, be described as essentially a philosophy of values. There are various problems connected with value. For instance, it may be asked whether we desire things because they are of value, or whether they are of value because we desire them. For want of space, we cannot consider such general questions here, however important and interesting they may be. We shall confine our attention to the values included in the well-known group of four, viz. dharma (virtue), artha (wealth), kāma (pleasure), and moksha (self-realization). We shall only observe, in passing, that values may be either instrumental or intrinsic. Thus in the example given above, water is an instrumental value; and the quenching of thirst by means of it is an intrinsic value. That is, though the term "value" is primarily used for the ends that are sought, often the means to their attainment are also, by courtesy, called so.

Though all the above four are ordinarily reckoned as values of life, a distinction is sometimes made within them, according to which only the first three are regarded so, excluding the last one of moksha. Early works like the Rāmāyana and the Mahābhārata, for example, often refer to them alone. But it would be wrong to conclude therefrom that the fourth value of moksha was now known at the time, for these epics and other early works themselves refer to it also. In fact, the ideal of moksha is at least as old as the Upanishads. The restriction of the name of "value" to "the aggregate of three" or the tri-varga, as this group is designated, probably only means that the writers of the works in question address themselves chiefly to the common people, for whom the final ideal of moksha is of little immediate interest. Whatever the reason for this inner distinction may be, it is a convenient one; and we shall adopt it in our treatment of the subject here.

INSTRUMENTAL AND PSYCHOLOGICAL VALUES— ARTHA AND KĀMA

To take up the tri-varga for consideration first: In this group of three, artha may be said to stand for economic value; kāma, for psychological value; and dharma, for moral value. To speak in the main, artha is an instrumental value, for it is helpful in satisfying one or other of the diverse needs of life. Their satisfaction is kāma, which is an intrinsic value, since it does not admit of the question "why?" We may, for example, ask why we seek food; but we cannot similarly ask for what we seek, the satisfaction arising from the partaking of it. We describe it as a "psychological value," not in its usual sense of subjective value in general, but in that of an end which satisfies the natural impulses of an individual as such. These two values of artha and kāma are sought not only by man, but by all sentient creatures. The only difference is that, while man can seek them knowingly, the other creatures do so instinctively. In this distinction, we find the characteristic feature of purushārthas or "human values," viz. that they represent ends that are *consciously* pursued by man. When they are sought otherwise by him, as they sometimes are, they may remain values but cease to be purushārthas. The possibility of his seeking them unconsciously is due to the fact that man combines in himself the character of an animal and that of a self-conscious agent—that he is not merely a spiritual but also a natural being. The wants which are common to man and the lower animals and whose urge is natural, rather than spiritual, are self-preservation and the propagation of offspring, or, as it may otherwise be stated, race-preservation.

MORAL VALUE—DHARMA

The case is quite different as regards dharma, for its appeal is restricted to man. While it is virtually unknown to the lower animals, man may be said to be innately aware of it. In this consists its uniqueness as compared with the other two values of artha and kāma, and we shall presently see in what respect it is superior to them. We have rendered it as "moral value"; and some forms of Indian thought, like early Buddhism, will bear us out completely. But in others, especially the so-called orthodox systems, the connotation of the term is much wider, for they include under it not only moral but also religious values, such as are detailed in the ritualistic portions of the Vedas. But, in accordance with a principle recognized from very early times, viz. that ceremonial is of little avail to those who are morally impure, the practice of virtue becomes a necessary condition of ritualistic life. We also find it stated in some ancient works of this tradition that, as between ritual and virtue, the latter is certainly to be preferred. The Mahābhārata, in a familiar verse, declares that "speaking the truth is far better than celebrating many horse-sacrifices." Gautama, one of the oldest among the law-givers, places what he terms the "virtues of the soul" (ātma-guna), like kindness and purity, above mere ceremonial. These are the reasons why we have rendered the term as "moral value," and we shall confine our attention in what follows solely to that aspect of dharma.

The notion of dharma, thus restricted, is so familiar that it is hardly necessary to refer to examples of virtues whose cultivation it signifies. Yet to give a general idea of them, we shall refer to one of the several lists of them found in old works. Yājnavalkya, in the Smriti which goes by his name, reckons them as nine—non-injury, sincerity, honesty, cleanliness, control of the senses, charity, self-restraint, love, and forbearance. It will be seen that some of these, like non-injury and charity, have a reference to the good of others or are altruistic, while others, like sincerity and self-restraint, serve to develop one's own character and will. It should not, however, be thought that this division into self-regarding and other-regarding virtues is a hard and fast one; for, as an individual has no life of his own independently of society, the former has a bearing on the latter, as surely as the latter has on the former.

RELATION OF DHARMA TO KĀMA

What is the relation of dharma to artha and kāma? Or, as artha is ordinarily but a means to kāma, we may narrow the scope of our question and ask, "What is the relation of dharma to kāma?" If kāma stands for pleasure, as stated above, we may say that it is desired by all, for pleasure is always welcome to everyone. Indeed, we cannot help desiring our own felicity. But not everything desired is necessarily *desirable*. A sick person may long for a certain kind of food, but it may not at all be advisable for him to partake of it from the standpoint of his physical well-being. That is, kāma, while it may be an object of desire, may not always be desirable; and, though appearing to be a true value of life, it may not really be so or may even prove to be a disvalue. How then can we distinguish these two kinds of kāma? To speak with reference only to the tri-varga which we are now considering, dharma furnishes the necessary criterion. That variety of kāma is a true value, which is in accord with the requirements of dharma, but not any other. In thus helping us to discriminate between good and bad kāma or in rationalizing life, as we might put it, consists the superiority of dharma, which is thus reckoned as the highest of the three values. This conception of dharma as a regulative principle is so important in the philosophy of conduct that all the Shastras and all the higher literature of India (the latter, though only impliedly) emphasize it. That is, for example, what Sri Krishna means when he says in the Gītā, "Dharmāviruddhah . . . kāmo'smi" (I am kāma, not at strife with dharma).[1]

DHARMA AS A MEANS AND AN END

Having considered the general nature of dharma and its relation to kāma, and therefore also to artha, which commonly is but a means to it, we may ask whether its function is limited to regulating the pursuit of these two values or whether it has any purpose of its own. There are two answers to be given to this question.

(1) The popular view, and probably also the older of the two, is that it has a purpose of its own. In this view, then, dharma is conceived as an instrumental value. A steadfast pursuit of it, in its double aspect of self-regarding and other-regarding virtues, results in one's good here as well as elsewhere; and this good—whether it stands for worldly happiness or heavenly bliss—is, as a whole, designated abhyudaya or "prosperity." Further, it is believed that dharma not only leads to the good, but that it does so invariably. Here is

[1] Bhagavad-Gītā, VII.11.

another reason for its superiority over the other two values, whose pursuit may or may not be successful. But it should be added that, for the attainment of the fruit of dharma, one may have to wait for long. The important point, however, is that it is sure to yield its fruit at some time, even though it be after many vicissitudes. It is the possible postponement of the result to an indefinite future that explains the common indifference of men towards dharma, notwithstanding their awareness of its excellence. It is this human shortsightedness that Vyasa, for example, has in his mind when, in concluding the Mahābhārata, he says, "Here I am, crying out with uplifted arms that dharma brings with it both artha and kāma; but no one listens to me." [2] The same feeling of sad astonishment at human folly is echoed in a common saying that "People want the fruits of dharma, but not dharma itself."

(2) The other view is that dharma is an intrinsic value, and therefore an end in and for itself. It is maintained by some Mimamsakas, viz. those of the Prabhakara school. They ridicule the idea that virtue should appeal to man's interest for being practised. That would be to look upon man as a creature of inclination and forget that he is a moral agent, who has the power to do what he ought and to abstain from doing what he ought not. Further, they allege that such a view makes dharma not only a means, but also a means to the admittedly inferior value of kāma, by making it minister to the doer's felicity. However unexceptionable the kāma pursued may be in its nature, and whatever altruistic activity it may incidentally involve, it finally stands for a subjective end or, in plainer terms, for self-love. If there is a moral principle, it must be absolute in the sense that it has nothing to do with our likes and dislikes and that it should be followed solely out of respect for

[2] Mahābhārata, XVIII.5.62.

it. It is the nature of dharma, they say, to be thus ultimate. Here we have the well-known principle of practising virtue *for its own sake*; and the student of Western philosophy will see in it a general kinship with Kant's teaching of the "categorical imperative," that is, a command about which there is nothing contingent or conditional.

This will, no doubt, appear at first as a very exalted view of dharma or "duty," if we may use that term instead, worthy to evoke our admiration. But it is really untenable, because it is based upon unsound psychology. It assumes that voluntary activity is possible without any end in view or, to put the same in another way, that it forms its own end (svayam-prayojana-bhūta). But how can anything be its own consequence? To accept such a view, as Shankara observes, changes what is put forward as a gospel of duty into a "gospel of drudgery." [3] For, in that case, devotion to duty would mean present toil; and dereliction of it, future evil, so that whether a person does his duty or leaves it undone, he has only trouble as his lot in life. Hence this view of dharma has not come to prevail. It was once for all given up in India when Mandana, a contemporary of Shankara, enunciated the principle that "nothing prompts a man to acts of will, but what is a means to some desired end."

DHARMA SUBSERVES MOKSHA

So much about the tri-varga. When we shift our standpoint from the system of the three values to that of the four (catur-varga) including moksha, we find the conception of dharma undergoing a profound change, which makes it superior to that in either of the above views. It continues here to be regarded as an instrumental value, as in the first of them,

---

[3] See Shankara's commentary on Bhagavad-Gītā, III.1; IV.18.

but the end which it is taken to serve is not the agent's "prosperity." It is rather the purification of one's character or, as the term used for it in Sanskrit means, "the cleansing of one's mind" (sattva-shuddhi) by purging it of all lower or selfish impulses. This cleansing is effected through the performance of the duties for which dharma stands in the manner taught in the Gītā, that is, without any thought whatsoever of their fruit. Thus, if the former view commends partial abnegation of kāma and thereby rationalizes life's activities, as we have said, the present one commends its total abnegation and thus spiritualizes them. Its true character of a higher value is restored to dharma here, for, in contrast with the other view, it wholly ceases to be subservient to kāma. The weakness of that view, then, is not in its conception of dharma as a means to an end, but only in its insistence that the end is some form of happiness for the doer. In this rejection of "prosperity" or personal benefit as the aim, the present view resembles that of the Prabhakara school; but, at the same time, it differs vitally from that view in holding that dharma has an end, and thus denying that there can be any voluntary activity without an appropriate motive. It is this changed conception of dharma that has come to prevail in Indian philosophy, and not either of the above.

AIDS TO MOKSHA—MORALITY AND KNOWLEDGE

But it may be said that moral purification or the conquest of the lower self is too negative in its nature to prompt voluntary activity. So it is necessary to add that actually, in this view, self-conquest is only the immediate end of dharma, while its final aim is moksha or self-realization.[4] This is the ultimate

---

[4] The ultimate goal is God-realization in theistic doctrines; but it, too, is to be achieved, generally speaking, through self-realization.

value; and its conception is quite positive, since it consists not merely in subjugating the lower self, but also in growing into the higher one; it implies also the transcending of the narrow, grooved life and the gaining of a larger, ampler life. This change in the older view of dharma or its transvaluation, viz. that it is a means to moksha, is already made in the Upanishads.[5] But it is not the only means and requires, as indicated by our characterization of the final goal, to be supported by a knowledge of what the higher or true self is. And it cannot be known fully and well, unless it is known in its relation to the rest of reality. This knowledge of the self in relation to its environment, social and physical, represents philosophic truth. Like the good, then, the true also is here conceived as an instrumental value, both alike being means to moksha.[6] The several systems differ in the place they assign to these two means in the scheme of life's discipline. But it will suffice for our purpose to say, following Shankara, that a successful pursuit of the good is required as a condition indispensable for the pursuit of the true.

We have seen that seeking the good is essentially for the purification of character. The search after the true is for removing our ignorance (avidyā) about the ultimate reality, which is the necessary implication of all our efforts to philosophize. But for such ignorance, man's desire to know the nature of reality, which is so natural to him, would be wholly unintelligible. This desire, so far as it is theoretical, is satisfied when we learn the final truth and are intellectually convinced of it. But intellectual conviction is not all that is needed for reaching the goal, since the actual effects of the ignorance are

---

[5] Bridhadāranyaka Upanishad, IV.4.22.

[6] This does not mean that the good and the true should not be pursued for their own sake. What is meant is only that they find their fulfilment in self-realization.

directly experienced by us in daily life and require, if they are to be removed, an equally direct experience of the truth about reality. For example, most of us feel the empirical self to be the true Self, while the fact, according to many of the systems, is that it is not so. But a mere intellectual conviction, which is what is commonly meant by philosophic truth, is scarcely of use in dismissing such beliefs. A perceptual illusion, for instance, is dispelled only by a perceptual experience of the fact underlying the illusion and not, say, by a hearsay knowledge of it. Seeing, as they say, is believing. Hence all the Indian schools prescribe a proper course of practical discipline to bring about this consummation, viz. transforming a mere intellectual conviction into direct experience. The chief element in it is dhyāna or yoga which means learning to steady the mind and, thereafter, constantly dwelling upon the truth, of which one has been intellectually convinced, until it culminates in direct experience. It is then that the aspirant realizes himself and becomes spiritually free.

NATURE OF MOKSHA

What is the exact nature of this ultimate ideal called moksha? It is held by some to be a state of absolute bliss; and by others, as one merely of absence of all pain and suffering. The distinction depends upon a difference in the conception of the self in the various systems. Bliss or joy is intrinsic to it, according to some, and it therefore naturally reveals itself when the self is released from bondage. According to others, neither bliss nor its opposite belongs to the self, and it is therefore without either in the condition of moksha when its true nature is restored to it. Before describing this condition further, it is necessary to refer briefly to an objection that is sure to occur to the reader at the above characterization of moksha in terms of pleasure and absence of pain, viz. that the ideal is hedonistic—a view which is now regarded as psychologically quite faulty. This is an objection which, on a superficial view, applies to the whole of the Indian theory of value; but whatever the answer to that general objection may be, the charge of hedonism does not, in the least, affect the conception of the ultimate value with which we are now concerned. For the pleasure for which it stands should be unmixed, and there should be no lapse from it when it is once attained—conditions which the kind of pleasure the hedonist has in view does not, and is not meant to, satisfy. In fact, moksha means absolute or unconditioned bliss (or, alternatively, absence of suffering), which is vastly different from the pleasure that hedonism holds to be the supreme end of life.

Now to revert to the consideration of the nature of moksha. Shankara has remarked that attaining the goal of life signifies nothing more than perfecting the means to it.[7] That is to say, the end here is not external to the means, but is only the means stabilized. This gives us a clue as regards the kind of life which a knower leads, and enables us thereby to grasp the exact meaning of moksha. We have mentioned two aids to the attainment of the goal, pursuing the good and acquiring a knowledge of the true self. Corresponding to these, the life of the knower, broadly speaking, will be characterized by two features. In the first place, it will be entirely free from the tyranny of the egoistic self, and therefore also free from the feverish activity for gratifying personal desires, which can never be completely gratified. In the second place, it will be marked by an unshakable conviction in the unity of all, and consequently by love for others—love for them, not as equals but as essentially one with oneself. Such love will necessarily

---

[7] See commentary on Bhagavad-Gītā, II.55.

prompt the freed man to work for their good, for while there is nothing that he wants for himself, he sees them immersed in so much ignorance and suffering. No doubt, he was doing unselfish work even before he became free; but that was, more or less, the result of conscious strife. Now it becomes quite spontaneous. This is in monistic schools. In pluralistic systems also, the same will be the case, the only difference being that the enlightened person will help others, prompted by pity or compassion rather than love in the above sense. Thus, whether it be in monistic or pluralistic schools, the knower, after gaining enlightenment and freedom for himself, will strive to spread that enlightenment among others and secure for them the same freedom, so far as it lies in his power. There is in this regard the magnanimous example of Buddha who, we may remark by the way, is only one instance among several that have appeared in the spiritual history of India. Hence, though the final aim of life or the ultimate value is here stated to be self-realization, it is really very much more, for it also signifies doing one's utmost to secure universal good.

We have described the state of moksha from the standpoint of what is called jīvanmukti or "liberation while one is still alive," for it is sure to make a better appeal to the modern mind. This ideal, however, is not accepted in all the systems, but only in some like the Advaita, Sānkhya-yoga, and Buddhism. The others insist that spiritual freedom will not actually be attained until after physical death. It is known as videhamukti. But even these systems may be said to admit jīvanmukti in fact, though not in name, for they postulate final release in the case of an enlightened person as soon as he leaves his physical body, implying thereby that there is nothing more to be done by him for attaining moksha. The distinction between the two views reduces itself finally to whether or not the discipline prescribed for the spiritual aspirant should as such (that is, under a sense of constraint) continue in the interval between the dawn of true knowledge and the moment of physical death. According to those who do not accept the ideal of jīvanmukti, it should continue, while according to the rest, it need not.

INDIAN OPTIMISM

The question that now remains to ask is whether such an ideal can be achieved at all. In one sense, the question is not legitimate, because moksha, standing as it does for a progressive attainment, is being realized at every stage. But it may be taken to mean whether the process of self-realization is an endless one or has a culminating stage; and if it has such a stage, whether it is attainable. All the Indian systems, including the non-Vedic ones, are of opinion that this process is directed to a definite goal, and that that goal can assuredly be achieved. According to them, the evil of samsāra or bondage carries with it the seeds of its own destruction, and it is sooner or later bound to be superseded by the good. In other words, none of the Indian schools is finally pessimistic, and the present-day criticism that they are "gospels of woe" is entirely wrong. We have more than one interesting indication in the Sanskrit language of this faith of the Indian in the ultimate goodness and rationality of the world. The Sanskrit word *sat*, as noticed by Max Müller long ago, means not only "the real" but also "the good." Similarly, the word bhavya, we may add, means not only "what will happen in the future" but also "what is auspicious," implying that the best is yet to be.

Besides the ultimate value of self-realization, we have referred to truth and goodness. But the latter are only two of the three, including beauty, which are now grouped together and are termed the "trinity of values." Aesthetic value, however, is not being treated in the present paper.

S. Radhakrishnan

Mysticism and Ethics in Hindu Thought

Any ethical theory must be grounded in metaphysics, in a philosophical conception of the relation between human conduct and ultimate reality. As we think ultimate reality to be, so we behave. Vision and action go together. If we believe absurdities, we shall commit atrocities. A self-sufficient humanism has its own metaphysical presuppositions. It requires us to confine our attention to the immediate world of space and time and argues that moral duty consists in conforming to nature and modelling our behaviour in accordance with the principles of her working. It attempts to perfect the causes of human life by purely natural means. The subject of ethics is treated as a branch of sociology or a department of psychology. Scientific materialism and mystical nationalism are two types of humanist ethics, interpreted in a narrow sense. They look upon man as a purely natural phenomenon whose outlook is rigorously confined by space and time. They encourage a cynical subservience to nature and historical process and an acquiescence in the merely practicable. Renunciation, self-sacrifice, disinterested service of humanity are not stimulated by the workings of natural law.

An abundance of material things will not help to make life more interesting. The rich of the world are among those who find life stale, flat, and unprofitable. Even the social conscience that urges us to extend the benefits of a material civilization cannot be accounted for by the principles of scientific naturalism. The material basis, while essential, is still too narrow for real living. The collective myths of Nazism, Fascism, and Communism propose to make life seem rich and significant by asking us to banish all considerations of reason and humanity and to worship the State. Man is not merely an emotional being. The Nation-State falls short of the human and the universal and constitutes a deadly menace to the growth of the universal in man which is postulated with increasing force by the advance of science and which the well-being of human society demands.

The question has its centre in the nature of man. Is he only a body which can be fed, clothed, and housed, or is he also a spirit that can aspire? The feeling of frustration experienced even by those who are provided with all the comforts and conveniences which a material civilization can supply indicates that man does not live by bread or emotional excitement alone. Besides, progress is not its own end. If it is the ultimate reality, it cannot ever be completed. We can draw nearer and nearer the goal, but cannot reach it. Its process has neither a beginning nor an end. It starts nowhere and leads nowhere. It has no issue, no goal. Senseless cycles of repetition cannot give meaning to life. It may be argued that, although the universe may have no purpose, items in the universe such as nations and individuals may have their purposes. The rise and fall of nations, the growth and crash of individuals may be quite interesting, and the universe may be viewed as an infinite succession of finite purposes. This cannot be regarded as a satisfactory goal of ethics. Does not the humanist hope to build a terrestrial paradise inhabited by a perfect race of artists and thinkers? What is the good of telling us that though our sun, moon, and stars will share in the destruction of earthly life, other suns, moons, and stars will arise? We long for a good which is never left behind and never superseded. Man's incapacity to be satisfied with what is merely relative and remain permanently within the boundaries of the finite and empirical reality cannot be denied. Man stands before the shrine of his own mystery. He enters it the moment he becomes aware of his own eternity. Apart from eternity there is nothing that can, strictly speaking, be called human. A meaningful ethical ideal must be transcendent to the immediate flow of events.

Again, in view of the enigmatic character of the actual, is moral life possible? There are some thinkers who exhort us to do what is right even though we may not know whether it can be realized or not. Moral enthusiasm is possible only if our motive includes the expectation of being able to contribute to the achievement of moral ideals. If we are not certain that active service of the ideals will further their actualization, we cannot be sure of their worthwhileness.

We cannot help asking ourselves whether our ideals are mere private dreams of our own or bonds created by society, or even aspirations characteristic of the human species. Only a philosophy which affirms that they are rooted in the universal nature of things can give depth and fervour to moral life, courage and confidence in moral difficulties. We need to be fortified by the conviction that the service of the ideals is what the cosmic scheme demands of us, that our loyalty or disloyalty to them is a matter of the deepest moment not only to ourselves or to society, or even to the human species, but to the nature of things. If ethical thought is profound, it will give a cosmic motive to morality. Moral consciousness must include a conviction of the reality of ideals. If the latter is religion, then ethical humanism is acted religion. When man realizes his essential unity with the whole of being, he expresses this unity in his life. Mysticism and ethics, other-worldliness and worldly work go together. In the primitive religions we have this combination. Otherworldliness appears as māna, which the savage derives from an innate sense of some mysterious power within the phenomena and behind the events of the visible world, and morality appears as taboo, and the sense of sacredness in things and persons, which with its inhibitions controls the whole range of his conduct. In the higher religions of mankind, belief in the transcendent and work in the natural have grown together in close intimacy and interaction. Religion is the soul's attitude, response, and adjustment in the presence of the supreme realities of the transcendent order; ethics deal with the right adjustment of life on earth, especially in human society. Both are motived by a desire to live in the light of ideals. If we are satisfied with what exists, there is no meaning in "ought"; if we are a species of passing phenomena, there is no meaning in religion. Religion springs from the conviction that there is another world beyond the visible and the temporal with which man has dealings, and ethics require us to act in this world with the compelling vision of another. With our minds anchored in the beyond we are to strive to make the actual more nearly like what it ought to be. Religion alone can give assurance and wider reference to ethics and a new meaning to human life. We make moral judgments about individual lives and societies simply because we are spiritual beings, not merely social animals.

If there is one doctrine more than another which is characteristic of Hindu thought, it is the belief that there is an interior depth to the human soul, which, in its essence, is uncreated and deathless and absolutely real. The spirit in man is different from the individual ego; it is that which animates and exercises the individual, the vast background of his being in which all individuals lie. It is the core of all being, the inner thread by being strung on which the world exists. In the soul of man are conflicting tendencies: the attraction of the infinite, which abides for ever, changeless, unqualified, untouched by the world; and the fascination of the finite, that which like the wind-beaten surface of the waters is never for a moment the same. Every human being is a potential spirit and represents, as has been well said, a hope of God and is not a mere fortuitous concourse of episodes like the changing forms of clouds or the patterns of a kaleidoscope. If the feeling for God were not in man, we could not implant it any more than we could squeeze blood from a stone. The heart of religion is that man truly belongs to another order, and the meaning of man's life is to be found not in this world but in more than historical reality. His highest aim is release from the historical succession denoted by birth and death. So long as he is lost in the historical process without a realization of the super-historical goal, he is only "once born" and is liable to sorrow. God and not the world of history is the true environment of our souls. If we overlook this important fact, and make ethics or world affirmation independent of religion or world negation, our life and thought become condescending, though this condescension may take the form of social service or philanthropy. But it is essentially a form of self-assertion and not real concern for the well-being of others. If goodwill, pure love, and disinterestedness are our ideals, then our ethics must be rooted in other-worldliness. This is the great classical tradition of spiritual wisdom. The mystery cults of Greece had for their central doctrine that man's soul is of divine origin and is akin to the spirit of God. The influence of these mystery cults on Socrates and Plato is unmistakable. When Jesus tells Nicodemus that until a man is begotten from above he cannot see or enter the Kingdom of God, when Paul declares that "he that soweth to the flesh shall of the flesh reap corruption; but he that soweth to the spirit shall of the spirit reap everlasting life," they are implying that our natural life is mortal and it is invaded by sin and death, and that the life of spirit is immortal. St. John in the First Epistle says: "the world passeth away, and the lust thereof: but he that doeth the will of God abideth for ever." We are amphibious beings, according to Plotinus. We live on earth and in a world of spirit.

Gandhi on His Mission

I do not consider myself worthy to be mentioned in the same breath with the race of prophets. I am a humble seeker after truth. I am impatient to realize myself, to attain moksha in this very existence. My national service is part of my training for freeing my soul from the bondage of flesh. Thus considered, my service may be regarded as purely selfish. I have no desire for the perishable kingdom of earth. I am striving for the Kingdom of Heaven which is moksha. To attain my end it is not necessary for me to seek the shelter of a cave. I carry one about me, if I would but know it. A cave-dweller can build castles in the air whereas a dweller in a palace like Janak has no castles to build. The cave-dweller who hovers round the world on the wings of thought has no peace. A Janak though living in the midst of "pomp and circumstance" may have peace that passeth understanding. For me the road to salvation lies through incessant toil in the service of my country and there-through of humanity. I want to identify myself with everything that lives. In the language of the Gītā I want to live at peace with both friend and foe. Though therefore a Mussulman or a Christian or a Hindu may despise me and hate me, I want to love him and serve him even as I would love my wife or son though they hate me. So my patriotism is for me a stage in my journey to the land of eternal freedom and peace. Thus it will be seen that for me there are no politics devoid of religion. They subserve religion. Politics bereft of religion are a death-trap because they kill the soul.

Radhakrishnan on Dharma

Dharma is a word of protean significance. It is derived from the root dhr (to uphold, to sustain, to nourish). It is the norm which sustains the universe, the principle of a thing in virtue of which it is what it is. In the Vedas, it is used to denote religious rites. The Chandogya Upanishad speaks of the three branches of the dharma, relating to the duties of the householder, the hermit and the student. When the Tattiriya Upanishad asks us to practice dharma, it refers to the duties of the stage of life to which we belong. In this sense it is employed by the Bhagavad-Gītā and Manu. It is, for the Buddhist, one of the three jewels (triratna), along with the Buddha and the sangha or the community. According to the Purva Mimamsa, it is a desirable object defined by a direction. The *Vaishesika Sutra* defines dharma as that from which happiness and beatitude result. For our purposes, we may define dharma as the whole duty of man in relation to the fourfold purposes of life (dharma, artha, kāma and moksha) by members of the four groups (caturvarna) and the four stages (caturashrama). While the supreme aim of social order is to train human beings for a state of spiritual perfection and sanctity, its essential aim is directed, by reason of its temporal ends, towards such a development of social conditions as will lead the mass of people to a level of moral, material and intellectual life in accord with the good and peace of all, as these conditions assist each person in the progressive realization of his life and liberty.

Sri Aurobindo on Dharma

Dharma is both that which we hold to and that which holds together our inner and outer activities. In its primary sense it means a fundamental law of our nature which secretly conditions all our activities, and in this sense each being, type, species, individual group has its own dharma. Secondly, there is the divine nature which has to develop and manifest in us, and in this sense dharma is the law of the inner workings by which that grows in our being. Thirdly, there is the law by which we govern our outgoing thought and action and our relations with each other so as to help best both our own growth and that of the human race towards the divine ideal.

Radhakrishnan on Religion

Religion is not so much a revelation to be attained by us in faith as an effort to unveil the deepest layers of man's being and get into enduring contact with them.

Muhammad Iqbal,
"Your Own Heart Is Your Candle"

All creatures yearn for Self-hood freed:
To bloom is every atom's greed!
Life without self-fruition—death;
Who builds the Self, him the gods speed.
The mustard-seed grows to a hill
With it: without, the hill a seed.
The stars stumble and do not meet—
To all being, severance is decreed;
Pale is the moon of night's last hour
No interclasps of friendship feed.
Your own heart is your candle: you
Yourself are all the light you need;
You are the sole truth of this world,
All else some conjuror's passes breed.
The thorns of the desert bring forth knowledge:
Lament no more, if your feet bleed.

Muhammad Iqbal, "A New Shrine"

I'll tell you truth, O Brahmin, if I may make so bold:
These idols in your temples—these idols have grown old.
From them you have learned hatred of those who share
   your life,
An Allah to *His* preachers has taught mistrust and strife;
Disgusted, from your temple and our shrine I have run,
Now both our preachers' sermons and your old myths I
   shun.
In shapes of stone you fancied God's dwelling-place: I see
In each speck of my country's poor dust, a deity.
Come, let us lift this curtain of alien thoughts again,
And reunite the severed, and wipe division's stain:
Too long has lain deserted the heart's warm habitation;
Let us build in this homeland a new temple's foundation!
And let our shrine be taller than all shrines of this globe,
With lofty pinnacles touching the skirts of heaven's robe;
And there at every sunrise let our sweet chanting move
The hearts of all who worship, and pour the wine of love;
Strength and peace too shall blend in the hymns the
   votary sings—
For in love lies salvation to all earth's living things.

Karma-yoga

Introduction

As the frail, determined Mahatma trekked along the dusty roads of rural India, he was sustained by his belief in the saving power of selfless action as taught in the Bhagavad-Gītā:

> I find a solace in the Bhagavad-Gītā that I miss even in the Sermon on the Mount. When disappointment stares me in the face and all alone I see not one ray of light, I go back to the Bhagavad-Gītā. I find a verse here and a verse there and I immediately begin to smile in the midst of overwhelming tragedies—and my life has been full of external tragedies—and if they have left no visible, no indelible scar on me, I owe it all to the teachings of the Bhagavad-Gītā.[1]

The ability to endure disappointment is precisely what Arjuna learned from Krishna; truly selfless action removes the pain of tragedy—or makes all tragedy external—by removing the ego-involvement in the fruits of action.

In response to Arjuna's refusal to act in accordance with his caste duty (varna-dharma), Krishna first establishes the true meaning of action (karma-yoga) and then places karma-yoga in relation to bhakti. The initial problem, which is essentially an ethical dilemma, is solved in the third chapter, verses 4, 8, 9:

[1] M. K. Gandhi, *Young India* (1925), pp. 1078–79.

Not by abstention from actions does a man gain freedom, and not by mere renunciation does he attain perfection.

Perform thy alloted work, for action is superior to inaction; even the maintenance of thy body cannot be accomplished without action.

This world is in bondage to karma, unless it is performed for the sake of sacrifice. For the sake of that, O son of Kunti, perform thy action free from attachment.

Ultimately, however, action for the sake of sacrifice should be performed in devotion to Krishna. In this respect, karma-yoga presupposes bhakti; selfless action is a way to liberation precisely because Krishna, the avatar who "comes into being age after age for the establishment of dharma," [2] uses such action for his divine purpose. Thus, the man of ritual action, the man whose action expresses the divine will, is closer to perfection than either the ascetic or the wise man:

And of all yogins, the one who, full of faith, worships Me with his inner self abiding in Me, he is thought by Me to be the most disciplined. [3]

The preeminence of bhakti-yoga, however, is a poor basis on which to build a social and political revolution. While karma-yoga is clearly affirmed in the Gītā, the historical exigencies of modern India called for a dramatic recovery of the values associated with karma-yoga. Modern interpreters, especially those involved in the Independence Movement, have emphasized the ideal of action not only as an antidote to the nonhistorical and quietist aspects of the Indian religious and philosophical traditions, but also as a positive spur to national resurgence.

[2] Bhagavad-Gītā, IV, 8.
[3] *Ibid.*, VI, 47.

Although Gandhi did not begin working in India until 1914, his interpretation of the Gītā had a fixed angle more than two decades earlier. Writing in a 1931 issue of *Young India*, Gandhi explained:

> Even in 1888–89, when I first became acquainted with the Gītā, I felt that it was not a historical work, but that, under the guise of physical warfare, it described the duel that perpetually went on in the hearts of mankind, and that physical warfare was brought in merely to make the description of the internal duel more alluring. This preliminary intuition became more confirmed on a closer study of religion and the Gītā.

Gandhi's well-known affinity with the Gītā was due at least in part to its practical advice concerning the national struggle in which he and his countrymen were engaged throughout the last three decades of his life. According to Gandhi, the Indian Nationalist Movement was as much an internal or spiritual problem as a social or political problem. The Gītā expressed this truth for Gandhi by showing that the historical crisis which triggered Arjuna's dilemma was actually a crisis of Arjuna's interior life:

> The fight is there, but the fight as it is going on within. The Pandavas and the Kauravas are the forces of good and evil within. The war is the war between Jekyll and Hyde, God and Satan, going on in the human breast. The internal evidence in support of this interpretation is there in the work itself and in the Mahābhārata of which the Gītā is a minute part. It is not a history of war between two families, but the history of man—the history of the spiritual struggle of man.[4]

Then, in a passage which is more descriptive of his own moral

[4] M. K. Gandhi, *Hindu Dharma*, Ahmedabad: Navajivan Publishing House, 1950, pp. 158–59.

philosophy than of the Gītā, Gandhi argues that the central teaching of the Gītā is the renunciation of the fruits of action, "but renunciation of fruit in no way means indifference to the result." [5] For Gandhi, any result that involved violence would be incompatible with the renunciation of the fruit of action; indeed, the desire for fruit is the root cause of untruth and himsā (violence).[6] Reluctantly granting that "according to the letter of the Gītā it is possible to say that warfare is consistent with renunciation of fruit," Gandhi nevertheless concludes:

> After forty years' unremitting endeavor fully to enforce the teaching of the Gītā in my own life, I have, in all humility, felt that perfect reverence is impossible without perfect observance of ahimsā in every shape and form.[7]

Gandhi's novel claim that the Gītā essentially teaches ahimsā was of course frequently contested; in response to one critic, Gandhi explained that "the question put is eternal and everyone who has studied the Gītā must needs find out his own solution." [8] Gandhi's solution, which emerged during fifty years of "experimenting with truth," is outlined in the three selections in this chapter.

When Gandhi renders God, Love, and Truth as interchangeable terms, he is not so much offering a philosophical definition as emphasizing the unity of the social, moral, and spiritual aspects of life and thought. One could argue that Gandhi is simply spinning out analytic or tautological statements, or that he is simply expressing a feeling for these terms.

[5] M. K. Gandhi, in Mahadev Desai, ed., trans., *The Gospel of Selfless Action or the Gītā according to Gandhi*, Ahmedabad: Navajivan Publishing House, 1946, p. 131.

[6] *Ibid.*, p. 132.

[7] *Ibid.*, pp. 133–34.

[8] *Hindu Dharma*, p. 133.

To Gandhi, such a criticism misses the larger truth of experience—namely, that years of selfless activity reveal the unity of the search for God, Truth, and Love. According to Gandhi's method, a genuine search for truth must be based on humility and discipline. In this he follows the standard Indian theory of yoga which is based on vairagya (nonattachment) and abhyāsa (constant practice). This combination, rather than a theory or belief, will yield the experience of God, Truth, and Love.

According to Gandhi's experiment on selfless and nonviolent action, the means or method of an action is identical with the end or result of an action. In the Nationalist Movement, for example, the proper means had to be nonviolent resistance if the result was to be a peaceful and worthy achievement. Using violent means to achieve independence would leave India violent, and consequently as bound spiritually as it had been politically and economically. An independence won by—and limited by—violence would be as different from an independence peacefully won as war is from peace. A violent means will yield a violent result, or the need for more violence; a nonviolent means, on the other hand, will eventually lead to complete nonviolence.

The identity of means and ends applies to all human actions, but Gandhi believes that its most significant instance is the case of nonviolence (or ahimsā). In his question-and-answer session in Europe in 1931, Gandhi defended nonviolence as a means-ends of absolute value—more valuable than the survival of the state or its citizens. Like Bertrand Russell, who proposed in 1915 that England should disarm and refuse to resist an armed invasion, no matter how barbarous, Gandhi contends that people should allow themselves to be annihilated rather than resist by violence. The end in this dramatic case is the transformation of both parties; Gandhi argues that by this courageous and virtuous means, sacrificial agents would advance humanity one step closer to the point at which the cycle of violence would be ended.

Gandhi's insistence on nonviolence in the face of an enemy attack well reveals his philosophy of nonviolence and his hope for humanity. Both Gandhi and Vinoba Bhave insist, however, that the true meaning of karma-yoga is in the struggle of daily life. The Gandhian tradition requires constant discipline; individuals can nonviolently withstand attacks on mind and body only to the extent that they have gained control of their own egoistic desires. In this sense, karma-yoga is the discipline, or means-end, of replacing individual preferences by objective needs. The karma-yogin acts according to what needs to be done, not what he or she happens to want. When Krishna, as avatar, enters the human arena to restore order (dharma), he acts as a karma-yogin: he continues in action because others need him to do so. The result for the karma-yogin is the bliss of Krishna, the bliss of a complete and perfectly satisfied being. The karma-yogin both serves as a model of the highest ideal—whether love, selflessness, or nonattachment—and produces the most beneficial results for all concerned.

Since an ethical principle can always be bent to serve one's selfish interest, the ideal of the karma-yogin certainly does not solve the problem of ethical conduct. But when coupled with or embodied in the example of inspiring individuals like Gandhi and Bhave, this ideal gains considerable force as a guide for moral action. In theoretical terms, the ideal of karma-yoga resembles Kant's categorical imperative, but when backed by the lifelong and dramatic example of Gandhi, Bhave, and other great souls of modern India, it more closely resembles the ideal of love depicted in the Christian gospels.

Mohandas K. Gandhi

Truth and God

[Replying to a question asked of him at a meeting in Switzerland on his way back from the Round Table Conference in London, 1931, Gandhiji said:]

You have asked me why I consider that God is Truth. In my early youth I was taught to repeat what in Hindu scriptures are known as one thousand names of God. But these one thousand names of God were by no means exhaustive. We believe—and I think it is the truth—that God has as many names as there are creatures and, therefore, we also say that God is nameless and since God has many forms we also consider Him formless, and since He speaks to us through many tongues we consider Him to be speechless and so on. And so when I came to study Islam I found that Islam too had many names for God. I would say with those who say God is Love, God is Love. But deep down in me I used to say that though God may be Love, God is Truth, above all. If it is possible for the human tongue to give the fullest description of

God, I have come to the conclusion that for myself, God is Truth. But two years ago I went a step further and said that Truth is God. You will see the fine distinction between the two statements, viz. that God is Truth and Truth is God. And I came to that conclusion after a continuous and relentless search after Truth which began nearly fifty years ago. I then found that the nearest approach to Truth was through love. But I also found that love has many meanings in the English language at least and that human love in the sense of passion could become a degrading thing also. I found too that love in the sense of ahimsā had only a limited number of votaries in the world. But I never found a double meaning in connection with truth and even atheists had not demurred to the necessity or power of Truth. But in their passion for discovering truth the atheists have not hesitated to deny the very existence of God—from their own point of view rightly. And it was because of this reasoning that I saw that rather than say that God is Truth I should say that Truth is God. I recall the name of Charles Bradlaugh who delighted to call himself an atheist, but knowing as I do something of him, I would never regard him as an atheist. I would call him a God-fearing man, though I know that he would reject the claim. His face would redden if I would say "Mr. Bradlaugh, you are a truth-fearing man, and so a God-fearing man." I would automatically disarm his criticism by saying that Truth is God, as I have disarmed criticisms of many a young man. Add to this the great difficulty that millions have taken the name of God and in His name committed nameless atrocities. Not that scientists very often do not commit cruelties in the name of truth. I know how in the name of truth and science inhuman cruelties are perpetrated on animals when men perform vivisection. There are thus a number of difficulties in the way, no matter how you describe God. But the human mind is a limited thing, and you have to labour under limitations when you think of a being or entity who is beyond the power of man to grasp.

And then we have another thing in Hindu philosophy, viz. God alone is and nothing else exists, and the same truth you find emphasized and exemplified in the Kalma of Islam. There you find it clearly stated—that God alone is and nothing else exists. In fact the Sanskrit word for Truth is a word which literally means that which exists—Sat. For these and several other reasons that I can give you I have come to the conclusion that the definition, "Truth is God," gives me the greatest satisfaction. And when you want to find Truth as God the only inevitable means is Love, i.e. non-violence, and since I believe that ultimately the means and the end are convertible terms, I should not hesitate to say that God is Love.

"What then is Truth?"

A difficult question [said Gandhiji], but I have solved it for myself by saying that it is what the voice within tells you. How, then, you ask, different people think of different and contrary truths? Well, seeing that the human mind works through innumerable media and that the evolution of the human mind is not the same for all, it follows that what may be truth for one may be untruth for another, and hence those who have made these experiments have come to the conclusion that there are certain conditions to be observed in making those experiments. Just as for conducting scientific experiments there is an indispensable scientific course of instruction, in the same way strict preliminary discipline is necessary to qualify a person to make experiments in the spiritual realm. Every one should, therefore, realize his limitations before he speaks of his inner voice. Therefore we have the belief based upon experience, that those who would make individual search after truth as God, must go through several vows, as for instance, the vow of truth, the vow of brahmacharya (purity)—for you cannot possibly divide your love for Truth and God with anything else—the vow of non-violence, of poverty and non-possession. Unless you impose on yourselves the five vows you may not embark on the experiment at all. There are several other conditions prescribed, but I must not take you through all of them. Suffice it to say that those who have made these experiments know that it is not proper for every one to claim to hear the voice of conscience, and it is because we have at the present moment everybody claiming the right of conscience without going through any discipline whatsoever and there is so much untruth being delivered to a bewildered world, all that I can, in true humility, present to you is that truth is not to be found by anybody who has not got an abundant sense of humility. If you would swim on the bosom of the ocean of Truth you must reduce yourself to a zero. Further than this I cannot go along this fascinating path.

First appeared in *Young India* on December 31, 1931.

Means and Ends

Reader: Why should we not obtain our goal, which is good, by any means whatsoever, even by using violence? Shall I think of the means when I have to deal with a thief in the house? My duty is to drive him out anyhow. You seem to admit that we have received nothing, and that we shall receive nothing by petitioning. Why, then, may we not do so by using brute force? And, to retain what we may receive we shall keep up the fear by using the same force to the extent that it may be necessary. You will not find fault with a continuance of force to prevent a child from thrusting its foot into fire? Somehow or other we have to gain our end.

Editor: Your reasoning is plausible. It has deluded many. I have used similar arguments before now. But I think I know better now, and I shall endeavour to undeceive you. Let us first take the argument that we are justified in gaining our end by using brute force because the English gained theirs by using similar means. It is perfectly true that they used brute force and that it is possible for us to do likewise, but by using similar means we can get only the same thing that they got. You will admit that we do not want that. Your belief that there is no connection between the means and the end is a great mistake. Through that mistake even men who have been considered religious have committed grievous crimes. Your reasoning is the same as saying that we can get a rose through planting a noxious weed. If I want to cross the ocean, I can do so only by means of a vessel; if I were to use a cart for that purpose, both the cart and I would soon find the bottom. "As is the God, so is the votary," is a maxim worth considering. Its meaning has been distorted and men have gone astray. The means may be likened to a seed, the end to a tree; and there is just the same inviolable connection between the means and the end as there is between the seed and the tree. I am not likely to obtain the result flowing from the worship of God by laying myself prostrate before Satan. If, therefore, any one were to say: "I want to worship God; it does not matter that I do so by means of Satan," it would be set down as ignorant folly. We reap exactly as we sow. The English in 1833 obtained greater voting power by violence. Did they by using brute force better appreciate their duty? They wanted the right of voting, which they obtained by using physical force. But real rights are a result of performance of duty; these rights they have not obtained. We, therefore, have before us in England the force of everybody wanting and insisting on his rights, nobody thinking of his duty. And, where everybody wants rights, who shall give them to whom? I do not wish to imply that they do no duties. They don't perform the duties corresponding to those rights; and as they do not perform that particular duty, namely, acquire fitness, their rights have proved a burden to them. In other words, what they have obtained is an exact result of the means they adopted. They used the means corresponding to the end. If I want to deprive you of your watch, I shall certainly have to fight for it; if I want to buy your watch, I shall have to pay for it; and if I want a gift, I shall have to plead for it; and, according to the means I employ, the watch is stolen property, my own property, or a donation. Thus we see three different results from three different means. Will you still say that means do not matter?

Now we shall take the example given by you of the thief to be driven out. I do not agree with you that the thief may be driven out by any means. If it is my father who has come to steal I shall use one kind of means. If it is an acquaintance I shall use another; and in the case of a perfect stranger I shall use a third. If it is a white man, you will perhaps say you will use means different from those you will adopt with an Indian thief. If it is a weakling, the means will be different from those to be adopted for dealing with an equal in physical strength; and if the thief is armed from top to toe, I shall simply remain quiet. Thus we have a variety of means between the father and the armed man. Again, I fancy that I should pretend to be sleeping whether the thief was my father or that strong armed man. The reason for this is that my father would also be armed and I should succumb to the strength possessed by either and allow my things to be stolen. The strength of my father would make me weep with pity; the strength of the armed man would rouse in me anger and we should become enemies. Such is the curious situation. From these examples we may not be able to agree as to the means to be adopted in each case. I myself seem clearly to see what should be done in all these cases, but the remedy may frighten you. I therefore hesitate to place it before you. For the time being I will leave you to guess it, and if you cannot, it is clear you will have to adopt different means in each case. You will also have seen that any means will not avail to drive away the thief. You will have to adopt means to fit each case. Hence it follows that your duty is not to drive away the thief by any means you like.

Let us proceed a little further. That well-armed man has stolen your property; you have harboured the thought of his act; you are filled with anger; you argue that you want to punish that rogue, not for your own sake, but for the good of your neighbours; you have collected a number of armed men, you want to take his house by assault; he is duly informed of it, he runs away; he too is incensed. He collects his brother robbers, and sends you a defiant message that he will commit robbery in broad daylight. You are strong, you do not fear him, you are prepared to receive him. Meanwhile, the robber pesters your neighbours. They complain before you. You reply that you are doing all for their sake, you do not mind that your own goods have been stolen. Your neighbours reply that the robber never pestered them before, and that he commenced his depredations only after you declared hostilities against him. You are between Scylla and Charybdis. You are full of pity for the poor men. What they say is true. What are you to do? You will be disgraced if you now leave the robber alone. You therefore, tell the poor men: "Never mind. Come, my wealth is yours, I will give you arms, I will teach you how to use them; you should belabour the rogue; don't you leave him alone." And so the battle grows; the robbers increase in numbers; your neighbours have deliberately put themselves to inconvenience. Thus the result of wanting to take revenge upon the robber is that you have disturbed your own peace; you are in perpetual fear of being robbed and assaulted; your courage has given place to cowardice. If you will patiently examine the argument, you will see that I have not overdrawn the picture. This is one of the means. Now let us examine the other. You set this armed robber down as an ignorant brother; you intend to reason with him at a suitable opportunity; you argue that he is, after all, a fellow man; you do not know what prompted him to steal. You, therefore, decide that, when you can, you will destroy the man's motive for stealing. Whilst you are thus reasoning with yourself, the man comes again to steal. Instead of being angry with him you take pity on him. You think that this stealing habit must be a disease with him. Henceforth, you, therefore, keep your doors and windows open, you change your sleeping-place, and you keep your things in a manner most accessible to him. The robber comes again and is confused as all this is new to him; nevertheless, he takes away your things. But his mind is agitated. He inquires about you in the village, he comes to learn about your broad and loving heart, he repents, he begs your pardon, returns you your things, and leaves off the stealing habit. He becomes your servant, and you will find for him honourable employment. This is the second method. Thus, you see, different means have brought about totally different results. I do not wish to deduce from this that robbers will act in the above manner or that all will have the same pity and love like you, but I only wish to show that fair means alone can produce fair results, and that, at least in the majority of cases, if not indeed in all, the force of love and pity is infinitely greater than the force of arms. There is harm in the exercise of brute force, never in that of pity.

Now we will take the question of petitioning. It is a fact

beyond dispute that a petition, without the backing of force, is useless. However, the late Justice Ranade used to say that petitions served a useful purpose because they were a means of educating people. They give the latter an idea of their condition and warn the rulers. From this point of view, they are not altogether useless. A petition of an equal is a sign of courtesy; a petition from a slave is a symbol of his slavery. A petition backed by force is a petition from an equal and, when he transmits his demand in the form of a petition, it testifies to his nobility. Two kinds of force can back petitions. "We shall hurt you if you do not give this," is one kind of force; it is the force of arms, whose evil results we have already examined. The second kind of force can thus be stated: "If you do not concede our demand, we shall be no longer your petitioners. You can govern us only so long as we remain the governed; we shall no longer have any dealings with you." The force implied in this may be described as love-force, soul-force, or, more popularly but less accurately, passive resistance.[1] This force is indestructible. He who uses it perfectly understands his position. We have an ancient proverb which literally means: "One negative cures thirty-six diseases." The force of arms is powerless when matched against the force of love or the soul.

Now we shall take your last illustration, that of the child thrusting its foot into fire. It will not avail you. What do you really do to the child? Supposing that it can exert so much physical force that it renders you powerless and rushes into fire, then you cannot prevent it. There are only two remedies open to you—either you must kill it in order to prevent it from perishing in the flames, or you must give your own life because you do not wish to see it perish before your very eyes. You

[1] Finding the word misleading, Gandhiji later called the same force Satyagraha or nonviolent resistance.—Ed.

will not kill it. If your heart is not quite full of pity, it is possible that you will not surrender yourself by preceding the child and going into the fire yourself. You, therefore, helplessly allow it to go to the flames. Thus, at any rate, you are not using physical force. I hope you will not consider that it is still physical force, though of a low order, when you would forcibly prevent the child from rushing towards the fire if you could. That force is of a different order and we have to understand what it is.

Remember that, in thus preventing the child, you are minding entirely its own interest, you are exercising authority for its sole benefit. Your example does not apply to the English. In using brute force against the English, you consult entirely your own, that is the national, interest. There is no question here either of pity or of love. If you say that the actions of the English, being evil, represent fire, and that they proceed to their actions through ignorance, and that therefore they occupy the position of a child and that you want to protect such a child, then you will have to overtake every evil action of that kind by whomsoever committed and, as in the case of the evil child, you will have to sacrifice yourself. If you are capable of such immeasurable pity, I wish you well in its exercise.

On Non-Violence

QUESTIONS IN PARIS AND GENEVA

"In the method we are adopting in India, fraud, lying, deceit and all the ugly brood of violence and untruth have absolutely no room. Everything is done openly and above board, for truth hates secrecy. The more open you are, the more truthful you are likely to be. There is no such thing as defeat or despair in the dictionary of a man who bases his life on truth and non-violence. And yet the method of non-violence is not in any shape or form a passive or inactive method. It is essentially an active movement, much more active than the one involving the use of sanguinary weapons. Truth and non-violence are perhaps the activest forces you have in the world. A man who wields sanguinary weapons and is intent upon destroying those whom he considers his enemies, does at least require some rest and has to lay down his arms for a while in every twenty-four hours. He is, therefore, essentially inactive, for a certain part of the day. Not so the votary of truth and non-violence, for the simple reason that they are not external weapons. They reside in the human breast and they are actively working their way whether you are awake or whether you are asleep, whether you are walking leisurely or playing an active game. The panoplied warrior of truth and non-violence is ever and incessantly active."

"How then can one be effectively non-violent? By simply refusing to take up arms?"

"I would say that merely to refuse military service is not enough. To refuse to render military service when the particular time arrives is to do the thing after all the time for combating the evil is practically gone. Military service is only a symptom of the disease which is deeper. I suggest to you that those who are not on the register of military service are equally participating in the crime if they support the State otherwise. He or she who supports a State organized in the military way—whether directly or indirectly—participates in the sin. Each man old or young takes part in the sin by contributing to the maintenance of the State by paying taxes. That is why I said to myself during the war that so long as I ate wheat supported by the army whilst I was doing everything short of being a soldier, it was best for me to enlist in the army and be shot; otherwise I should retire to the mountains and eat food grown by nature. Therefore, all those who want to stop military service can do so by withdrawing all co-operation. Refusal of military service is much more superficial than non-co-operation with the whole system which supports the State. But then one's opposition becomes so swift and so effective that you run the risk of not only being marched to jail, but of being thrown into the streets."

"Then may not one accept the non-military services of the State?"

"Now," said Gandhiji, "you have touched the tenderest spot in human nature. I was faced with the very question as author of the non-co-operation movement. I said to myself, there is no State either run by Nero or Mussolini which has not good points about it, but we have to reject the whole, once we decide to non-co-operate with the system. There are in our country grand public roads, and palatial educational institutions, said I to myself, but they are part of a system which crushes the nation. I should not have anything to do with them. They are like the fabled snake with a brilliant jewel on its head, but which has fangs full of poison. So I came to the conclusion that the British rule in India had crushed the spirit of the nation and stunted its growth, and so I decided to deny myself all the privileges—services, courts, titles. The policy would vary with different countries but sacrifice and self-denial are essential."

"But is there not a big difference between an independent nation and a subject nation? India may have a fundamental quarrel with an alien Government, but how can the Swiss quarrel with their State?"

"Difference there undoubtedly is," said Gandhiji. "As a

member of a subject nation I could best help by shaking myself rid of my subjection. But here I am asked as to how best to get out of a military mentality. You are enjoying your amenities on condition that you render military service to the State. There you have to get the State rid of its military mentality."

In answer to a similar question at another meeting Gandhiji said: "Non-co-operation in military service and service in non-military matters are not compatible. Definitely military service is an ill-chosen word. You are all the while giving military service by deputy because you are supporting a State which is based on military service. In Transvaal and other countries some are debarred from military service, but they have to pay money to the State. You will have to extend the scope of non-co-operation to your taxes."

"How could a disarmed neutral country allow other nations to be destroyed? But for our army which was waiting ready at our frontier during the last war we should have been ruined."

"At the risk of being considered a visionary or a fool I must answer this question in the only manner I know. It would be cowardly of a neutral country to allow an army to devastate a neighbouring country. But there are two ways in common between soldiers of war and soldiers of non-violence, and if I had been a citizen of Switzerland and a President of the Federal State what I would have done would be to refuse passage to the invading army by refusing all supplies. Secondly, by re-enacting a Thermopylae in Switzerland, you would have presented a living wall of men and women and children and invited the invaders to walk over your corpses. You may say that such a thing is beyond human experience and endurance. I say that it is not so. It was quite possible. Last year in Gujarat women stood lathi charges unflinchingly and in Peshawar thousands stood hails of bullets without resorting to violence. Imagine these men and women staying in front of an army requiring a safe passage to another country. The army would be brutal enough to walk over them, you might say. I would then say you will have done your duty by allowing yourself to be annihilated. An army that dares to pass over the corpses of innocent men and women would not be able to repeat that experiment. You may, if you wish, refuse to believe in such courage on the part of the masses of men and women, but then you would have to admit that non-violence is made of sterner stuff. It was never conceived as a weapon of the weak, but of the stoutest hearts."

"Is it open to a soldier to fire in the air and avoid violence?"

"A soldier who having enlisted himself flattered himself that he was avoiding violence by shooting in the air did no credit to his courage or to his creed of non-violence. In my scheme of things such a man would be held to be guilty of untruth and cowardice both—cowardice in that in order to escape punishment he enlisted, and untruth in that he enlisted to serve as soldier and did not fire as expected. Such a thing discredits the cause of waging war against war. The War Resisters have to be like Caesar's wife—above suspicion. Their strength lies in absolute adherence to the morality of the question."

First appeared in *Young India* on December 31, 1931.

Vinoba Bhave

The Yoga of Action

THE INFINITE GAINS OF RENUNCIATION OF FRUIT

Brothers, in the Second Chapter, we glanced over the whole of the philosophy of life. Now, in the Third Chapter, we shall explain this philosophy more clearly. We began by considering principles; now we shall go into detail. In the previous Chapter we discussed karma-yoga (the way of action). The great thing in karma-yoga is giving up the fruit of one's actions. Yes, in karma-yoga one surrenders the fruit; but the question arises: Does the fruit come to one, nevertheless, or does it not? Thus the Third Chapter says that the karma-yogi, by giving up the fruit of his action, does not lose it, but paradoxically enough gains it in infinite measure.

Here one is reminded of the story of Lakshmi (the goddess of prosperity). It was her svayamvara (the day when she was to choose her husband). All the devas and danavas had come with hopes raised high; Lakshmi had not proclaimed her vow before. She came into the assembly and said, "I shall garland only the man who has no desire for me." But then, they were all greedy people. So Lakshmi began to search for the desireless one whom she could choose. Now there appeared before her the form of Lord Vishnu lying peacefully on the serpent, Sesha. She put the wedding garland round His neck and to this day she sits there, stroking His feet. Ramaa (the goddess of beauty) becomes the slave of him who does not hanker after her. That is the wonder of it.

The ordinary man puts up a bristling hedge around his fruits; but by doing so, he loses the infinite fruit that should have been his. The worldly man, after endless toil, receives a small reward; but the karma-yogi, though he may do little, receives immense benefit. The difference is due only to a bhavana (an inward attitude). Tolstoy says somewhere: People talk a lot about the sacrifice of Jesus Christ; but no one knows how much the worldly man runs about every day of his life and grows dry within! He carries on his back the burden of two donkeys and capers about. Is not his suffering much greater, his plight far worse, than Jesus Christ's?

The worldly people also do much penance; but it is in pursuit of low aims. We reap what we sow; as is the desire, so is the fruit. The world will not pay more for our wares than the price we ourselves mark on them. Sudama went to the Lord Krishna with a gift of flattened rice. The handful of rice may not be worth even a pie, but to Sudama it seemed beyond price, for his devotion went with it. It was charmed rice. Every grain of it was charged with his love. However cheap a thing may be, the mantra, the charm, increases its value, its power. What, after all, is the weight of a currency note? If we burn it, we might, perhaps, be able to warm a drop of water. But the stamp on it gives it its value.

This is the whole beauty of karma-yoga also. Action is like the currency note. Its value is that of the *bhavana* (the feeling behind it), the stamp it bears, not that of the karma or outward action, the piece of paper. In a way, what I am telling you is the secret of image-worship itself. There is great beauty in the idea of worshipping an image. Who can break this image? This image, in the beginning, was merely a piece of stone. I put life into it. I filled it with my bhavana, my feeling. How can anyone destroy my feeling? Stones can be smashed, but not feelings. When I withdraw my feelings from the image, then what remains will be mere stone; a thing which anyone can break to pieces.

In other words, then, action is a piece of stone, or a piece of paper. My mother scribbled three or four lines on a piece of paper and sent it off to me; another gentleman sent me a long discursive fifty-page letter. Now, which is more weighty? But the feeling in my mother's few lines is beyond measure; it is sacred. The other stuff cannot stand comparison with it. Action must be moistened with love, filled with feeling (bhavana). We set a price on the labourer's work, and pay him his due wages. But a ritual gift (dakshina) is not given like that. One sprinkles water on the dakshina, before giving it away.

Here, one does not ask how much is given. The important question is whether it was moistened or not—whether there was love in it or not. There is an entertaining passage in the Manusmrti. A student lived twelve years in his Master's house. He went there an animal, and came out a man. Now what fee was he to give his Master? In olden days, the fees were not collected in advance. After studying for twelve years, one gave the teacher what was proper. Manu says, "Give the Master one or two leaves and flowers, a fan or a pair of sandals, or a water-pot." Don't think this is a joke; for whatever is to be given, should be given with the knowledge that it is a symbol of faith. What, after all, is the weight of a flower? But in the eyes of devotion, it is equal to all creation. "With a single leaf of tulasi, Rukmini weighed Giridhar, the Lord who lifted up a mountain." Satyabhama's ponderous jewellery was of no avail. But when mother Rukmini laid a tulasi leaf, filled with devotion, on the scale, the thing was done. The tulasi leaf was charged with magic. It was no longer a common leaf. This is true of the action of the karma-yogi too.

Suppose two men go for a bath in the Ganga. One of them says, "What is this Ganga that people talk so much about? Take two parts of hydrogen and one of oxygen; combine the two gases—it becomes Ganga. What else is there in the Ganga?" The other says, "The Ganga flows from the lovely lotus-feet of Lord Vishnu. She has dwelt in the matted hair of Shiva. Thousands of seers, both ascetic and kingly, have done penance near her. Countless holy acts have been performed by her side. Such is the sacred Ganga, my mother." Filled with this bhavana (feeling), he bathes in the river. The oxygen-hydrogen-wallah also bathes. Both derive the benefit of physical cleansing. But the devotee (bhakta) gets the benefit of mental purification as well. Even a buffalo, if it bathes in the Ganga, will achieve physical cleanliness. The dirt of the body will go. But how wash the mind of its taint? One got the slight benefit of physical cleanliness; the other, in addition, gained the invaluable fruit of inward purity.

When, after bathing, a man performs Suryanamaskar (a strenuous form of Sun worship), he will, of course, get the benefit of physical exercise. It is not for the sake of bodily health that he performs Suryanamaskar, but he does it as worship (upasana). Of course he gains good health, but the brightness of his intellect also increases. While he grows healthier, God as the Sun (Suryanarayan) also grants him greater awareness and imaginative power.

The action is the same; but a distinction arises from the difference in bhavana (in the inward attitude). The action of the man who seeks spiritual good opens out the soul; the action of the worldly man serves to bind it. If the karma-yogi is a farmer, he will till the land, considering it his svadharma. His stomach will of course be filled; but he does not work for filling his stomach. He looks upon food as a means by which he keeps his body fit for the task of tilling the land. The end is svadharma and food is the means. But to the farmer who is not a karma-yogi, filling his stomach is the end, and his svadharma, farming, is the means. The two attitudes are thus opposed to each other.

In describing the qualities of the sthitaprajna (the steadfast seer) in the Second Chapter, this distinction has been brought out in a striking way. When others are awake, the karma-yogi is asleep; and when others are asleep, the karma-yogi is awake. Just as we take good care to keep our stomach filled, the karma-yogi is watchful lest even one moment should slip past without action. If he too eats, it is out of necessity. Because there is no help for it, he puts some food into his stomach. The worldly man finds joy in eating; the yogi finds it a hardship. So he does not take pleasure in every morsel, as he tastes it. He eats with self-restraint. The night of the one is the day of the other; and the day of the one is the night of the other. In other words, the thing in which one finds joy, in it the other finds pain, and vice versa. Though the actions of the worldly man and the karma-yogi look alike, the karma-yogi's distinction is that he has given up attachment to the fruit of his action, and finds joy in the action itself. The yogi, like the worldly man, eats, drinks, sleeps. But his bhavana, his attitude to these actions, is different. That is why, though there are sixteen chapters of the Gītā left, still, at the very beginning, the figure of the steadfast seer, the sthitaprajna, the embodiment of self-control, is placed before us.

The similarity and the difference between the actions of the worldly man and those of the karma-yogi are immediately apparent. Suppose the karma-yogi is engaged in the care of cows. With what outlook does he do it? His bhavana (attitude) is that, by his service to the cows, society will get its fill of milk; and that, through the cow, he will forge for himself a link of love with the lower orders of creation. He does not do it for his wages. The wages come to him all right; but the real joy and pleasure are in this pure bhavana, this spiritual outlook.

The karma-yogi's action unites him with all creation. If we will not eat without first watering the tulasi plant, we create, by this resolve, a bond of love between ourselves and the vegetable kingdom. How can I eat, while leaving the tulasi hungry? Learning in this way to identify ourselves with the cow and the tulasi, we must attain oneness with the whole universe. In the Mahābhārata war, everybody, at sunset, leaves the field for evening prayer, but Lord Krishna unyokes the horses from the chariot, gives them water, rubs them down, removes the burrs from their bodies. What joy the Lord finds in this service! In describing this, the poet knows no weariness. Picture it to yourself. The Lord Parthasarathi (the Lord as Arjuna's charioteer) feeds the horses from his yellow silk (pitambar), which he has filled with grain. And thus you will experience in imagination the joy of karma-yoga. Take it that every act is a noble, spiritual, consecrated act. Take khadi work itself. Does the man who hawks khadi (home-spun cloth) in the streets, with a bundle on his back, never get tired? No, because he is absorbed in the thought that he has to feed the millions of his brothers and sisters in this country who are naked and starving. Selling this yard of khadi makes him one with Daridranarayana (God in the form of the poor).

VARIED BENEFITS OF KARMA-YOGA

In the yoga of desireless action, there is a miraculous power. By such action, both the individual and society are richly blessed. The life of the man who follows his svadharma runs the even tenor of its course. But, because he is always absorbed in action, his body keeps pure and healthy. And, as a result of his action, the society in which he lives prospers too. The karma-yogi farmer will not cultivate opium or tobacco just because it will fetch a lot of money, for he has related his work to the welfare of society. Action done as svadharma confers nothing but benefit on the community. The trader who believes that his business is for the good of society will never deal in foreign fineries. His business advances the welfare of society. The karma-yogi forgets himself and lives in identity with the community around him. Any society into which such karma-yogis are born will maintain order, prosperity and goodwill.

The result of the karma-yogi's action is that while his life goes on smoothly, his body and mind are radiant; and society too prospers. Besides these two benefits, he also receives the great gift of chitta-suddhi, purity of mind. "Purity through action," it is called. Action is a means to inward purity; but not the routine action of everybody. What brings about inward purity is the "charged" action of the karma-yogi. The Mahābhārata tells the story of the merchant Tuladhar (the balance-holder). A Brahmin called Jajali goes to him to find true knowledge. Tuladhar says to him, "Brother, it is necessary to keep the beam of this balance always even." By constantly doing this external action, Tuladhar's mind too had become straight and sensitive. Whether a child comes into the shop, or a grown-up person, his beam remains level for all, leaning neither this way nor that. One's action transforms one's mind. The karma-yogi's work is a form of prayer (japa). His mind is purified by it, and the clear mind receives the image of jnana, true knowledge. Through his many separate actions, the karma-yogi, in the end, attains true knowledge. From the arm of the balance Tuladhar got mental poise. As Sena, the barber, cleaned other people's heads, wisdom came to him. "Look, I remove the dirt from others' heads, but have I ever removed the dirt from my own head, from my own mind?" The language of the spirit came to him through his work. As he weeds his field, the karma-yogi gets the idea of removing the weeds of habit and passion from his heart. Gora the potter kneads and moulds the raw clay and gives baked pots to the people; from this he learns the lesson that his own life too is a pot that needs to be baked. He can test with his fingers if a pot is baked or raw; he thus becomes a judge of saintliness. From this it is evident that the karma-yogi, through the terms of his own trade or occupation, gains knowledge of perfection. What was their trade but a school of the spirit? These actions of theirs were nothing but worship, nothing but service. Viewed from without, these actions looked worldly, but inwardly, in reality, they were spiritual.

Another great benefit flows from the actions of the karma-yogi: Society has before it an ideal. In a community, it happens that one man is born before and another after. It becomes the responsibility of the one who was born earlier to set an example to those who come later. It is the responsibility of the elder brother to the younger brother, of the parent to the children, of the leader to his followers, of the teacher to his pupils, to set an example through his actions. And who but the karma-yogi is unceasingly devoted to his work, for in work only he sees joy. Thus false vanity loses ground in society. Though the karma-yogi is contented within himself, he cannot live at all without work. Tukaram says, "What if I have found

God by singing his praises, by bhajan? Should I therefore give up my bhajan? After all, bhajan has now become my nature."

> "Having first kept good company,
> Tuka became Pandurang.
> Why break the thread of bhajan?
> Why change one's very nature?"

The karma-yogi has climbed up the steps of action and reached the top; but he does not even then lift his foot off the step. He cannot shake off action. Work has become second nature to his limbs. In this way he continues to show to society the great use and value of the steps—of service through performing svadharma.

It is indeed a great thing to rid society of falsehood. Through hypocrisy and deceit, society decays. If the jnāni, the man of wisdom, were to sit in silence, others too would follow his example and sit with folded hands. The jnāni, with eternal contentment, loses himself in inner happiness, and remains quiet; but the other, though inwardly weeping, becomes inactive. One is at rest because he is happy at heart; the other too is at rest though his mind is shrunken! This state is terrifying. It encourages vanity and hypocrisy. That is why all the saints, even after reaching the heights, have with good reason held on to the means, the apron-strings of action, have kept on performing their karma till death. The mother delights in her children's games with their dolls. Though she knows that it is only make-believe, she joins in and creates in the children interest in the game. If she takes no part, the children would find no fun in it. If the karma-yogi, because he is contented, gives up action, others, even though they have the need for it, will also give up action and therefore remain with hungry, joyless hearts.

Therefore the karma-yogi, like the ordinary man, goes on

working. He does not think that he is in any way an exceptional person. He exerts himself infinitely more than other men. It is not necessary to put a stamp on any action and mark it as spiritual. There is no need to advertise one's action. If you are a perfect brahmachari (a seeker of the real), then let your actions show a hundred times more zest than other men's. Even though you get less food, do much more work; let society get more and more out of you. Let your brahmacharya be seen in your conduct and dealings, as the fragrance of sandal spreads far and wide.

The essence of the matter is that the karma-yogi, by surrendering the desire for fruit, receives an infinite reward. His life proceeds evenly. He is radiant in body and mind. The society in which he moves is happy. He attains inward purity and also jnāna. And society being rid of hypocrisy and deceit, the ideal of a perfect life comes within our reach. This, experience proves, is the greatness of karma-yoga.

OBSTACLES IN THE COURSE OF KARMA-YOGA

The karma-yogi does his work much better than others, because work to him is prayer, worship, ritual; work itself is a mode of worship (puja). I performed puja. After the puja I received the food offered during the worship, as prasada (a token of grace). But is this the reward, the payment for my puja? If a man performs puja for the sake of the food, he will of course get immediately this part of prasada. But through the act of puja, the karma-yogi seeks to get the reward of the vision of God. He does not estimate his action so cheap that it can merely fetch him a portion of the food offering. He is not prepared to mark such a low price on his action. He does not apply such gross measure to his actions. When a man's outlook is gross, the fruit he receives will also be gross. There is a proverb among farmers—"Sow deep, but sow moist." It is not enough to sow deep; there must be moisture in the soil too. With both depth and moisture in the soil, the yield will be enormous. So, the action should be "deep," i.e., well-culti-vated. And, it should also be moist with the love of God, with a sense of dedication. The karma-yogi's actions are sown deep, and surrendered to God.

We have developed some absurd ideas about the spirit. People imagine that once a man has become spiritual, there is no more need for him to move hand or foot, or do any work. They say, "What sort of religious man is this, who ploughs the fields and weaves khādi?" But nobody asks how a spiritual man can eat food. The God of the karma-yogi brushes down horses. At the Pandavas' Rajasuya sacrifice He clears the leaf plates after the feast. He goes out into the forest to graze cows. If the Lord of Dvaraka went back to Gokul again, He would tend cows, playing on His flute. So the saints have pictured a karma-yogi God who rubs horses down, takes cows out to graze, drives a chariot, cleans dishes and mops up floors. And they themselves have done the work of a tailor, or a potter, or a weaver, or a gardener, or a trader, or a barber or a cobbler. Doing these things, they have found themselves and become free.

People slip from the religious observance of karma-yoga for two reasons. In this connection, we must remember the specific nature of our indriyas. Our senses are caught up in dualities, such as likes and dislikes. For the things we want we feel an attachment, or fondness, and an aversion for other things. Thus attachment and aversion, desire and anger, gnaw into a man and eat him up. How noble, how beautiful, how infinitely rewarding karma-yoga is! But desire and anger tie round our necks this perpetual rattle, "Take this, and leave that," and we trail this behind us day and night. That is why, at the end of this Chapter, the Lord rings the warning bell, so that we may shake off this encumbrance and save ourselves. The karma-yogi should become, like the sthitaprajna, an embodiment of self-control.

Vivekananda on Karma-yoga

Karma-yoga is attaining through unselfish work of that freedom which is the goal of all human nature. Every selfish action, therefore, retards our reaching the goal, and every unselfish action takes us toward the goal; this is why the only definition that can be given of morality is this: That which is selfish is immoral, and that which is unselfish is moral.

Gandhi on the Gītā

While on the one hand it is beyond dispute that all action binds, on the other hand it is equally true that all living beings have to do some work whether they will or not. Here all activity, whether mental or physical, is to be included in the term action. Then how is one to be free from the bondage of action, even though he may be acting? The manner in which the Gītā has solved the problem is, to my knowledge, unique. The Gītā says: "Do your alloted work but renounce its fruit—be detached and work—have no desire for reward and work."

This is the unmistakable teaching of the Gītā. He who gives up action falls. He who gives up only the reward rises. But renunciation of fruit in no way means indifference to the result. In regard to every action one must know the result that is expected to follow, the means thereto, and the capacity for it. He, who, being thus equipped, is without desire for the result, and is yet wholly engrossed in the due fulfilment of the task before him, is said to have renounced the fruits of his action.

Sri Aurobindo on Karma-yoga

There is a mighty law of life, a great principle of human evolution, a body of spiritual knowledge and experience of which India has always been destined to be guardian, exemplar and missionary. This is the sanātana dharma, the eternal religion. Under the stress of alien impacts she has largely lost hold not of the structure of that dharma, but of its living reality. For the religion of India is nothing if it is not lived. It has to be applied not only to life, but to the whole of life; its spirit has to enter into and mould our society, our politics, our literature, our science, our individual character, affections and aspirations. To understand the heart of this dharma, to experience it as a truth, to feel the high emotions to which it rises and to express and execute it in life is what we understand by karma-yoga. We believe that it is to make the yoga the ideal of human life that India rises today; by the yoga she will get the strength to realize her freedom, unity and greatness, by the yoga she will keep the strength to preserve it. It is a spiritual revolution we forsee and the material is only its shadow and reflex.

Aesthetics

Introduction

"Raso vai sah," says the Taittiriya Upanishad. "Brahman is of the nature of rasa." Elsewhere in the Upanishads the joy of God realization (Brahmananda) and the taste of aesthetic experience (rasasvadana) are described as "twin brothers" (sahodarah). In India religion, philosophy, and art have always been inseparable aspects of a single, unified cultural tradition. That is why the classical philosophical systems lean so heavily on poetic, metaphorical, and allegorical descriptions, while the arts of sculpture, painting, music, even architecture, are so much permeated by metaphysical and religious concepts. Indian culture is essentially experience-oriented. Religion, philosophy, art—all these are of significance only if they are lived, not if they are merely thought about or analyzed.

This distinctively aesthetic flavor of Indian culture was carried over from ancient to medieval times. In medieval India, religion and philosophy practically dissolved into poetry. The saint-poets of the various linguistic regions not only preserved the philosophical and religious heritage but enlarged and enriched it through ever new creative expression. It is not surprising, therefore, that the outstanding thinkers of modern India show such deep sensitiveness to beauty. Rabindranath

Tagore and Ananda Coomaraswamy are directly associated with the aesthetic approach to life. Sri Aurobindo's poetic achievement, which was for many decades overshadowed by his fame as a sage and a philosopher, is now being widely recognized. Jawaharlal Nehru had in him a poetic streak which distinguished his writings and speeches from those of other statesmen of the modern age. Even Mahatma Gandhi was not indifferent to the aesthetic side of life. He valued the beauty of nature more than man-made art, and he refused to separate beauty from truth. One may or may not accept his viewpoint, but his aesthetic sensitiveness cannot be doubted. Nehru once said of the Mahatma: "He may not have been an artist, but his life itself is a supreme work of art."

The principle of harmony is the axis around which Tagore's aesthetic ideas revolve. This is an inclusive principle in which truth, beauty, love, and joy appear as different movements of a single symphony. What we describe as "discord" is merely the imperfect realization of harmony, just as nonbeing is merely the inadequate expression of Being. Tagore looks upon ugliness not as the opposite of beauty but as the distorted expression of beauty in our life. Ugliness arises when the eternal law of harmony is violated. When we "detach beauty" and try to "hold it apart," we do not get a true aesthetic experience because our world becomes divided. Beauty cannot be sought in uniqueness or "startling singularity" but in the "unassuming harmony of common objects." But through exaggeration—the poet is here thinking of extreme realists—"even commonness becomes aggressively uncommon" and defeats its own purpose.

Tagore describes art as the response of the finite man to the "call of the Real." This Real is viewed not as abstract, impersonal Being but as something "supremely personal."

Only a vivid sense of the Real can bring us joy. But the Real eludes us so long as we are caught up in a whirlpool of sensations and egoistic cravings. Great art releases us from the manifestations of our lower nature. It brings inward freedom. "We must have the perfect emancipation of heart which gives us the power to stand at the innermost centre of things, and taste that fulness of joy which is Brahma's." The sentence just quoted gives us a good insight into the entire Indian viewpoint which Tagore so effortlessly represents. "Perfect emancipation" is the ultimate goal of all endeavor including aesthetic creativity. When the poet refers to "the power to stand at the innermost centre of things," and again to "tasting the fulness of Brahma's joy," he is merely elaborating the fundamental principle of harmony from two different sides. Beauty, like life, is one. It is also many-faceted. There is a place in it for movement and rest, for the flowers of spring and the fruits of autumn, for Urvashi's passion and Lakshmi's grace.

Ananda Coomaraswamy is usually remembered for his fabulous erudition, which he employed in a variety of fields with meticulous precision. But sometimes one tends to overlook the fact that Coomaraswamy was wholly faithful to the Indian view according to which scholarship is of little value unless it illumines the totality of life. In the essay in this section, Coomaraswamy has taken up a specific aesthetic phenomenon and has examined it in the light of what he calls the "idealistic conception of reality." The title of the essay, "The Origin and Use of Images," is deceptively simple. In discussing Indian religious sculpture, Coomaraswamy shows how the absolute monism of the Vedanta, in which the concept of a "God with attributes" is transcended, can be reconciled with the personal God who is the object of devotion and love; and how this reconciliation is expressed in the worship of deities. Here we have a concrete illustration of the convergence of the philosophical, the religious, and the aesthetic impulses. The philosopher grasps the inevitability of the use of imagery. "God Himself makes concessions to our mortal nature, taking the forms imagined by his worshippers, making Himself as we are so that we may be as He is." The entire tradition represents a "continuity ranging from the contemplation of the Absolute to the physical service of an image made of clay." In this tradition there is "an ultimate acceptance of every aspect of God conceived by man, and of every ritual devised by his devotion."

The divine form is a mental construct. It is visualized, conceived and then worshipped. Aesthetic excellence is achieved only when the true nature of the object of worship is understood. Ideally speaking, "Such gnosis is possible only to the perfected yogin, the jīvanmukta. Dhyāna has to be realized in samādhi. To worship the Divine, *be* the Divine."

While Coomaraswamy speaks as an avowed exponent of the traditional Indian standpoint, quoting chapter and verse, Krishnamurti refuses to lean on any concept that has been "handed down." His plea is for complete spontaneity. And yet many of his comments are imbued by the same spirit which animates the ideas of Tagore and Coomaraswamy. He too, in his own way, emphasizes harmony. "True creativity cannot exist where there is conflict." And conflict arises because of possessiveness. The more acquisitive we become, the less sensitive we are to the rhythm of the whole. "Only when we understand our relationship with others, and with nature, does sensitivity come. It comes with love." We are constantly seeking—even in art—new thrills and excitements. This craving for ever new sensations makes our minds dull and our hearts weary. "Since our hearts are withered, and we have forgotten how to be kindly, how to look at the stars, at the trees, at the reflections on the water, we require the stimulation of pictures, and jewels, and books and endless amusements."

The remedy lies in inwardness of understanding. "To cultivate the outer without understanding the inner must inevitably build up those values which lead men to destruction and sorrow." When there is inner harmony and peace, our creativity no longer needs artificial stimulants. Our love of beauty can then express itself with perfect ease and naturalness: "in a song, in a smile, or in silence." But most of us, alas, have no inclination to be silent!

Ananda Coomaraswamy

The Origin and Use of Images in India

> It may be said that images are to the Hindu worshipper
> what diagrams are to the geometrician.—Rao, *Elements of*
> *Hindu Iconography*

Few of those who condemn idolatry, or make its suppression a
purpose of missionary activity, have ever seriously envisaged
the actual use of images, in historical or psychological
perspective, or surmised a possible significance in the fact that
the vast majority of men of all races, and in all ages, including
the present, Protestants, Hebrews, and Muslims being the
chief exceptions, have made use of more or less anthropomorphic images as aids to devotion. For these reasons it may be not
without value to offer an account of the use of images in India,
as far as possible in terms of thought natural to those who
actually make use of such images. This may at least conduce to
a realization of the truth enunciated by an incarnate Indian
deity, Krishna, that "the path men take from every side is
Mine."

In explaining the use of images in India, where the method is regarded as edifying, it should not be inferred that Hindus or Buddhists are to be represented *en masse* as less superstitious than other peoples. We meet with all kinds of stories about images that speak, or bow, or weep; images receive material offerings and services, which they are said to "enjoy"; we know that the real presence of the deity is invited in them for the purpose of receiving worship; on the completion of an image, its eyes are "opened" by a special and elaborate ceremony. Thus, it is clearly indicated that the image is to be regarded as if animated by the deity.

Obviously, however, there is nothing peculiarly Indian here. Similar miracles have been reported of Christian images; even the Christian church, like an Indian temple, is a house dwelt in by God in a special sense, yet it is not regarded as his prison, nor do its walls confine his omnipresence, whether in India or in Europe.

Further, superstition, or realism, is inseparable from human nature, and it would be easy to show that this is always and everywhere the case. The mere existence of science does not defend us from it; the majority will always conceive of atoms and electrons as real things, which would be tangible if they were not so small, and will always believe that tangibility is a proof of existence; and are fully convinced that a being, originating at a given moment of time, may yet, as that same being, survive eternally in time. He who believes that phenomena of necessity stand for solid existing actualities, or that there can exist any empirical consciousness or individuality without a material (substantial) basis, or that anything that has come into being can endure as such forever, is an idolater, a fetishist. Even if we should accept the popular Western view of Hinduism as a polytheistic system, it could not be maintained that the Indian icon is in any sense a fetish.

As pointed out by Guénon, "Dans l'Inde, en particulier, une image symbolique representant l'un ou l'autre des 'attributs divins,' et qui est appelée pratika, n'est point une 'idole,' car elle n'a jamais été prise pour autre chose que ce qu'elle est réellement, un support de méditation et un moyen auxiliaire de realization" * (*Introduction à l'étude des doctrines hindoues,* p. 209). A good illustration of this is to be found in the Divyavadana, Chapter XXVI, where Upagupta compels Mara, who as a yaksha has the power of assuming shapes at will, to exhibit himself in the shape of the Buddha. Upagupta bows down, and Mara, shocked at this apparent worship of himself, protests. Upagupta explains that he is not worshipping Mara, but the person represented—"just as people venerating earthen images of the undying angels, do not revere the clay as such, but the immortals represented therein." [1] Here we have the case of an individual who has passed beyond individuality, but is yet represented according to human needs by an image. The principle is even clearer in the case of the images of the angels; the image per se is neither God nor any angel, but merely an aspect or hypostasis (avastha) of God, who is in the last analysis without likeness (amurta), not determined by form (arupa), trans-form (para-rupa). His various forms or emanations are conceived by a process of symbolic filiation. To conceive of Hinduism as a polytheistic system is in itself a naïveté of which only a Western student, inheriting Graeco-

* "In India, in particular, a symbolic image represents one or another of the 'divine attributes,' which is called pratika, for it is neither an 'idol,' nor does it take on any qualities from that thing which it really is, an aid to meditation and a supplementary means toward realization."

[1] Cf. the *Hermeneia* of Athos, §445, cited by Fichtner, *Wandmalereien der Athosklöster* (1931), p. 15: "All honor that we pay the image, we refer to the Archetype, namely Him whose image it is. . . . In no wise honor we the colors or the art, but the archetype in Christ, who is in Heaven. For as Basilius says, the honoring of an image passes over to its prototype."

Roman concepts of "paganism" could be capable; the Muhammadan view of Christianity as polytheism could be better justified than this.

In fact, if we consider Indian religious philosophy as a whole, and regard the extent to which its highest conceptions have passed as dogmas into the currency of daily life, we shall have to define Hindu civilization as one of the least superstitious the world has known. Māyā is not properly *de*lusion, but strictly speaking creative power, sakti, the principle of manifestation; *de*lusion, moha, is to conceive of appearances as things in themselves, and to be attached to them as such without regard to their procession.

In the Bhagavad-Gītā, better known in India than the New Testament in Europe, we are taught of the Real, that "This neither dies nor is it born; he who regardeth This as a slayer, he who thinketh This is slain, are equally unknowing." Again and again, from the Upanishads to the most devotional theistic hymns the Godhead, ultimate reality, is spoken of as unlimited by any form, not to be described by any predicate, unknowable. Thus, in the Upanishads, "He is, by that alone is He to be apprehended" (cf. "I am that I am"); in the words of the Shaiva hymnist Mānikka Vāshagar, "He is passing the description of words, not comprehensible by the mind, not visible to the eye or other senses." Similarly in later Buddhism, in the Vajrayāna (Sūnyavāda) system, we find it categorically stated that the divinities, that is, the personal God or premier angel in all His forms, "are manifestations of the essential nature of non-being"; the doctrine of the only reality of the Void (Behmen's "Abyss") is pushed to the point of an explicit denial of the existence of any Buddha or any Buddhist doctrine.

Again, whereas we are apt to suppose that the religious significance of Christianity stands or falls with the actual historicity of Jesus, we find an Indian commentator (Nilakantha) saying of the Krishna Līlā, believed historical by most Hindus, that the narration is not the real point, that this is not an historical event, but is based upon eternal truths, on the actual relation of the soul to God, and that the events take place, not in the outer world, but in the heart of man. Here we are in a world inaccessible to higher criticism, neither of superstition on the one hand, nor of cynicism on the other. It has been more than once pointed out that the position ⁀f Christianity could well be strengthened by a similar emancipation from the historical point of view, as was to a large extent actually the case with the Schoolmen.

As for India, it is precisely in a world dominated by an idealistic concept of reality, and yet with the approval of the most profound thinkers, that there flourished what we are pleased to call idolatry. Mānikka Vāshagar, quoted above, constantly speaks of the attributes of God, refers to the legendary accounts of His actions, and takes for granted the use and service of images. In Vajrayāna Buddhism, often though not quite correctly designated as nihilistic, the development of an elaborate pantheon, fully realized in material imagery, reaches its zenith. Shankara himself, one of the most brilliant intellects the world has known, interpreter of the Upanishads and creator of the Vedanta system of pure monism accepted by a majority of all Hindus and analogous to the idealism of Kant, was a devout worshipper of images, a visitor to shrines, a singer of devotional hymns.

True, in a famous prayer, he apologizes for visualizing in contemplation One who is not limited by any form, for praising in hymns One who is beyond the reach of words, and for visiting Him in sacred shrines, who is omnipresent. Actually, too, there exist some groups in Hinduism (the Sikhs, for example) who do not make use of images. But if even he who knew could not resist the impulse to love,—and love requires an object of adoration, and an object must be conceived in word or form,—how much greater must be the necessity of that majority for whom it is so much easier to worship than to know. Thus the philosopher perceives the inevitability of the use of imagery, verbal and visual, and sanctions the service of images. God Himself makes like concession to our mortal nature, "taking the forms imagined by His worshipers," making Himself as we are that we may be as He is.

The Hindu Īshvara (Supreme God) is not a jealous God, because all gods are aspects of Him, imagined by His worshippers; in the words of Krishna: "When any devotee seeks to worship any aspect with faith, it is none other than Myself that bestows that steadfast faith, and when by worshipping any aspect he wins what he desires, it is none other than Myself that grants his prayers. Howsoever men approach Me, so do I welcome them, for the path men take from every side is Mine." Those whose ideal is less high attain, indeed, of necessity to lesser heights; but no man can safely aspire to higher ideals than are pertinent to his spiritual age. In any case, his spiritual growth cannot be aided by a desecration of his ideals; he can be aided only by the fullest recognition of these ideals as retaining their validity in any scheme, however profound. This was the Hindu method; Indian religion adapts herself with infinite grace to every human need. The collective genius that made of Hinduism a continuity ranging from the contemplation of the Absolute to the physical service of an image made of clay did not shrink from an ultimate acceptance of every aspect of God conceived by man, and of every ritual devised by his devotion.

We have already suggested that the multiplicity of the forms of images, coinciding with the development of monotheistic Hinduism, arises from various causes, all ultimately referable to the diversity of need of individuals and groups. In particular, this multiplicity is due historically to the inclusion of all pre-existing forms, all local forms, in a greater theological synthesis, where they are interpreted as modes or emanations (vyūha) of the supreme Īshvara; and subsequently, to the further growth of theological speculation. In the words of Yāska, "We see actually that because of the greatness of God, the one principle of life is praised in various ways. Other angels are the individual members of a unique Self" (*Nirukta*, VII, 4): cf. Ruysbroeck, *Adornment* . . . , Ch. XXV, "because of His incomprehensible nobility and sublimity, which we cannot rightly name nor wholly express, we give Him all these names."

Iconolatry, however, was not left to be regarded as an ignorant or useless practice fit only for spiritual children; even the greatest, as we have seen, visited temples, and worshipped images, and certainly these greatest thinkers did not do so blindly or unconsciously. A human necessity was recognized, the nature of the necessity was understood, its psychology systematically analyzed, the various phases of image worship, mental and material, were defined, and the variety of forms explained by the doctrines of emanation and of gracious condescension.

In the first place, then, the forms of images are not arbitrary. Their ultimate elements may be of popular origin rather than priestly invention, but the method is adopted and further developed within the sphere of intellectual orthodoxy. Each conception is of human origin, notwithstanding that the natural tendency of man to realism leads to a belief in actually existent heavens where the Angel appears as he is represented. In the words of Shukracarya, "the characteristics of images are determined by the relation that subsists between the adorer and the adored"; in those cited by Gopālabhatta from an unknown source, the present spiritual activity of the worshiper, and the actual existence of a traditional iconography, are reconciled as follows—"Though it is the devotion (bhakti) of the devotee that causes the manifestation of the image of the Blessed One (Bhagavata), in this matter (of iconography) the procedure of the ancient sages should be followed." [2]

The whole problem of symbolism (pratika, "symbol") is discussed by Shankara, Commentary on the Vedanta Sutras, I, 1, 20. Endorsing the statement that "all who sing here to the harp, sing Him," he points out that this "Him" refers to the highest Lord only, who is the ultimate theme even of worldly songs. And as to anthropomorphic expressions in scripture, "we reply that the highest Lord may, when he pleases, assume a bodily shape formed of Māyā, in order to gratify his devout worshipers"; but all this is merely analogical, as when we say that the Brahman abides here or there, which in reality abides only in its own glory (cf. *ibid.*, I, 2, 29). The representation of the invisible by the visible is also discussed by Deussen, *Philosophy of the Upanishads*, pp. 99–101.

Parenthetically, we may remark that stylistic sequences (change of aesthetic form without change of basic shape) are a revealing record of changes in the nature of religious experience; in Europe, for example, the difference between a thirteenth-century and a modern Madonna betrays the passage from passionate conviction to facile sentimentality. Of this, however, the worshipper is altogether unaware; from the

[2] "It is for the advantage (artha) of the worshippers (upasaka) (and not by any intrinsic necessity) that the Brahman—whose nature is intelligence (cin-maya), beside whom there is no other, who is impartite and incorporeal—is aspectually conceived (rupa-kalpana)," Ramopanishad, text cited by Bhattacharya, *Indian Images*, p. xvii. That is to say the image, as in the case of any other "arrangement of God," has a merely logical, not an absolute validity. "Worship" (upasana) has been defined as an "intellectual operation (manasa-vyapara) with respect to the Brahman with attributed-qualities (saguna)."

standpoint of edification, the value of an image does not depend on its aesthetic qualities. A recognition of the significance of stylistic changes, in successive periods, important as it may be for us as students of art, is actually apparent only in disinterested retrospect; the theologian, proposing means of edification, has been concerned only with the forms of images. Stylistic changes correspond to linguistic changes: we all speak the language of our own time without question or analysis.

Let us consider now the processes actually involved in the making of images. Long anterior to the oldest surviving images of the supreme deities we meet with descriptions of the gods as having limbs, garments, weapons or other attributes; such descriptions are to be found even in the Vedic lauds and myths. Now in theistic Hinduism, where the method of yoga is employed, that is, focused attention leading to the realization of identity of consciousness with the object considered, whether or not this object be God, these descriptions, now called dhyāna mantrams or trance formulae, or alternatively, sādhanās, means, provide the germ from which the form of the deity is to be visualized. For example, "I worship our gentle lady Bhuvaneshvarī, like the risen sun, lovely, victorious, destroying defects in prayer, with a shining crown on her head, three-eyed and with swinging earrings adorned with diverse gems, as a lotus-lady, abounding in treasure, making the gestures of charity and giving assurance. Such is the dhyānam of Bhuvaneshvarī" (a form of Devī). To the form thus conceived imagined flowers and other offerings are to be made. Such interior worship of a mantra-body or correspondingly imagined form is called subtle (sūkshma), in contradistinction to the exterior worship of a material image, which is termed gross (sthula), though merely in a descriptive, not a deprecatory, sense.

Further contrasted with both these modes of worship is that

called para-rūpa, "trans-form," in which the worship is paid directly to the deity as he is in himself. This last mode no doubt corresponds to the ambition of the iconoclast, but such gnosis is in fact only possible, and therefore only permissible, to the perfected yogin and veritable jīvanmukta, who is so far as he himself is concerned set free from all name and aspect, whatever may be the outward appearance he presents. Had the iconoclast in fact attained to such perfection as this, he could not have been an iconoclast.

In any case it must be realized, in connection with the gross or subtle modes of worship, that the end is only to be attained by an identification of the worshipper's consciousness with the form under which the deity is conceived: nādevo devam yajet, "only as the angel can one worship the angel," and so devo bhūtvā devam yajet, "to worship the Angel become the Angel." Only when the dhyānam is thus realized in full samādhi (the consummation of yoga, which commences with focused attention) is the worship achieved. Thus, for example, with regard to the form of Natarāja, representing Shiva's cosmic dance, in the words of Tirumular,

> The dancing foot, the sound of the tinkling bells,
> The songs that are sung, and the various steps,
> The forms assumed by our Master as He dances,
> Discover these in your own heart, so shall your bonds be broken.

When, on the other hand, a material image is to be produced for purposes of worship in a temple or elsewhere, this as a technical procedure must be undertaken by a professional craftsman, who may be variously designated shilpin, "craftsman," yogin, "yogi," sādhaka, "adept," or simply rūpakāra or pratimākāra, "imager." Such a craftsman goes through the whole process of self-purification and worship, mental visualization and identification of consciousness with the form evoked, and then only translates the form into stone or metal. Thus the trance formulae become the prescriptions by which the craftsman works, and as such they are commonly included in the Shilpa Shāstras, the technical literature of craftsmanship. These books in turn provide invaluable data for the modern student of iconography.

Technical production is thus bound up with the psychological method known as yoga. In other words the artist does not resort to models but uses a mental construction, and this condition sufficiently explains the cerebral character of the art, which everyone will have remarked for himself. In the words of the encyclopaedist Shukracarya, "One should set up in temples the images of angels who ire the objects of his devotion, by mental vision of their att ibutes; it is for the full achievement of this yoga-vision that the proper lineaments of images are prescribed; therefore the mortal imager should resort to trance-vision, for thus and no otherwise, and surely not by direct perception, is the end to be attained."

The proper characteristics of image; are further elucidated in the Shilpa Shāstras by a series of car ons known as tālamāna or pramāna, in which are prescribed the ideal proportions proper to the various deities, whether conceived as Kings of the World, or otherwise. These propertions are expressed in terms of a basic unit, just as we speal of a figure having so many "heads"; but the corresponding Indian measure is that of the "face," from the hair on the forehe id to the chin, and the different canons are therefore designate l Ten-face, Nine-face, and so on down to the Five-face car on suitable for minor deities of dwarfish character. These ideal proportions correspond to the character of the aspec of the angel to be represented, and complete the exposi ion of this character otherwise set forth by means of facial expression, attributes, costume, or gesture. And as Shukracary a says further, "Only an image made in accordance with the canon can be called beautiful; some may think that beautiful which corresponds to their own fancy, but that not in accordance with the canon is unlovely to the discerning eye." And again, "Even the misshapen image of an angel is to be preferred to that of a man, however attractive the latter may be"; because the representations of the angels are means to spiritual ends, not so those which are only likenesses of human individuals. "When the consciousness is brought to rest in the form (nāma, "name," "idea"), and sees only the form, then, inasmuch as it rests in the form, aspectual perception is dispensed with and only the reference remains; one reaches then the world-without-aspectual-perception, and with further practice attains to liberation from all hindrances, becoming adept." [3] Here, in another language than our own, are contrasted ideal and realistic art: the one a means to the attainment of fuller consciousness, the other merely a means to pleasure. So too might the anatomical limitations of Giotto be defended as against the human charm of Raphael.

It should be further understood that images differ greatly in the degree of their anthropomorphism. Some are merely symbols, as when the Bodhi tree is used to represent the Buddha at the time of the Enlightenment, or when only the feet of the Lord are represented as objects of worship. A very important iconographic type is that of the yantra, used especially in the Shakta systems; here we have to do with a purely geometrical form, often for instance composed of interlocking triangles, representing the male and female, static and kinetic aspects of the Two-in-One. Further, images in the

---

[3] Verses cited in the *Trimsika* of Vasubandhu; see *Bibliothèque de l'École des Hautes Études*, fasc. 245, 1925, and Lévi, "Matériaux pour l'Étude du Système Vijnaptimātra," *ibid.*, fasc. 260 (Paris, 1932), p. 119.

round may be avyakta, non-manifest, like a lingam; or vyaktavyakta, partially manifest, as in the case of a mukha-lingam; or vyakta, fully manifest in "anthromorphic" or partly theriomorphic types.[4] In the last analysis all these are equally ideal, symbolic forms.

In the actual use of a material image, it should always be remembered that it must be prepared for worship by a ceremony of invocation (āvahana); and if intended only for temporary use, subsequently desecrated by a formula of dismissal (visarjana). When not in pūjā, that is before consecration or after desecration, the image has no more sacrosanct character than any other material object. It should not be supposed that the deity, by invocation and dismissal, is made to come or go, for omnipresence does not move; these ceremonies are really projections of the worshipper's own mental attitude toward the image. By invocation he announces to himself his intention of using the image as a means of communion with the Angel; by dismissal he announces that his service has been completed, and that he no longer regards the image as a link between himself and the deity.

It is only by a change of viewpoint, psychologically equivalent to such a formal desecration, that the worshipper, who naturally regards the icon as a devotional utility, comes to regard it as a mere work of art to be sensationally regarded as such. Conversely, the modern aesthetician and Kunsthistoriker, who is interested only in aesthetic surfaces and sensations, fails to conceive of the work as the necessary product of a given determination, that is, as having purpose and utility. Of

---

[4] The stage of partial manifestation is compared to that of the "blooming" of a painting. The term "bloom" or "blossom" (unmil) is used to describe the "coming out" of a painting as the colors are gradually applied (Maheshvarananda, *Maharthamanjari*, p. 44, and my "Further References to Indian Painting," *Artibus Asiae*, p. 127, 1930–1932, item 102).

these two, the worshipper, for whom the object was made, is nearer to the root of the matter than the aesthetician who endeavors to isolate beauty from function.[5]

[5] Cf. my "Hindu Sculpture," in *The League,* vol. V, no. 3 (New York, 1933).

Rabindranath Tagore

The Realisation of Beauty

Things in which we do not take joy are either a burden upon our minds to be got rid of at any cost; or they are useful, and therefore in temporary and partial relation to us, becoming burdensome when their utility is lost; or they are like wandering vagabonds, loitering for a moment on the outskirts of our recognition, and then passing on. A thing is only completely our own when it is a thing of joy to us.

The greater part of this world is to us as if it were nothing. But we cannot allow it to remain so, for thus it belittles our own self. The entire world is given to us, and all our powers have their final meaning in the faith that by their help we are to take possession of our patrimony.

But what is the function of our sense of beauty in this process of the extension of our consciousness? Is it there to separate truth into strong lights and shadows, and bring it before us in its uncompromising distinction of beauty and ugliness? If that were so, then we should have to admit that this sense of beauty creates a dissension in our universe and sets up a wall of hindrance across the highway of communication that leads from each individual thing to all things.

But that cannot be true. As long as our realisation is incomplete a division necessarily remains between things known and unknown, pleasant and unpleasant. But in spite of the dictum of some philosophers man does not accept any arbitrary and absolute limit to his knowable world. Every day his science is penetrating into the region formerly marked on his map as unexplored or inexplorable. Our sense of beauty is similarly engaged in ever pushing on its conquests. Truth is everywhere, therefore everything is the object of our knowledge. Beauty is omnipresent, therefore everything is capable of giving us joy.

In the early days of his history man took everything as a phenomenon of life. His science of life began by creating a sharp distinction between life and non-life. But as it is proceeding farther and farther the line of demarcation between the animate and inanimate is growing more and more dim. In the beginning of our apprehension these sharp lines of contrast are helpful to us, but as our comprehension becomes clearer they gradually fade away.

The Upanishads have said that all things are created and sustained by an infinite joy. To realise this principle of creation we have to start with a division—the division into the beautiful and the nonbeautiful. Then the apprehension of beauty has to come to us with a vigorous blow to awaken our consciousness from its primitive lethargy, and it attains its object by the urgency of the contrast. Therefore our first acquaintance with beauty is in her dress of motley colours, that affects us with its stripes and feathers, nay, with its disfigurements. But as our acquaintance ripens, the apparent discords are resolved into modulations of rhythm. At first we detach beauty from its surroundings, we hold it apart from the rest, but at the end we realise its harmony with all. Then the music of beauty has no more need of exciting us with loud noise; it renounces violence, and appeals to our heart with the truth that it is meekness that inherits the earth.

In some stage of our growth, in some period of our history, we try to set up a special cult of beauty, and pare it down to a narrow circle, so as to make it a matter of pride for a chosen few. Then it breeds in its votaries affectations and exaggerations, as it did with the Brahmins in the time of the decadence of Indian civilisation, when the perception of the higher truth fell away and superstitions grew up unchecked.

In the history of aesthetics there also comes an age of emancipation when the recognition of beauty in things great and small becomes easy, and when we see it more in the unassuming harmony of common objects than in things startling in their singularity. So much so, that we have to go through the stages of reaction when in the representation of beauty we try to avoid everything that is obviously pleasing and that has been crowned by the sanction of convention. We are then tempted in defiance to exaggerate the commonness of commonplace things, thereby making them aggressively uncommon. To restore harmony we create the discords which are a feature of all reactions. We already see in the present age the sign of this aesthetic reaction, which proves that man has at last come to know that it is only the narrowness of perception which sharply divides the field of his aesthetic consciousness into ugliness and beauty. When he has the power to see things detached from self-interest and from the insistent claims of the lust of the senses, then alone can he have the true vision of the beauty that is everywhere. Then only can he see that what is unpleasant to us is not necessarily unbeautiful, but has its beauty in truth.

When we say that beauty is everywhere we do not mean

that the word ugliness should be abolished from our language, just as it would be absurd to say that there is no such thing as untruth. Untruth there certainly is, not in the system of the universe, but in our power of comprehension, as its negative element. In the same manner there is ugliness in the distorted expression of beauty in our life and in our art which comes from our imperfect realisation of Truth. To a certain extent we can set our life against the law of truth which is in us and which is in all, and likewise we can give rise to ugliness by going counter to the eternal law of harmony which is everywhere.

Through our sense of truth we realise law in creation, and through our sense of beauty we realise harmony in the universe. When we recognise the law in nature we extend our mastery over physical forces and become powerful; when we recognise the law in our moral nature we attain mastery over self and become free. In like manner the more we comprehend the harmony in the physical world the more our life shares the gladness of creation, and our expression of beauty in art becomes more truly catholic. As we become conscious of the harmony in our soul, our apprehension of the blissfulness of the spirit of the world becomes universal, and the expression of beauty in our life moves in goodness and love towards the infinite. This is the ultimate object of our existence, that we must ever know that "beauty is truth, truth beauty"; we must realise the whole world in love, for love gives it birth, sustains it, and takes it back to its bosom. We must have that perfect emancipation of heart which gives us the power to stand at the innermost centre of things and have the taste of that fulness of disinterested joy which belongs to Brahma.

Music is the purest form of art, and therefore the most direct expression of beauty, with a form and spirit which is one and simple, and least encumbered with anything extraneous. We seem to feel that the manifestation of the infinite in the finite forms of creation is music itself, silent and visible. The evening sky, tirelessly repeating the starry constellations, seems like a child struck with wonder at the mystery of its own first utterance, lisping the same word over and over again, and listening to it in unceasing joy. When in the rainy night of July the darkness is thick upon the meadows and the pattering rain draws veil upon veil over the stillness of the slumbering earth, this monotony of the rain patter seems to be the darkness of sound itself. The gloom of the dim and dense line of trees, the thorny bushes scattered in the bare heath like floating heads of swimmers with bedraggled hair, the smell of the damp grass and the wet earth, the spire of the temple rising above the undefined mass of blackness grouped around the village huts—everything seems like notes rising from the heart of the night, mingling and losing themselves in the one sound of ceaseless rain filling the sky.

Therefore the true poets, they who are seers, seek to express the universe in terms of music.

They rarely use symbols of painting to express the unfolding of forms, the mingling of endless lines and colours that goes on every moment on the canvas of the blue sky.

They have their reason. For the man who paints must have canvas, brush, and colour-box. The first touch of his brush is very far from the complete idea. And then when the work is finished and the artist is gone, the widowed picture stands alone, the incessant touches of love of the creative hand are withdrawn.

But the singer has everything within him. The notes come out from his very life. They are not materials gathered from outside. His idea and his expression are brother and sister; very often they are born as twins. In music the heart reveals itself immediately; it suffers not from any barrier of alien material.

Therefore though music has to wait for its completeness like any other art, yet at every step it gives out the beauty of the whole. As the material of expression even words are barriers, for their meaning has to be construed by thought. But music never has to depend upon any obvious meaning; it expresses what no words can ever express.

What is more, music and the musician are inseparable. When the singer departs, his singing dies with him; it is in eternal union with the life and joy of the master.

This world-song is never for a moment separated from its singer. It is not fashioned from any outward material. It is his joy itself taking never-ending form. It is the great heart sending the tremor of its thrill over the sky.

There is a perfection in each individual strain of this music, which is the revelation of completion in the incomplete. No one of its notes is final, yet each reflects the infinite.

What does it matter if we fail to derive the exact meaning of this great harmony? Is it not like the hand meeting the string and drawing out at once all its tones at the touch? It is the language of beauty, the caress, that comes from the heart of the world and straightway reaches our heart.

Last night, in the silence which pervaded the darkness, I stood alone and heard the voice of the singer of eternal melodies. When I went to sleep I closed my eyes with this last thought in my mind, that even when I remain unconscious in slumber the dance of life will still go on in the hushed arena of my sleeping body, keeping step with the stars. The heart will throb, the blood will leap in the veins, and the millions of living atoms of my body will vibrate in tune with the note of the harp-string that thrills at the touch of the master.

Rabindranath Tagore

Urvashi and Lakshmi

V. S. Naravane (translator)

At some mysterious moment,
During the churning of the primeval ocean,
Two women arose
From their bed in the boundless deep.
One was Urvashi, beautiful Urvashi,
Celestial nymph, queen of the passions.
The other was Lakshmi, kind and beneficent,
Mother of the universe, goddess of heaven.

Urvashi pours into April's cup the flaming wine of revelry.
She scatters with both hands the bright roses of spring,
Steals the peace from human hearts,
And bursts into the restless song of youth.

Then comes Lakshmi, soothing the passions,
Restoring to the earth autumn's serene joys:

Fruitful maturity, calm loveliness.
Her blessings bring perfection and abundance,
And her gentle smile overflows with the nectar of grace.
Lakshmi softly leads the world back
   to the temple of the Infinite
      at the sacred confluence of Life and Death.

J. Krishnamurti

Art, Beauty and Creation

Most of us are constantly trying to escape from ourselves; and as art offers a respectable and easy means of doing so, it plays a significant part in the lives of many people. In the desire for self-forgetfulness, some turn to art, others take to drink, while still others follow mysterious and fanciful religious doctrines.

When, consciously or unconsciously, we use something to escape from ourselves, we become addicted to it. To depend on a person, a poem, or what you will, as a means of release from our worries and anxieties, though momentarily enriching, only creates further conflict and contradiction in our lives.

The state of creativeness cannot exist where there is conflict, and the right kind of education should therefore help the individual to face his problems and not glorify the ways of escape; it should help him to understand and eliminate conflict, for only then can this state of creativeness come into being.

Art divorced from life has no great significance. When art is separate from our daily living, when there is a gap between our instinctual life and our efforts on canvas, in marble or in words, then art becomes merely an expression of our superficial desire to escape from the reality of what *is*. To bridge this gap is very arduous, especially for those who are gifted and technically proficient; but it is only when the gap is bridged that our life becomes integrated and art an integral expression of ourselves.

Mind has the power to create illusion; and without understanding its ways, to seek inspiration is to invite self-deception. Inspiration comes when we are open to it, not when we are courting it. To attempt to gain inspiration through any form of stimulation leads to all kinds of delusions.

Unless one is aware of the significance of existence, capacity or gift gives emphasis and importance to the self and its cravings. It tends to make the individual self-centered and separative; he feels himself to be an entity apart, a superior being, all of which breeds many evils and causes ceaseless strife and pain. The self is a bundle of many entities, each opposed to the others. It is a battlefield of conflicting desires, a center of constant struggle between the "mine" and the "not-mine"; and as long as we give importance to the self, to the "me" and the "mine," there will be increasing conflict within ourselves and in the world.

A true artist is beyond the vanity of the self and its ambitions. To have the power of brilliant expression, and yet be caught in worldly ways, makes for a life of contradiction and strife. Praise and adulation, when taken to heart, inflate the ego and destroy receptivity, and the worship of success in any field is obviously detrimental to intelligence.

Any tendency or talent which makes for isolation, any form of self-identification, however stimulating, distorts the expression of sensitivity and brings about insensitivity. Sensitivity is dulled when gift becomes personal, when importance is given to the "me" and the "mine"—*I* paint, *I* write, *I* invent. It is only when we are aware of every movement of our own thought and feeling in our relationship with people, with things and with nature, that the mind is open, pliable, not tethered to self-protective demands and pursuits; and only then is there sensitivity to the ugly and the beautiful, unhindered by the self.

Sensitivity to beauty and to ugliness does not come about through attachment; it comes with love, when there are no self-created conflicts. When we are inwardly poor, we indulge in every form of outward show, in wealth, power and possessions. When our hearts are empty, we collect things. If we can afford it, we surround ourselves with objects that we consider beautiful, and because we attach enormous importance to them, we are responsible for much misery and destruction.

The acquisitive spirit is not the love of beauty; it arises from the desire for security, and to be secure is to be insensitive. The desire to be secure creates fear; it sets going a process of isolation which builds walls of resistance around us, and these walls prevent all sensitivity. However beautiful an object may be, it soon loses its appeal for us; we get used to it, and that which was a joy becomes empty and dull. Beauty is still there, but we are no longer open to it, and it has been absorbed into our monotonous daily existence.

Since our hearts are withered and we have forgotten how to be kindly, how to look at the stars, at the trees, at the reflections on the water, we require the stimulation of pictures and jewels, of books and endless amusements. We are constantly seeking new excitements, new thrills, we crave an ever-increasing variety of sensations. It is this craving and its satisfaction that make the mind and heart weary and dull. As long as we are seeking sensation, the things that we call beautiful and ugly have but a very superficial significance. There is lasting joy only when we are capable of approaching all things afresh—which is not possible as long as we are bound up in our desires. The craving for sensation and gratification prevents the experiencing of that which is always new. Sensations can be bought, but not the love of beauty.

When we are aware of the emptiness of our own minds and hearts without running away from it into any kind of stimulation or sensation, when we are completely open, highly sensitive, only then can there be creation, only then shall we find creative joy. To cultivate the outer without understanding the inner must inevitably build up those values which lead men to destruction and sorrow.

Learning a technique may provide us with a job, but it will not make us creative; whereas, if there is joy, if there is the creative fire, it will find a way to express itself, one need not study a method of expression. When one really wants to write a poem, one writes it, and if one has the technique, so much the better; but why stress what is but a means of communication if one has nothing to say? When there is love in our hearts, we do not search for a way of putting words together.

Great artists and great writers may be creators, but we are not, we are mere spectators. We read vast numbers of books, listen to magnificent music, look at works of art, but we never directly experience the sublime; our experience is always through a poem, through a picture, through the personality of a saint. To sing we must have a song in our hearts; but having lost the song, we pursue the singer. Without an intermediary we feel lost; but we *must* be lost before we can discover anything. Discovery is the beginning of creativeness; and without creativeness, do what we may, there can be no peace or happiness for man.

We think that we shall be able to live happily, creatively, if we learn a method, a technique, a style; but creative happiness comes only when there is inward richness, it can never be attained through any system. Self-improvement, which is another way of assuring the security of the "me" and the "mine," is not creative, nor is it love of beauty. Creativeness comes into being when there is constant awareness of the ways of the mind, and of the hindrances it has built for itself.

The freedom to create comes with self-knowledge; but self-knowledge is not a gift. One can be creative without having any particular talent. Creativeness is a state of being in which the conflicts and sorrows of the self are absent, a state in which the mind is not caught up in the demands and pursuits of desire.

To be creative is not merely to produce poems, or statues, or children; it is to be in that state in which truth can come into being. Truth comes into being when there is a complete cessation of thought; and thought ceases only when the self is absent, when the mind has ceased to create, that is, when it is no longer caught in its own pursuits. When the mind is utterly still without being forced or trained into quiescence, when it is silent because the self is inactive, then there is creation.

The love of beauty may express itself in a song, in a smile, or in silence; but most of us have no inclination to be silent. We have not the time to observe the birds, the passing clouds, because we are too busy with our pursuits and pleasures. When there is no beauty in our hearts, how can we help the children to be alert and sensitive? We try to be sensitive to beauty while avoiding the ugly; but avoidance of the ugly makes for insensitivity. If we would develop sensitivity in the young, we ourselves must be sensitive to beauty and to ugliness, and must take every opportunity to awaken in them the joy there is in seeing, not only the beauty that man has created, but also the beauty of nature.

Rabindranath Tagore

From "Fireflies"

I touch God in my song
   as the hill touches the far-away sea
     with its waterfall.

The butterfly counts not months but moments,
   and has time enough.

Emancipation from the bondage of the soil
   is no freedom for the tree.

From "Stray Birds"

The fish in the water is silent, the animal on the earth is
noisy, the bird in the air is singing.

But Man has in him the silence of the sea, the noise of the earth and the music of the air.

Every child comes with the message that God is not yet discouraged of man

Be still, my heart, these great trees are prayers.

The mighty desert is burning for the love of a blade of grass who shakes her head and laughs and flies away.

That I exist is a perpetual surprise which is life.

Sri Aurobindo on Art

The first and lowest use of Art is the purely aesthetic, the second is the intellectual or educative, the third and highest the spiritual. By speaking of the aesthetic use as the lowest, we do not wish to imply that it is not of immense value to humanity, but simply to assign to it its comparative value in relation to the higher uses. The aesthetic is of immense importance and until it has done its work, mankind is not really fitted to make full use of Art on the higher planes of human development. Aristotle assigns a high value to tragedy because of its purifying force. He describes its effect as katharsis, a sacramental word of the Greek mysteries, which, in the secret discipline of the ancient Greek Tantrics, answered precisely to our cittashuddhi, the purification of the citta or mass of established ideas, feelings and actional habits in a man either by sanyama, rejection, or by bhoga, satisfaction, or by both. Aristotle was speaking of the purification of feelings, passions and emotions in the heart through imaginative treatment in poetry but the truth the idea contains is of much wider application and constitutes the justification of the aesthetic side of art. It purifies by beauty. The beautiful and the good are held by many thinkers to be the same and, though the idea may be wrongly stated, it is, when put from the right standpoint, not only a truth but the fundamental truth of existence. According to our own philosophy the whole world came out of ānanda and returns into ānanda, and the triple term in which ānanda may be stated is Joy, Love, Beauty. To see divine beauty in the whole world, man, life, nature, to love that which we have seen and to have pure unalloyed bliss in that love and that beauty is the appointed road by which mankind as a race must climb to God. That is the reaching to vidyā through avidyā, to the One Pure and Divine through the manifold manifestation of Him, of which the Upanishad repeatedly speaks. But the bliss must be pure and unalloyed, unalloyed by self-regarding emotions, unalloyed by pain and evil. The sense of good and bad, beautiful and un-beautiful, which afflicts our understanding and our senses, must be replaced by akhanda rasa, undifferentiated and unabridged delight in the delightfulness of things, before the highest can be reached. On the way to this goal full use must be made of the lower and abridged sense of beauty which seeks to replace the less beautiful by the more, the lower by the higher, the mean by the noble.

Education

Introduction

"She who is seated on a white lotus, wearing a beautiful white garment; she who holds a lute in her hand and has a garland of fresh white jasmine buds around her neck; she who is worshipped even by Brahma, Shiva and other gods—may that Sarasvati, Goddess of Learning, remove my ignorance."

This stanza from a popular hymn to Sarasvati is recited in India even today, as it has been recited for centuries, when a child is first entrusted to the care of a teacher, or when a class meets for the first time. It is significant that these ideas of beauty and grace, purity, simplicity, and holiness are associated with the goddess of learning. In the traditional Indian scheme of values, scholarship is not regarded as an end in itself, and education is looked upon as the molding of the complete man. In modern times two of India's outstanding thinkers, Rabindranath Tagore and Sri Aurobindo, have emphasized the integral nature of true education.

Tagore's work in the field of education is well known. The school he founded in 1901 at Shantiniketan, Bengal, which later developed into the international university of Vishva-Bharati, embodies Tagore's educational ideals. Sri Aurobindo's educational thought has received much less attention. Yet it is important to remember that as early as 1906 Tagore and Sri Aurobindo were jointly associated with a project for national education. The project was drawn up by Tagore on behalf of a council appointed by the Bengal National Congress. To implement this project, the Bengal National College was founded, of which Sri Aurobindo became the first principal.

The educational system established by the British in India was one-sided, and came in for sharp criticism from both Tagore and Sri Aurobindo. "The Western system of education," says Tagore, "is impersonal. . . . It dwells in the cold-storage compartments of lessons and the ice-packed minds of the schoolmasters. . . . The introduction of this education was not a part of the solemn marriage ceremony which was to unite the minds of East and West in mutual understanding. It represented an artificial method of training specially calculated to produce the carriers of the white man's burden." There was a time when India provided her children with a culture which was the product of her own thought and creation. But this culture was brushed aside by the educationists under British rule: "Our educated community is not a cultured community but a community of qualified candidates."

India must therefore return to her age-old ideal and look upon education as an expression of the complete truth about man: "Truth must not only inform but inspire. If the inspiration dies out, and only the information accumulates, then truth loses its infinity." This is what has happened in modern Indian education where "there is no communication of life and love." In establishing the school at Shantiniketan, Tagore had before him the clearly conceived goal of remedying this situation: "The educational institution which I have in mind has for its object the constant pursuit of truth, from which the imparting of truth naturally follows." A school must be "a place where knowledge could become living—that knowledge which not only has its substance and law but its atmosphere subtly informed by a creative personality."

In traditional Indian education, learning was not separated from living: "It flowed naturally through the social channels" and became "a system of widespread irrigation of culture." Through recitation of epics, myths, legends, and folk ballads, through choral singing, performance of popular plays, and even through the sharing of the simple chores of daily life, the perennial ideals that give stability to man's life were imparted to children not in a contrived or abstract manner but as something effortlessly imbibed. "Owing to this vital method of culture, the common people of India, though technically illiterate, have been made conscious of the sanctity of social relationships, entailing constant sacrifice and self-control, urged and supported by ideals collectively expressed in one word, dharma." We must, of course, take into account the complexities of modern life. But, Tagore insists, the fundamental truth of the unity of all facets of human life cannot be ignored: "All human complexities must harmonise with organic unity with life, failing which there will be endless conflicts." Modern man is ignoring this truth. He is bravely but mechanically bearing the burden of all the complications and conflicts that have resulted from his error. "To the gods, viewing this from on high, it must seem like the floundering of a giant who has got out of his depth and knows not how to swim." How prophetic and appropriate these remarks of Tagore's, made half a century ago, sound in today's confused human condition!

Sri Aurobindo's condemnation of the prevailing system of education was based on the same fundamental idea of unity— the unity of all sides of human nature, and the unity of man with the universe. Referring to the great achievements of ancient India, not only in philosophy and art but also in the natural sciences, Sri Aurobindo asks: "What was it that stood behind that civilisation, second to none in the massiveness of its outlines or the perfection of its details? Without a great and unique discipline, involving a perfect education of soul and mind, a result so immense and persistent would have been impossible." Much has been said about the ashrams and universities of ancient India. But Sri Aurobindo points out that the success of these traditional institutions would not have been possible without a fundamental principle based upon "a profound knowledge of human psychology and its subtle application to the method of intellectual training and instruction."

Elaborating this principle, Sri Aurobindo says: "The ancient Aryans knew that man was not separate from the universe, but a homogeneous part of it, as a wave is part of the ocean. An infinite energy, Prakriti, Māyā, or Shakti, pervades the world, pours itself into every name and form, and the clod, the plant, the insect, the animal, the man are, in their phenomenal existence, merely more or less efficient adharas of this energy." On this profound philosophical awareness, Sri Aurobindo bases his interpretation of all aspects of human endeavour, including education: "The same force which moves in the stars and the planets moves in us, and all our thought and action are merely its play and are born of the complexity of its functionings." It is not enough to realise that man is the adhara (support) of this universal energy. Man must continually endeavor to increase his capacity as an adhara. Such an increase is, in fact, the basic aim of evolution.

In the light of this explanation, it is easy to see that Sri Aurobindo's conception of national education was not based on the idea that merely by including the study of Indian philosophy or culture in the school curriculum the situation could be set right. His approach to the question was much deeper. And it brought him to the same general conclusion that Tagore had reached by a somewhat different road: "Information cannot be the foundation of intelligence; it can only be part of the material out of which the knower builds knowledge, the starting-point, the nucleus, of fresh discovery and enlarged creation. An education that confines itself to imparting information is no education."

Worshippers at Sarasvati's shrine must not therefore bring insignificant offerings. She smiles only when her devotees show the deepest understanding of the whole of existence. We must never forget, says Tagore, that Sarasvati is seated on a lotus flower. "The symbolic meaning of this is that she dwells in the centre of life and the heart of all existence, which opens itself in beauty to the light of heaven."

Sri Aurobindo

The Brain of India

A new centre of thought implies a new centre of education. The system prevailing in our universities is one which ignores the psychology of man, loads the mind laboriously with numerous little packets of information carefully tied with red tape, and, by the methods used in this loading process, damages or atrophies the faculties and instruments by which man assimilates, creates, and grows in intellect, manhood and energy. The new National Education, as inaugurated in Bengal, sought immensely to enlarge the field of knowledge to which the student was introduced, and in so far as it laid stress on experiment and observation, employed the natural and easy instrument of the vernacular and encouraged the play of thought on the subject of study, corrected the habit of spoiling the instruments of knowledge by the use of false methods. But many of the vicious methods and ideas employed by the old system were faithfully cherished by the new, and the domination of the Council by men wedded to the old lines was bound to spell a most unfavourable effect on the integrity of the system in its most progressive features. Another vital defect of the new education was that it increased the amount of information the student was required to absorb without strengthening the body and brain sufficiently to grapple with the increased mass of intellectual toil, and it shared with the old system the defect of ignoring the psychology of the race. The mere inclusion of the matter of Indian thought and culture in the field of knowledge does not make a system of education Indian, and the instruction given in the Bengal National College was only an improved European system, not Indian or National. Another error which has to be avoided and to which careless minds are liable, is the reactionary idea that in order to be national, education must reproduce the features of the old *tol* system of Bengal. It is not eighteenth century India, the India which by its moral and intellectual deficiencies gave itself into the keeping of foreigners, that we have to revive, but the spirit, ideals and methods of the ancient and mightier India in a yet more effective form and with a more modern organisation.

What was the secret of that gigantic intellectuality, spirituality and superhuman moral force which we see pulsating in the Ramayana and Mahābhārata, in the ancient philosophy, in the supreme poetry, art, sculpture and architecture of India? What was at the basis of the incomparable public works and engineering achievement, the opulent and exquisite industries, the great triumphs of science, scholarship, jurisprudence, logic, metaphysics, the unique social structure? What supported the heroism and self-abandonment of the Kshatriya, the Sikh and the Rajput, the unconquerable national vitality and endurance? What was it that stood behind that civilisation second to none, in the massiveness of its outlines or the perfection of its details? Without a great and unique discipline involving a perfect education of soul and mind, a result so immense and persistent would have been impossible. It would be an error to look for the secret of Aryan success in the details of the instruction given in the old Ashrams and universities so far as they have come down to us. We must know what was the principle and basis on which the details were founded. We shall find the secret of their success in a profound knowledge of human psychology and its subtle application to the methods of intellectual training and instruction.

At the basis of the old Aryan system was the all-important discipline of Brahmacharya. The first necessity for the building up of a great intellectual superstructure is to provide a foundation strong enough to bear it. Those systems of education which start from an insufficient knowledge of man, think they have provided a satisfactory foundation when they have supplied the student with a large or well-selected mass of information on the various subjects which comprise the best part of human culture at the time. The school gives the materials, it is for the student to use them,—this is the formula. But the error here is fundamental. Information cannot be the foundation of intelligence, it can only be part of the material out of which the knower builds knowledge, the starting-point, the nucleus of fresh discovery and enlarged creation. An education that confines itself to imparting knowledge, is no education. The various faculties of memory, judgment, imagination, perception, reasoning, which build the edifice of thought and knowledge for the knower, must not only be equipped with their fit and sufficient tools and materials, but trained to bring fresh materials and use more skilfully those of which they are in possession. And the foundation of the structure they have to build, can only be the provision of a fund of force and energy sufficient to bear the demands of a continually growing activity of the memory, judgment and creative power. Where is that energy to be found?

The ancient Aryans knew that man was not separate from

the universe, but only a homogeneous part of it, as a wave is part of the ocean. An infinite energy, Prakriti, Māyā or Shakti, pervades the world, pours itself into every name and form, and the clod, the plant, the insect, the animal, the man are, in their phenomenal existence, merely more or less efficient adharas of this Energy. We are each of us a dynamo into which waves of that energy have been generated and stored, and are being perpetually conserved, used up and replenished. The same force which moves in the star and the planet, moves in us, and all our thought and action are merely its play and born of the complexity of its functionings. There are processes by which man can increase his capacity as an adhara. There are other processes by which he can clear of obstructions the channel of communication between himself and the universal energy and bring greater and greater stores of it pouring into his soul and brain and body. This continual improvement of the adhara and increase in quantity and complexity of action of the informing energy, is the whole aim of evolution. When that energy is the highest in kind and the fullest in amount of which the human adhara is capable, and the adhara itself is trained utterly to bear the inrush and play of the energy, then is a man siddha, the fulfilled or perfect man, his evolution is over and he has completed in the individual that utmost development which the mass of humanity is labouring towards through the ages.

If this theory be correct, the energy at the basis of the operation of intelligence must be in ourselves and it must be capable of greater expansion and richer use to an extent practically unlimited. And this also must be a sound principle, that the more we can increase and enrich the energy, the greater will be potentially the range, power and activity of the functions of our mind and the consequent vigour of our intellectuality and the greatness of our achievement. This was the first principle on which the ancient Aryans based their education and one of the chief processes which they used for the increased storage of energy, was the practice of Brahmacharya.

The practice of Brahmacharya is the first and most necessary condition of increasing the force within and turning it to such uses as may benefit the possessor or mankind. All human energy has a physical basis. The mistake made by European materialism is to suppose the basis to be everything and confuse it with the source. The source of life and energy is not material but spiritual, but the basis, the foundation on which the life and energy stand and work, is physical. The ancient Hindus clearly recognised this distinction between kārana and pratishthā, the north pole and the south pole of being. Earth or gross matter is the pratishthā, Brahman or spirit is the kārana. To raise up the physical to the spiritual is Brahmacharya, for by the meeting of the two the energy which starts from one and produces the other is enhanced and fulfils itself.

This is the metaphysical theory. The application depends on a right understanding of the physical and psychological conformation of the human receptacle of energy. The fundamental physical unit is the retas, in which the tejas, the heat and light and electricity in a man, is involved and hidden. All energy is latent in the retas. This energy may be either expended physically or conserved. All passion, lust, desire wastes the energy by pouring it, either in the gross form or a sublimated subtler form, out of the body. Immorality in act throws it out in the gross form; immorality of thought in the subtle form. In either case there is waste, and unchastity is of the mind and speech as well as of the body. On the other hand, all self-control conserves the energy in the retas, and conservation always brings with it increase. But the needs of the physical body are limited and the excess of energy must create a surplus which has to turn itself to some use other than the physical. According to the ancient theory retas is jala or water, full of light and heat and electricity, in one word, of tejas. The excess of the retas turns first into heat or tapas which stimulates the whole system, and it is for this reason that all forms of self-control and austerity are called tapas or tapasyā because they generate the heat, or stimulus which is a source of powerful action and success; secondly, it turns to tejas proper, light, the energy which is at the source of all knowledge; thirdly, it turns to vidyut or electricity, which is at the basis of all forceful action whether intellectual or physical. In the vidyut again is involved the ojas, or prānashakti, the primal energy which proceeds from ether. The retas refining from jala to tapas, tejas and vidyut and from vidyut to ojas, fills the system with physical strength, energy and brain-power and in its last form of ojas rises to the brain and informs it with that primal energy which is the most refined form of matter and nearest to spirit. It is ojas that creates a spiritual force or vīrya, by which a man attains to spiritual knowledge, spiritual love and faith, spiritual strength. It follows that the more we can by Brahmacharya increase the store of tapas, tejas, vidyut and ojas, the more we shall fill ourselves with utter energy for the works of the body, heart, mind and spirit.

This view of the human soul was not the whole of the knowledge on which ancient Hinduism based its educational discipline. In addition it had the view that all knowledge is within and has to be evoked by education rather than instilled from outside. The constitution of man consists of three principles of nature sattva, rajas and tamas, the comprehensive, active and passive elements of universal action, which, in one of their thousandfold aspects, manifest as knowledge, passion and ignorance. Tamas is a constitutional dullness or passivity which obscures the knowledge within and creates ignorance, mental inertia, slowness, forgetfulness, disinclination to study, inability to grasp and distinguish. Rajas is an undisciplined activity which obscures knowledge by passion, attachment, prejudgment, predilection and wrong ideas. Sattva is an illumination which reveals the hidden knowledge and brings it to the surface where the observation can grasp and the memory record it. This conception of the constitution of the knowing faculty made the removal of tamas, the disciplining of rajas and the awakening of sattva the main problem of the teacher. He had to train the student to be receptive of illumination from within. The disciplining of rajas was effected by a strict moral discipline which induced a calm, clear, receptive state of mind, free from intellectual self-will and pride and the obscuration of passion,—the famous discipline of the brahmacārin which was the foundation of Aryan culture and Aryan morale; and the interference of wrong ideas was sought to be removed by strict mental submission to the teacher during the receptive period, when the body of ascertained knowledge or right ideas already in man's possession was explained to him and committed to memory. The removal of tamas was effected by the discipline of moral purity, which awakened the energy of tejas and electricity in the system and by the power of tapasyā trained it to be a reservoir of mental force and clarity. The awakening of illumination was actively effected by the triple method of repetition, meditation and discussion. Āvritti or repetition was meant to fill the recording part of the mind with the sabda or words, so that the artha or meaning might of itself rise from within: needless to say, a mechanical repetition was not likely to produce this effect. There must be that clear still receptivity and that waiting upon the word or thing with the contemplative part of the mind which is what the ancient Indians meant by dhyāna or meditation. All of us have felt, when studying a language, difficulties which seemed insoluble while grappling with a text suddenly melt away and a clear understanding arise without assistance from book or teacher after putting away the book from our mind for a brief period. Many of us have experienced also the strangeness of taking up a language or subject, after a brief discontinuance, to find that we understand it much better than when we took it up, know the meanings of words we had never met with before and can explain sentences which, before we discontinued the study, would have baffled our understanding. This is because the jnātā or knower within has had his attention called to the subject and has been busy in the interval drawing upon the source of knowledge within in connection with it. This experience is only possible to those whose sattwic or illuminative element has been powerfully aroused or consciously or unconsciously trained to action by the habit of intellectual clarity and deep study. The highest reach of the sattwic development is when one can dispense often or habitually with outside aids, the teacher or the text book, grammar and dictionary and learn a subject largely or wholly from within. But this is only possible to the yogin by a successful prosecution of the discipline of yoga.

Rabindranath Tagore

An Eastern University

Once upon a time we were in possession of such a thing as our own mind in India. It was living. It thought, it felt, it expressed itself. It was receptive as well as productive. That this mind could be of any use in the process, or in the end, of our education was overlooked by our modern educational dispensation. We are provided with buildings and books and other magnificent burdens calculated to suppress our mind. The latter was treated like a library-shelf solidly made of wood, to be loaded with leather-bound volumes of second-hand information. In consequence, it has lost its own colour and character, and has borrowed polish from the carpenter's shop. All this has cost us money, and also our finer ideas, while our intellectual vacancy has been crammed with what is described in official reports as Education. In fact, we have bought our spectacles at the expense of our eyesight.

In India our goddess of learning is Sarasvati. My audience in the West, I am sure, will be glad to know that her complexion is white. But the signal fact is that she is living and she is a woman, and her seat is on a lotus-flower. The symbolic meaning of this is, that she dwells in the centre of life and the heart of all existence, which opens itself in beauty to the light of heaven.

The Western education which we have chanced to know is impersonal. Its complexion is also white, but it is the whiteness of the white-washed class-room walls. It dwells in the cold-storage compartments of lessons and the ice-packed minds of the schoolmasters. The effect which it had on my mind when, as a boy, I was compelled to go to school, I have described elsewhere. My feeling was very much the same as a tree might have, which was not allowed to live its full life, but was cut down to be made into packing-cases.

The introduction of this education was not a part of the solemn marriage ceremony which was to unite the minds of the East and West in mutual understanding. It represented an artificial method of training specially calculated to produce the carriers of the white man's burden. This want of ideals still clings to our education system, though our Universities have latterly burdened their syllabus with a greater number of subjects than before. But it is only like adding to the bags of wheat the bullock carries to market; it does not make the bullock any better off. . . .

Universities should never be made into mechanical organisations for collecting and distributing knowledge. Through them the people should offer their intellectual hospitality, their wealth of mind to others, and earn their proud right in return to receive gifts from the rest of the world. But in the whole length and breadth of India there is not a single University established in the modern time where a foreign or an Indian student can properly be acquainted with the best products of the Indian mind. For that we have to cross the sea, and knock at the doors of France and Germany. Educational institutions in our country are India's alms-bowl of knowledge; they lower our intellectual self-respect; they encourage us to make a foolish display of decorations composed of borrowed feathers.

This it was that led me to found a school in Bengal, in face of many difficulties and discouragements, and in spite of my own vocation as a poet, who finds his true inspiration only when he forgets that he is a schoolmaster. It is my hope that in this school a nucleus has been formed, round which an indigenous University of our own land will find its natural growth—a University which will help India's mind to concentrate and to be fully conscious of itself; free to seek the truth and make this truth its own wherever found, to judge by its own standard, give expression to its own creative genius, and offer its wisdom to the guests who come from other parts of the world.

Man's intellect has a natural pride in its own aristocracy, which is the pride of its culture. Culture only acknowledges the excellence whose criticism is in its inner perfection, not in any external success. When this pride succumbs to some compulsion of necessity or lure of material advantage, it brings humiliation to the intellectual man. Modern India, through her very education, has been made to suffer this humiliation. Once she herself provided her children with a culture which was the product of her own ages of thought and creation. But it has been thrust aside, and we are made to tread the mill of passing examinations, not for learning anything, but for notifying that we are qualified for employments under organisations conducted in English. Our educated community is not a cultured community, but a community of qualified candidates. Meanwhile the proportion of possible employments to the number of claimants has gradually been growing narrower, and the consequent disaffection has been widespread. At last the very authorities who are responsible for this are blaming their victims. Such is the perversity of human nature. It bears its worst grudge against those it has injured.

It is as if some tribe which had the primitive habit of decorating its tribal members with birds' plumage were some day to hold these very birds guilty of the crime of being extinct. There are belated attempts on the part of our governors to read us pious homilies about disinterested love of learning, while the old machinery goes on working, whose product is not education but certificates. It is good to remind the fettered bird that its wings are for soaring; but it is better to cut the chain which is holding it to its perch. The most pathetic feature of the tragedy is that the bird itself has learnt to use its chain for its ornament, simply because the chain jingles in fairly respectable English. . . .

Where society is comparatively simple and obstructions are not too numerous, we can clearly see how the life-process guides education in its vital purpose. The system of folk-education, which is indigenous to India, but is dying out, was one with the people's life. It flowed naturally through the social channels and made its way everywhere. It is a system of widespread irrigation of culture. Its teachers, specially trained men, are in constant requisition, and find crowded meetings in our villages, where they repeat the best thoughts and express the ideals of the land in the most effective form. The mode of instruction includes the recitation of epics, expounding of the scriptures, reading from the Puranas, which are the classical records of old history, performance of plays founded upon the early myths and legends, dramatic narration of the lives of ancient heroes, and the singing in chorus of songs from the old religious literature. Evidently, according to this system, the best function of education is to enable us to realise that to live as a man is great, requiring profound philosophy for its ideal, poetry for its expression, and heroism in its conduct. Owing to this vital method of culture the common people of India, though technically illiterate, have been made conscious of the sanctity of social relationships, entailing constant sacrifice and self-control, urged and supported by ideals collectively expressed in one word, dharma.

Such a system of education may sound too simple for the complexities of modern life. But the fundamental principle of social life in its different stages of development remains the same; and in no circumstance can the truth be ignored that all human complexities must harmonise in organic unity with life, failing which there will be endless conflict. Most things in the civilised world occupy more than their legitimate space. Much of their burden is needless. By bearing this burden civilised man may be showing great strength, but he displays little skill. To the gods, viewing this from on high, it must seem like the flounderings of a giant who has got out of his depth and knows not how to swim. . . .

A most important truth, which we are apt to forget, is that a teacher can never truly teach unless he is still learning himself. A lamp can never light another lamp unless it continues to burn its own flame. The teacher who has come to the end of his subject, who has no living traffic with his knowledge, but merely repeats his lessons to his students, can only load their minds; he cannot quicken them. Truth not only must inform but inspire. If the inspiration dies out, and the information only accumulates, then truth loses its infinity. The greater part of our learning in the schools has been wasted because, for most of our teachers, their subjects are like dead specimens of once living things, with which they have a learned acquaintance, but no communication of life and love.

The educational institution, therefore, which I have in mind has primarily for its object the constant pursuit of truth, from which the imparting of truth naturally follows. It must not be a dead cage in which living minds are fed with food artificially prepared. It should be an open house, in which students and teachers are at one. They must live their complete life together, dominated by a common aspiration for truth and a need of sharing all the delights of culture. In former days the great master-craftsmen had students in their workshops where they co-operated in shaping things to perfection. That was the place where knowledge could become living—that knowledge which not only has its substance and law, but its atmosphere subtly informed by a creative personality. For intellectual knowledge also has its aspect of creative art, in which the man who explores truth expresses something which is human in him—his enthusiasm, his courage, his sacrifice, his honesty, and his skill. In merely academical teaching we find subjects, but not the man who pursues the subjects; therefore the vital part of education remains incomplete.

For our Universities we must claim, not labelled packages of truth and authorised agents to distribute them, but truth in its living association with her lovers and seekers and discoverers. Also we must know that the concentration of the mind-forces scattered throughout the country is the most important mission of a University, which, like the nucleus of a living cell, should be the centre of the intellectual life of the people.

The bringing about of an intellectual unity in India is, I am told, difficult to the verge of impossibility owing to the fact that India has so many different languages. Such a statement is as unreasonable as to say that man, because he has a diversity of limbs, should find it impossible to realise life's unity in himself, and that only an earthworm composed of a tail and nothing else could truly know that it had a body. . . .

If we were to take for granted, what some people maintain, that Western culture is the only source of light for our mind, then it would be like depending for daybreak upon some star, which is the sun of a far distant sphere. The star may give us light, but not the day; it may give us direction in our voyage of exploration, but it can never open the full view of truth before our eyes. In fact, we can never use this cold starlight for stirring the sap in our branches, and giving colour and bloom to our life. This is the reason why European education has become for India mere school lessons and no culture; a box of matches, good for the small uses of illumination, but not the light of morning, in which the use and beauty, and all the subtle mysteries of life are blended in one. . . .

The main river in Indian culture has flowed in four streams,—the Vedic, the Puranic, the Buddhist, and the Jain. It has its source in the heights of the Indian consciousness. But a river, belonging to a country, is not fed by its own waters alone. The Tibetan Brahmaputra is a tributary to the Indian Ganges. Contributions have similarly found their way to India's original culture. The Muhammadan, for example, has repeatedly come into India from outside, laden with his own stores of knowledge and feeling and his wonderful religious democracy, bringing freshet after freshet to swell the current. To our music, our architecture, our pictorial art, our literature, the Muhammadans have made their permanent and precious contribution. Those who have studied the lives and writings of our medieval saints, and all the great religious movements that sprang up in the time of the Muhammadan rule, know how deep is our debt to this foreign current that has so intimately mingled with our life.

So, in our centre of Indian learning, we must provide for the co-ordinate study of all these different cultures—, the Vedic, the Puranic, the Buddhist, the Jain, the Islamic, the Sikh and the Zoroastrian. The Chinese, Japanese and Tibetan will also have to be added; for, in the past, India did not remain isolated within her own boundaries. Therefore, in order to learn what she was, in her relation to the whole continent of Asia, these cultures too must be studied. Side by side with them must finally be placed the Western culture. For only then shall we be able to assimilate this last contribution to our common stock. A river flowing within banks is truly our own, and it can contain its due tributaries; but our relations with a flood can only prove disastrous.

There are some who are exclusively modern, who believe that the past is the bankrupt time, leaving no assets for us, but only a legacy of debts. They refuse to believe that the army which is marching forward can be fed from the rear. It is well to remind such persons that the great ages of renaissance in history were those when man suddenly discovered the seeds of thought in the granary of the past. . . .

So far I have dwelt only upon the intellectual aspect of Education. For, even in the West, it is the intellectual training which receives almost exclusive emphasis. The Western universities have not yet truly recognised that fulness of expression is fulness of life. And a large part of man can never find its expression in the mere language of words. It must therefore seek for its other languages,—lines and colours, sounds and movements. Through our mastery of these we not only make our whole nature articulate, but also understand man in all his attempts to reveal his innermost being in every age and clime. The great use of Education is not merely to collect facts, but to know man and to make oneself known to man. It is the duty of every human being to master, at least to some extent, not only the language of intellect, but also that personality which is the language of Art. It is a great world of reality for man,—vast and profound,—this growing world of his own creative nature. This is the world of Art. To be brought up in ignorance of it is to be deprived of the knowledge and use of that great inheritance of humanity, which has been growing and waiting for every one of us from the beginning of our history. It is to remain deaf to the eternal voice of Man, that speaks to all men the messages that are beyond speech. From the educational point of view we know Europe where it is scientific, or at best literary. So our notion of its modern culture is limited within the boundary lines of grammar and the laboratory. We almost completely ignore the aesthetic life of man, leaving it uncultivated, allowing weeds to grow there. Our newspapers are prolific, our meeting-places are vociferous; and in them we wear to shreds the things we have borrowed from our English teachers. We make the air dismal and damp with the tears of our grievances. But where are our arts, which, like the outbreak of spring flowers, are the spontaneous overflow of our deeper nature and spiritual magnificence?

Through this great deficiency of our modern education, we are condemned to carry to the end a dead load of dumb wisdom. Like miserable outcasts, we are deprived of our place in the festival of culture, and wait at the outer court, where the colours are not for us, nor the forms of delight, nor the songs. Ours is the education of a prison-house, with hard labour and with a drab dress cut to the limits of minimum decency and necessity. We are made to forget that the perfection of colour and form and expression belongs to the perfection of vitality,— that the joy of life is only the other side of the strength of life. The timber merchant may think that the flowers and foliage are mere frivolous decorations of a tree; but if these are suppressed, he will know to his cost that the timber too will fail.

During the Mogul period, music and art in India found a great impetus from the rulers, because their whole life—not merely their official life—was lived in this land; and it is the wholeness of life from which originates Art. But our English teachers are birds of passage; they cackle to us, but do not sing,—their true heart is not in the land of their exile.

Constriction of life, owing to this narrowness of culture, must no longer be encouraged. In the centre of Indian culture which I am proposing, music and art must have their prominent seats of honour, and not be given merely a tolerant nod of recognition. The different systems of music and different schools of art which lie scattered in the different ages and provinces of India, and in the different strata of society, and also those belonging to the other great countries of Asia, which had communication with India, have to be brought there together and studied. . . .

Before I conclude my paper, a delicate question remains to be considered. What must be the religious ideal that is to rule our centre of Indian culture? The one abiding ideal in the religious life of India has been Mukti, the deliverance of man's soul from the grip of self, its communion with the Infinite Soul through its union in ānanda with the universe. This religion of spiritual harmony is not a theological doctrine to be taught, as a subject in the class, for half an hour each day. It is the spiritual truth and beauty of our attitude towards our surroundings, our conscious relationship with the Infinite, and the lasting power of the Eternal in the passing moments of our life. Such a religious ideal can only be made possible by making provision for students to live in intimate touch with nature, daily to grow in an atmosphere of service offered to all creatures, tending trees, feeding birds and animals, learning to feel the immense mystery of the soil and water and air. . . .

In other words, this institution should be a perpetual creation by the co-operative enthusiasm of teachers and students, growing with the growth of their soul; a world in itself, self-sustaining, independent, rich with ever-renewing life, radiating life across space and time, attracting and maintaining round it a planetary system of dependent bodies. Its aim should lie in imparting life-breath to the complete man, who is intellectual as well as economic, bound by social bonds, but aspiring towards spiritual freedom and final perfection.

Sri Aurobindo on Education

The discovery that education must be a bringing out of the child's own intellectual and moral capacities to their highest possible value and must be based on the psychology of the child-nature was a step forward towards a more healthy because a more subjective system; but it still fell short because it still regarded him as an object to be handled and moulded by the teacher, to be educated. But at least there was a glimmering of the realisation that each human being is a self-developing soul and that the business of both parent and teacher is to enable and to help the child to educate himself, to develop his own intellectual, moral, aesthetic and practical capacities and to grow freely as an organic being, not to be kneaded and pressured into form like an inert plastic material. It is not yet realised what this soul is or that the true secret, whether with child or man, is to help him to find his deeper self, the real psychic entity within. That, if we ever give it a chance to come forward, and still more if we call it into the foreground as "the leader of the march set in our front," will itself take up most of the business of education out of our hands and develop the capacity of the psychological being towards a realisation of its potentialities of which our present mechanical view of life and man and external routine methods of dealing with them prevent us from having any experience or forming any conception. These new educational methods are on the straight way to this truer dealing. The closer touch attempted with the psychical entity behind the vital and physical mentality and an increasing reliance on its possibilities must lead to the ultimate discovery that man is inwardly a soul and a conscious power of the Divine and that the evocation of this real man within is the right object of education and indeed of all human life if it would find and live according to the hidden Truth and deepest law of its own being. That was the knowledge which the ancients sought to express through religious and social symbolism, and subjectivism is a road of return to the lost knowledge. First deepening man's inner experience, restoring perhaps on an unprecedented scale insight and self-knowledge to the race, it must end by revolutionising his social and collective self-expression.

Spiritual Discipline

Introduction

In his famous discussion of "The Holy Men of India," Carl Jung describes Ramana Maharshi as "the whitest spot on a white surface," less a unique phenomenon than the perfect "embodiment of spiritual India." In Ramana Maharshi, Jung finds "purest India, the breath of eternity, scorning and scorned by the world":

> It is the song of the ages, resounding, like the shrilling of crickets on a summer's night, from a million beings. This melody is built up on the one great theme, which veiling its monotony under a thousand colorful reflections, tirelessly and everlastingly rejuvenates itself in the Indian spirit, whose youngest incarnation is Sri Ramana himself.[1]

Jung correctly recognized that Ramana Maharshi typifies the holy men of India who for centuries have drowned "the world of multiplicity in the All and All-Oneness of Universal Being." As uniform as the Indian spiritual tradition may appear at first, however, Sri Ramana's fidelity to "India's ancient

[1] C. G. Jung, "The Holy Men of India," in *Psychology and Religion: West and East*, Vol. 11: *The Collected Works of C. G. Jung*, trans. R. F. C. Hull, New York: Pantheon Books, 1958, p. 579.

chants" is but one mode of contemporary Indian spirituality. Sri Aurobindo and Maharishi Mahesh Yogi, for example, represent quite different spiritual experiences from Ramana Maharshi—less traditional but no less true to Indian spirituality.

When Jung writes that Ramana Maharshi typifies a spirituality in which he "is right when he intones India's ancient chants, but wrong when he pipes any other tune," [2] he separates Sri Ramana from Sri Aurobindo, Maharishi Mahesh Yogi, and many other contemporary Indian spiritual personalities. Jung himself recognized that Ramakrishna, for example, revealed a more modern and perhaps more Western attitude toward the ego than the more conservatively Indian position of Sri Ramana. Similarly, Sri Aurobindo's position on the ego and on many equally important points diverges from the Vedantist, and consequently from Sri Ramana's, position. Finally Maharishi Mahesh Yogi does not present a systematic alternative or a spiritual experience comparable to those of Sri Ramana or Sri Aurobindo, but he offers a technique that may significantly help to bridge the gap between the masses of humanity and these two spiritual giants.

It may be said that Sri Ramana's entire system is based on his own realization of Self. He answered the question raised in the following selection, "Who am I?" when at the age of seventeen he experienced the identity of the "I" or ego with the Ātman or Universal Self. Even more remarkable than this experience was his ability to sustain its effects, i.e., to maintain the awareness of absolute unity throughout the fifty years during which he offered spiritual direction to all who sought his guidance.

[2] *Ibid.*, p. 578.

The key to Sri Ramana's guidance is the silence which can be achieved by inquiring into the thought, "Who am I?" In this way, the "I" can be seized, controlled, and shown to be a manifestation of Self; ultimately it can be shown that "I," along with the world, God, and other parts of reality, are all the Self. Silence allows this identity to be realized. But since silence is possible only by control of the desiring ego, one must begin with the thought of the ego and proceed until the familiar "I" is absorbed into the true, Universal Self.

Whereas Sri Ramana experienced spiritual liberation as a very young man, and offered an unrevised account of his permanent spiritual state, Sri Aurobindo's experience and its articulation evolved over the course of his spiritual life. Further, his experience, and his account of it, involved a wide variety of spiritual and cultural strains. His yoga system is as close to his own experience as is Sri Ramana's, but his experience was vastly more complex. If Sri Ramana is quintessentially Indian, Sri Aurobindo is trans-Indian: at the age when Ramana Maharshi realized the Self, the young Aurobindo Ghose was completing his studies at St. Paul's School in London and was about to enter Cambridge University. Twenty years of intense academic and political work separated Aurobindo from his total commitment to yoga. These diverse interests and activities continued to function in his spiritual life and thought, both in his own experience and in his message for historical transformation.

In the following selection, for example, Sri Aurobindo outlines the various yogas and argues that each is necessary for the full development of human spirituality. In direct contrast to Ramana Maharshi, Sri Aurobindo argues that union with the Divine cannot be an adequate goal of yoga, but that yoga and the yogin must aim at the transformation of each level of existence. "Integral" then, refers not only to a synthesis of several kinds of yoga, but equally to an integration of the spiritual and material orders of life. Yoga for Sri Aurobindo is the means and end of spiritual evolution.

By comparison with Sri Ramana and Sri Aurobindo, Maharishi Mahesh Yogi can be better understood as a guru or transmitter of spiritual teaching than as a spiritual source or phenomenon. Or it may simply be pointed out that Maharishi is performing an important practical work. In the long run, of course, the spiritual teaching of great souls like Sri Ramana and Sri Aurobindo will probably prove to be the most practical of all teachings, but Maharishi offers a more immediate solution to millions of Westerners for whom the experiences and teachings of avatars remains entirely out of reach.

Maharishi acknowledges that Transcendental Meditation (or TM) is derived from the standard method of meditation practiced for centuries in India and described in the Bhagavad-Gītā. But his original contribution is the method by which millions have learned an elementary yet effective way of meditating. Essentially, Transcendental Meditation consists of two points: first, the effort to experience thought in its finest possible state until the active or experiencing mind goes below the mental to the source of thought; second, the use of a mantra, or thought-sound, by which to lead the mind past meaning to a creative calm. It must be emphasized, however, that even Maharishi's own book-length description of this technique is dramatically less convincing than a sincere and consistent effort to practice it for several months. Although the elaborate scientific studies on behalf of Transcendental Meditation are fascinating and confirming, the most convincing test of it and most other claims in the Indian spiritual tradition is experience. Maharishi's approach to meditation is pragmatic not simply because his mission is to the West, but equally because his message is derived from a spiritual tradition based firmly on the primacy of experimentation and personal truth. Maharishi's Transcendental Meditation brings the most accessible and usable aspect of that rich tradition to millions of spiritual seekers in the West.

Ramana Maharshi

Who Am I?

"Who Am I?" was written at the same period as "Self-Enquiry" (ca. 1901). It began as answers to certain questions asked by Sivaprakasam Pillai, one of the early disciples. It was first published in the form of questions and answers but was later changed into the form of a connected exposition. The original work has been adopted in the present edition.

As all living beings desire to be happy always, without misery, as in the case of every one there is observed supreme love for one's self, and as happiness alone is the cause for love, in order to gain that happiness which is one's nature and which is experienced in the state of deep sleep where there is no mind, one should know one's self. For that, the path of knowledge, the inquiry of the form *"Who am I?"* is the principal means.

1. Who am I?

The gross body which is composed of the seven humours (dhātus), I am not; the five cognitive sense-organs, viz. the senses of hearing, touch, sight, taste, and smell, which apprehend their respective objects, viz. sound, touch, colour, taste, and odour, I am not; the five conative sense-organs, viz. the organs of speech, locomotion, grasping, excretion, and procreation, which have as their respective functions speaking, moving, grasping, excreting, and enjoying, I am not; the five vital airs, prāna, etc., which perform respectively the five functions of in-breathing, etc., I am not; even the mind which thinks, I am not; the nescience too, which is endowed only with the residual impressions of objects, and in which there are no objects and no functionings, I am not.

2. If I am none of these, then who am I?

After negating all of the above-mentioned as "not this" ("not this") that Awareness which alone remains—that I am.

3. What is the nature of Awareness?

The nature of Awareness is existence-consciousness-bliss.

4. When will the realization of the Self be gained?

When the world which is what-is-seen has been removed, there will be realization of the Self which is the seer.

5. Will there not be realization of the Self even while the world is there (taken as real)?

There will not be.

6. Why?

The seer and the object seen are like the rope and the snake. Just as the knowledge of the rope which is the substrate will not arise unless the false knowledge of the illusory serpent goes, so the realization of the Self which is the substrate will not be gained unless the belief that the world is real is removed.

7. When will the world which is the object seen be removed?

When the mind, which is the cause of all cognitions and of all actions, becomes quiescent, the world will disappear.

8. What is the nature of the mind?

What is called "mind" is a wondrous power residing in the Self. It causes all thoughts to arise. Apart from thoughts, there is no such thing as mind. Therefore, thought is the nature of mind. Apart from thoughts, there is no independent entity called the world. In deep sleep there are no thoughts, and there is no world. In the states of waking and dream, there are thoughts, and there is a world also. Just as the spider emits the thread (of the web) out of itself and again withdraws it into itself, likewise the mind projects the world out of itself and again resolves it into itself. When the mind comes out of the Self, the world appears. Therefore, when the world appears (to be real), the Self does not appear; and when the Self appears (shines), the world does not appear. When one persistently inquires into the nature of the mind, the mind will end leaving the Self (as the residue). What is referred to as the Self is the Ātman. The mind always exists only in dependence on something gross; it cannot stay alone. It is the mind that is called the subtle body or the soul (jiva).

9.   What is the path of inquiry for understanding the nature of the mind?

That which rises as "I" in this body is the mind. If one inquires as to where in the body the thought "I" rises first, one would discover that it rises in the heart. That is the place of the mind's origin. Even if one thinks constantly "I," "I," one will be led to that place. Of all the thoughts that arise in the mind, the "I" thought is the first. It is only after the rise of this that the other thoughts arise. It is after the appearance of the first personal pronoun that the second and third personal pronouns appear; without the first personal pronoun there will not be the second and third.

10.   How will the mind become quiescent?

By the inquiry "Who am I?" The thought "Who am I?" will destroy all other thoughts, and, like the stick used for stirring the burning pyre, it will itself in the end get destroyed. Then, there will arise Self-realization.

11. What is the means for constantly holding on to the thought "Who am I?"

When other thoughts arise, one should not pursue them, but should inquire: "To whom did they arise?" It does not matter how many thoughts arise. As each thought arises, one should inquire with diligence, "To whom has this thought arisen?". The answer that would emerge would be "to me." Thereupon if one inquires "Who am I?" the mind will go back to its source; and the thought that arose will become quiescent. With repeated practice in this manner, the mind will develop the skill to stay in its source. When the mind that is subtle goes out through the brain and the sense-organs, the gross names and forms appear; when it stays in the heart, the names and forms disappear. Not letting the mind go out, but retaining it in the Heart is what is called "inwardness" (antar-mukha). Letting the mind to go out of the Heart is known as "externalization" (bahir-mukha). Thus, when the mind stays in the Heart, the "I" which is the source of all thoughts will go, and the Self which ever exists will shine. Whatever one does, one should do without the egoity "I." If one acts in that way, all will appear as of the nature of Shiva (God).

12. Are there no other means for making the mind quiescent?

Other than inquiry, there are no adequate means. If through other means it is sought to control the mind, the mind will appear to be controlled, but will again go forth. Through the control of breath also, the mind will become quiescent; but it will be quiescent only so long as the breath remains controlled, and when the breath resumes the mind also will again start moving and will wander as impelled by residual impressions. The source is the same for both mind and breath. Thought, indeed, is the nature of the mind. The thought "I" is the first thought of the mind; and that is egoity. It is from that whence egoity originates that breath also originates. Therefore, when the mind becomes quiescent, the breath is controlled, and when the breath is controlled, the mind becomes quiescent. But in deep sleep, although the mind becomes quiescent, the breath does not stop. This is because of the will of God, so that the body may be preserved and other people may not be under the impression that it is dead. In the state of waking and in samadhi, when the mind becomes quiescent the breath is controlled. Breath is the gross form of mind. Till the time of death, the mind keeps breath in the body; and when the body dies, the mind takes the breath along with it. Therefore, the exercise of breath-control is only an aid for rendering the mind quiescent (manonigraha); it will not destroy the mind (mano-nasa).

Like the practice of breath-control, meditation on the forms of God, repetition of mantras, restriction on food, etc., are but aids for rendering the mind quiescent.

Through meditation on the forms of God and through repetition of mantras, the mind becomes one-pointed. The mind will always be wandering. Just as when a chain is given to an elephant to hold in its trunk it will go along grasping the chain and nothing else, so also when the mind is occupied with a name or form it will grasp that alone. When the mind expands in the form of countless thoughts, each thought becomes weak; but as thoughts get resolved, the mind becomes one-pointed and strong; for such a mind Self-inquiry will become easy. Of all the restrictive rules, that relating to the taking of sattvic food in moderate quantities is the best; by observing this rule, the sattvic quality of mind will increase, and that will be helpful to Self-inquiry.

13. The residual impressions (thoughts) of objects appear

unending like the waves of an ocean. When will all of them be removed?

As the meditation on the Self rises higher and higher, the thoughts will get destroyed.

14. Is it possible for the residual impressions of objects that come from beginningless time, as it were, to be resolved, and for one to remain as the pure Self?

Without yielding to the doubt "Is it possible, or not?" one should presistently hold on to the meditation on the Self. Even if one be a great sinner, one should not worry and weep, "O! I am a sinner, how can I be saved?"; one should completely renounce the thought "I am a sinner"; and concentrate keenly on meditation on the Self; then, one would surely succeed. There are not two minds—one good and the other evil; the mind is only one. It is the residual impressions that are of two kinds—auspicious and inauspicious. When the mind is under the influence of auspicious impressions it is called good; and when it is under the influence of inauspicious impressions it is regarded as evil.

The mind should not be allowed to wander towards worldly objects and what concerns other people. However bad other people may be, one should bear no hatred for them. Both desire and hatred should be eschewed. All that one gives to others one gives to one's self. If this truth is understood who will not give to others? When one's self arises all arises; when one's self becomes quiescent all becomes quiescent. To the extent we behave with humility, to that extent there will result good. If the mind is rendered quiescent, one may live anywhere.

15. How long should inquiry be practised?

As long as there are impressions of objects in the mind, so long the inquiry "Who am I?" is required. As thoughts arise they should be destroyed then and there in the very place of their origin, through inquiry. If one resorted to contemplation of the Self unintermittently, until the Self was gained, that alone would do. As long as there are enemies within the fortress, they will continue to sally forth; if they are destroyed as they emerge, the fortress will fall into our hands.

16. What is the nature of the Self?

What exists in truth is the Self alone. The world, the individual soul, and God are appearances in it, like silver in mother-of-pearl; these three appear at the same time, and disappear at the same time.

The Self is that where there is absolutely no "I" thought. That is called "Silence." The Self itself is the world; the Self itself is "I"; the Self itself is God; all is Shiva, the Self.

17. Is not everything the work of God?

Without desire, resolve, or effort, the sun rises; and in its mere presence, the sun-stone emits fire, the lotus blooms, water evaporates; people perform their various functions and then rest. Just as in the presence of the magnet the needle moves, it is by virtue of the mere presence of God that the souls governed by the three (cosmic) functions or the fivefold divine activity perform their actions and then rest, in accordance with their respective karmas. God has no resolve; no karma attaches itself to Him. This is like worldly actions not affecting the sun, or like the merits and demerits of the other four elements not affecting the all-pervading ether.

18. Of the devotees, who is the greatest?

He who gives himself up to the Self that is God is the most excellent devotee. Giving one's self up to God means remaining constantly in the Self without giving room for the rise of any thoughts other than the thought of the Self.

Whatever burdens are thrown on God, He bears them. Since the supreme power of God makes all things move, why should we, without submitting ourselves to it, constantly worry ourselves with thoughts as to what should be done and how, and what should not be done and how not? We know that the train carries all loads, so after getting on it why should we carry our small luggage on our head to our discomfort, instead of putting it down in the train and feeling at ease?

19. What is non-attachment?

As thoughts arise, destroying them utterly without any residue in the very place of their origin is non-attachment. Just as the pearl-diver ties a stone to his waist, sinks to the bottom of the sea and there takes the pearls, so each one of us should be endowed with non-attachment, dive within himself and obtain the Self-Pearl.

20. Is it not possible for God and the Guru to effect the release of a soul?

God the the Guru will only show the way to release; they will not by themselves take the soul to the state of release.

In truth, God and the Guru are not different. Just as the prey which has fallen into the jaws of a tiger has no escape, so those who have come within the ambit of the Guru's gracious look will be saved by the Guru and will not get lost; yet, each one should by his own effort pursue the path shown by God or Guru and gain release. One can know oneself only with one's eye of knowledge, and not with somebody else's. Does he who is Rāma require the help of a mirror to know that he is Rāma?

21. Is it necessary for one who longs for release to inquire into the nature of the categories (tattvas)?

Just as one who wants to throw away garbage has no need to analyse it and see what it is, so one who wants to know the Self has no need to count the number of categories or inquire into their characteristics; what he has to do is to reject altogether the categories that hide the Self. The world should be considered like a dream.

22. Is there no difference between waking and dream?

Waking is long and a dream short; other than this there is

no difference. Just as waking happenings seem real while awake, so do those in a dream while dreaming. In dream the mind takes on another body. In both waking and dream states thoughts, names and forms occur simultaneously.

23. Is it any use reading books for those who long for release?

All the texts say that in order to gain release one should render the mind quiescent; therefore their conclusive teaching is that the mind should be rendered quiescent; once this has been understood there is no need for endless reading. In order to quieten the mind one has only to inquire within oneself what one's Self is; how could this search be done in books? One should know one's Self with one's own eye of wisdom. The Self is within the five sheaths; but books are outside them. Since the Self has to be inquired into by discarding the five sheaths, it is futile to search for it in books. There will come a time when one will have to forget all that one has learned.

24. What is happiness?

Happiness is the very nature of the Self; happiness and the Self are not different. There is no happiness in any object of the world. We imagine through our ignorance that we derive happiness from objects. When the mind goes out, it experiences misery. In truth, when its desires are fulfilled, it returns to its own place and enjoys the happiness that is the Self. Similarly, in the states of sleep, samadhi, and fainting, and when the object desired is obtained or the object disliked is removed, the mind becomes inward-turned, and enjoys pure Self-Happiness. Thus the mind moves without rest, alternately going out of the Self and returning to it. Under the tree the shade is pleasant; out in the open the heat is scorching. A person who has been going about in the sun feels cool when he reaches the shade. Some one who keeps on going from the shade into the sun and then back into the shade is a fool. A wise man stays permanently in the shade. Similarly, the mind of the one who knows the truth does not leave Brahman. The mind of the ignorant, on the contrary, revolves in the world, feeling miserable, and for a little time returns to Brahman to experience happiness. In fact, what is called the world is only thought. When the world disappears, i.e. when there is no thought, the mind experiences happiness; and when the world appears, it goes through misery.

25.   What is wisdom-insight (jnāna-drishti)?

Remaining quiet is what is called wisdom-insight. To remain quiet is to resolve the mind in the Self. Telepathy, knowing past, present and future happenings and clairvoyance do not constitute wisdom-insight.

26.   What is the relation between desirelessness and wisdom?

Desirelessness is wisdom. The two are not different; they are the same. Desirelessness is refraining from driving the mind towards any object. Wisdom means the appearance of no object. In other words, not seeking what is other than the Self is detachment or desirelessness; not leaving the Self is wisdom.

27.   What is the difference between inquiry and meditation?

Inquiry consists in retaining the mind in the Self. Meditation consists in thinking that one's self is Brahman, existence-consciousness-bliss.

28.   What is release?

Inquiring into the nature of one's self that is in bondage, and realizing one's true nature is release.

Sri Aurobindo

The Principle of the Integral Yoga

The principle of yoga is the turning of one or of all powers of our human existence into a means of reaching the divine Being. In an ordinary yoga one main power of being or one group of its powers is made the means, vehicle, path. In a synthetic yoga all powers will be combined and included in the transmuting instrumentation.

In hathayoga the instrument is the body and life. All the power of the body is stilled, collected, purified, heightened, concentrated to its utmost limits or beyond any limits by asana and other physical processes; the power of the life too is similarly purified, heightened, concentrated by asana and pranayama. This concentration of powers is then directed towards that physical centre in which the divine consciousness sits concealed in the human body. The power of life, nature-power, coiled up with all its secret forces asleep in the lowest nervous plexus of the earth-being,—for only so much escapes into waking action in our normal operations as is sufficient for the limited uses of human life,—rises awakened through centre after centre and awakens, too, in its ascent and passage the forces of each successive nodus of our being, the nervous life, the heart of emotion and ordinary mentality, the speech, sight, will, the higher knowledge, till through and above the brain it meets with and it becomes one with the divine consciousness.

In rajayoga the chosen instrument is the mind. Our ordinary mentality is first disciplined, purified and directed towards the divine Being, then by a summary process of asana and pranayama the physical force of our being is stilled and concentrated, the life-force released into a rhythmic movement capable of cessation and concentrated into a higher power of its upward action, the mind, supported and strengthened by this greater action and concentration of the body and life upon which it rests, is itself purified of all its unrest and emotion and its habitual thought-waves, liberated from distraction and dispersion, given its highest force of concentration, gathered up into a trance of absorption. Two objects, the one temporal, the other eternal, are gained by this discipline. Mind-power develops in another concentrated action abnormal capacities of knowledge, effective will, deep light of reception, powerful light of thought-radiation which are altogether beyond the narrow range of our normal mentality; it arrives at the yogic or occult powers around which there has been woven so much quite dispensable and yet perhaps salutary mystery. But the one final end and the one all-important gain is that the mind, stilled and cast into a concentrated trance, can lose itself in the divine consciousness and the soul be made free to unite with the divine Being.

The triple way takes for its chosen instruments the three main powers of the mental soul-life of the human being. Knowledge selects the reason and the mental vision and it makes them by purification, concentration and a certain discipline of a God-directed seeking its means for the greatest knowledge and the greatest vision of all, God-knowledge and God-vision. Its aim is to see, know and be the Divine. Works, action selects for its instrument the will of the doer of works; it makes life an offering of sacrifice to the Godhead and by purification, concentration and a certain discipline of subjection to the divine Will a means for contact and increasing unity of the soul of man with the divine Master of the universe. Devotion selects the emotional and aesthetic powers of the soul and by turning them all Godward in a perfect purity, intensity, infinite passion of seeking makes them a means of God-possession in one or many relations of unity with the Divine Being. All aim in their own way at a union or unity of the human soul with the supreme Spirit.

Each yoga in its process has the character of the instrument it uses; thus the Hathayogic process is psycho-physical, the rajayogic mental and psychic, the way of knowledge is spiritual and cognitive, the way of devotion spiritual, emotional and aesthetic, the way of works spiritual and dynamic by action. Each is guided in the ways of its own characteristic power. But all power is in the end one, all power is really soul-power. In the ordinary process of life, body and mind this truth is quite obscured by the dispersed, dividing and distributive action of Nature which is the normal condition of all our functionings, although even there it is in the end evident; for all material energy contains hidden the vital, mental, psychic, spiritual energy and in the end it must release these forms of the one Shakti, the vital energy conceals and liberates into action all the other forms, the mental supporting itself on the life and body and their powers and functionings contains undeveloped or only partially developed the psychic and the spiritual power of the being. But when by yoga any of these powers is taken up from the dispersed and distributive action, raised to its highest degree, concentrated, it becomes manifest soul-power and reveals the essential unity. Therefore the hathayogic process has too its pure psychic and spiritual result, the rajayogic arrives by psychic means at a spiritual consummation. The triple way may appear to be altogether mental and spiritual in its way of seeking and its objectives, but it can be attended by results more characteristic of the other paths, which offer themselves in a spontaneous and involuntary flowering, and for the same reason, because soul-power is all-power and where it reaches its height in one direction its other possibilities also begin to show themselves in fact or in incipient potentiality. This unity at once suggests the possibility of a synthetic yoga.

Tantric discipline is in its nature a synthesis. It has seized on the large universal truth that there are two poles of being whose essential unity is the secret of existence, Brahman and Shakti, Spirit and Nature, and that Nature is power of the spirit or rather is spirit as power. To raise nature in man into manifest power of spirit is its method and it is the whole nature that it gathers up for the spiritual conversion. It includes in its system of instrumentation the forceful hathayogic process and especially the opening up of the nervous centres and the passage through them of the awakened Shakti on her way to her union with the Brahman, the subtler stress of the rajayogic purification, meditation and concentration, the leverage of will-force, the motive power of devotion, the key of knowledge. But it does not stop short with an effective assembling of the different powers of these specific yogas. In two directions it enlarges by its synthetic turn the province of the yogic method. First, it lays its hand firmly on many of the main springs of human quality, desire, action and it subjects them to an intensive discipline with the soul's mastery of its motives as a first aim and their elevation to a diviner spiritual level as its final utility. Again, it includes in its objects of yoga not only liberation,[1] which is the one all-mastering preoccupation of the specific systems, but a cosmic enjoyment[2] of the power of the Spirit, which the others may take incidentally on the way, in part, casually, but avoid making a motive or object. It is a bolder and larger system.

In the method of synthesis which we have been following, another clue of principle has been pursued which is derived from another view of the possibilities of yoga. This starts from the method of Vedanta to arrive at the aim of the Tantra. In the tantric method Shakti is all-important, becomes the key to the finding of spirit; in this synthesis spirit, soul is all-important, becomes the secret of the taking up of Shakti. The Tantric method starts from the bottom and grades the ladder of ascent upwards to the summit; therefore its initial stress is upon the action of the awakened Shakti in the nervous system of the body and its centres; the opening of the six lotuses is the opening up of the ranges of the power of Spirit. Our synthesis takes man as a spirit in mind much more than a spirit in body and assumes in him the capacity to begin on that level, to spiritualise his being by the power of the soul in mind opening itself directly to a higher spiritual force and being and to perfect by that higher force so possessed and brought into action the whole of his nature. For that reason our initial stress has fallen upon the utilisation of the powers of soul in mind and the turning of the triple key of knowledge, works and love in the locks of the spirit; the hathayogic methods can be dispensed with,—though there is no objection to their partial use,—the rajayogic will only enter in as an informal element. To arrive by the shortest way at the largest development of spiritual

[1] mukti
[2] bhukti

power and being and divinise by it a liberated nature in the whole range of human living is our inspiring motive.

The principle in view is a self-surrender, a giving up of the human being into the being, consciousness, power, delight of the Divine, a union or communion at all the points of meeting in the soul of man, the mental being, by which the Divine himself, directly and without veil master and possessor of the instrument, shall by the light of his presence and guidance perfect the human being in all the forces of the Nature for a divine living. Here we arrive at a farther enlargement of the objects of the yoga. The common initial purpose of all yoga is the liberation of the soul of man from its present natural ignorance and limitation, its release into spiritual being, its union with the highest self and Divinity. But ordinarily this is made not only the initial but the whole and final object: enjoyment of spiritual being there is, but either in a dissolution of the human and individual into the silence of self-being or on a higher plane in another existence. The Tantric system makes liberation the final, but not the only aim; it takes on its way a full perfection and enjoyment of the spiritual power, light and joy in the human existence, and even it has a glimpse of a supreme experience in which liberation and cosmic action and enjoyment are unified in a final overcoming of all oppositions and dissonances. It is this wider view of our spiritual potentialities from which we begin, but we add another stress which brings in a completer significance. We regard the spirit in man not as solely an individual being travelling to a transcendent unity with the Divine, but as a universal being capable of oneness with the Divine in all souls and all Nature and we give this extended view its entire practical conse-quence. The human soul's individual liberation and enjoyment of union with the Divine in spiritual being, consciousness and delight must always be the first object of the yoga; its free enjoyment of the cosmic unity of the Divine becomes a second object; but out of that a third appears, the effectuation of the meaning of the divine unity with all beings by a sympathy and participation in the spiritual purpose of the Divine in humanity. The individual yoga then turns from its separateness and becomes a part of the collective yoga of the divine Nature in the human race. The liberated individual being, united with the Divine in self and spirit, becomes in his natural being a self-perfecting instrument for the perfect outflowering of the Divine in humanity.

This outflowering has its two terms; first, comes the growth out of the separative human ego into the unity of the spirit, then the possession of the divine nature in its proper and its higher forms and no longer in the inferior forms of the mental being which are a mutilated translation and not the authentic text of the original script of divine Nature in the cosmic individual. In other words, a perfection has to be aimed at which amounts to the elevation of the mental into the full spiritual and supramental nature. Therefore this integral yoga of knowledge, love and works has to be extended into a yoga of spiritual and gnostic self-perfection. As gnostic knowledge, will and ānanda are a direct instrumentation of spirit and can only be won by growing into the spirit, into divine Being, this growth has to be the first aim of our yoga. The mental being has to enlarge itself into the oneness of the Divine before the Divine will perfect in the soul of the individual its gnostic outflowering. That is the reason why the triple way of knowledge, works and love becomes the keynote of the whole yoga, for that is the direct means for the soul in mind to rise to its highest intensities where it passes upward into the divine oneness. That too is the reason why the yoga must be integral. For if immergence in the Infinite or some close union with the Divine were all our aim, an integral yoga would be superfluous, except for such greater satisfaction of the being of man as we may get by a self-lifting of the whole of it towards its Source. But it would not be needed for the essential aim, since by any single power of the soul-nature we can meet with the Divine; each at its height rises up into the infinite and absolute, each therefore offers a sufficient way of arrival, for all the hundred separate paths meet in the Eternal. But the gnostic being is a complete enjoyment and possession of the whole divine and spiritual nature; and it is a complete lifting of the whole nature of man into its power of a divine and spiritual existence. Integrality becomes then an essential condition of this yoga.

At the same time we have seen that each of the three ways at its height, if it is pursued with a certain largeness, can take into itself the powers of the others and lead to their fulfilment. It is therefore sufficient to start by one of them and find the point at which it meets the other at first parallel lines of advance and melts into them by its own widenings. At the same time a more difficult, complex, wholly powerful process would be to start, as it were, on three lines together, on a triple wheel of soul-power. But the consideration of this possibility must be postponed till we have seen what are the conditions and means of the yoga of self-perfection. For we shall see that this also need not be postponed entirely, but a certain preparation of it is part of and a certain initiation into it proceeds by the growth of the divine works, love and knowledge.

Maharishi Mahesh Yogi

How to Contact Being

The science of being not only affirms the theory of one absolute element at the basis of the entire creation but also provides a systematic way whereby any man may experience directly the essential nature of transcendental, absolute Being.

First we shall consider from a theoretical point of view the possibility of directly experiencing the Absolute, and then we shall consider the practical results of such an experience in day-to-day life.

We have seen that Being lies in the transcendental field of absolute existence beyond the subtlest stratum of creation. To experience this transcendental reality it is necessary for our attention to be led through all the subtle strata of creation; arriving at the subtlest level, it will transcend that experience and come to the field of transcendental Being.

What do we find on the gross level of creation? We find gross things to see with the eyes, gross words or sounds to hear with the ears, gross odours to smell with the nose, varieties of sensations to feel with the sense of touch and varieties of flavours to taste with the tongue. We think, and normally the process of thinking seems to have no connection with these senses of perception. But the process of thinking does include one or many of these senses.

Our experience in the field of perception shows that we experience gross and subtle things. We use our eyes to see, our ears to hear and so on; but we know there is a limit to what the eyes can see, the ears hear and the tongue taste. This marks the limit of the experience of gross creation.

The eyes can see forms as long as the forms do not become refined beyond a certain point. The ears can hear sounds within a certain frequency range. The nose can smell odours as long as they are gross enough. This is the case with all the senses of perception. They are only able to experience gross objects.

Thus we understand that our experience is ordinarily limited to the gross field of creation. The subtle fields are beyond our ordinary range of experience. We know that there are forms much finer than those which the eyes can see and that these may be observed through the microscope. We know that there are sounds which the ears cannot hear but which may be heard with the help of amplifiers. This shows that there exist subtle strata of creation with which we are not familiar because our ordinary capacity for experience is limited to the gross. Therefore to experience transcendental Being it is necessary to develop the faculty of experience.

If we could develop our faculty of experience through any of the senses, or develop our ability to experience thought before it reaches the conscious level of the mind, and if this ability to experience thought could be so developed that it reached the source of thought, then, having transcended the source, it would be possible to reach the transcendental state of pure Being. In this way, by progressively experiencing finer states of creation through any one of the senses until the finest experience is transcended, the state of Being is reached.

Since Being is by nature transcendental, It does not belong to the range of any of the senses of perception. Only when sensory perception has come to an end can the transcendental field of Being be reached. As long as we experience through the senses we are in the relative field. Therefore Being cannot be experienced through any of the senses. This shows that through whichever sense of experience we proceed we must first reach the ultimate limit of experience through that sense. Then, transcending that, we will reach a state of consciousness in which the experiencer no longer experiences.

The word experiencer implies a relative state; it is a relative word. For the experiencer to exist there has to be an object of experience. The experiencer and the object of experience are both relative. When we have transcended the experience of the subtlest object, the experiencer is left by himself without an experience, without an object of experience and without the process of experiencing. When the subject is left without an object of experience, having transcended the subtlest state of the object, he steps out of the process of experiencing and arrives at the state of Being. The mind is then found in the state of Being which is beyond the relative field.

The state of Being is neither a state of objective nor of subjective existence, because both these states belong to the relative field of life. When the subtlest state of objective experience has been transcended, then the individual's subjectivity merges into the Transcendent. This state of consciousness is known as pure existence, the state of absolute Being.

This is how, by bringing the attention to the field of the Transcendent, it is possible to contact and experience Being. It cannot be experienced on the level of thinking because, as far as thinking goes, this is still a field of relative existence; the whole field of sensory perception lies within relative existence.

The transcendental state of Being lies beyond all seeing, hearing, touching, smelling and tasting—beyond all thinking and beyond all feeling. This state of the unmanifested, absolute, pure consciousness of Being is the ultimate state in life. It is easily experienced through the system of transcendental meditation.

TRANSCENDENTAL MEDITATION

The process of bringing the attention to the level of transcendental Being is known as the system of transcendental meditation.

In the practice of transcendental meditation a suitable thought is selected, and the technique for experiencing it in its initial stages of development enables the conscious mind to arrive systematically at the source of thought, the field of Being.

THE MAIN PRINCIPLE

We have seen that Being is the state of eternal and absolute existence and that the way to experience Being is to experience from the gross to the subtle states of creation until the mind arrives at the Transcendent.

We have seen that we could proceed through any sense of perception. For example, through the sense of sight we could gradually experience increasingly subtle forms until eventually our eyes reached a point where they were unable to perceive a form beyond a certain degree of subtlety. If we close our eyes and train the inner eye—the eye of the mind—to perceive the object at the point where we failed to perceive it through our open eyes, we would have a mental image of the object. If there were a way to experience the finer states of that mental image, to experience its finest state and transcend it, we would then reach the state of Being. Likewise, through any sense of perception we could begin to experience an object and eventually arrive at the transcendental state of Being.

Through the experience of a thought we can experience the subtle states of thinking and, transcending them, are certain to arrive at the transcendental state of Being.

Thinking is, in itself, the subtle state of speech. When we speak our words are audible, but if we do not speak, the words do not become perceptible. Thus we find that thought is a subtle form of sound.

The process of thinking starts from the deepest, most refined level of consciousness and becomes grosser as it develops. Eventually it becomes gross enough to be perceived on the surface level of consciousness, the ordinary level of thinking. An analogy will clarify this principle.

A thought starts from the deepest level of consciousness, from the deepest level of the ocean of mind, as a bubble starts at the bottom of the sea. As the bubble rises, it gradually becomes bigger. When it comes to the surface of the water it is perceived as a bubble.

Mind is like an ocean. The surface layers of the mind function actively while the deeper levels remain silent. The functioning surface level of the ocean of mind is called the conscious mind. Any thought at the surface level is consciously cognized, and it is at this level that thoughts are appreciated as thoughts.

A thought starts from the deepest level of consciousness and rises through the whole depth of the ocean of mind until it finally appears as a conscious thought at the surface. Thus we find that every thought stirs the whole range of the depth of consciousness but is consciously appreciated only when it reaches the conscious level; all its earlier stages of development are not appreciated. That is why we say that, for all practical purposes, the deeper levels of the ocean of consciousness are as though silent.

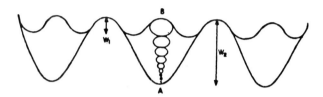

Referring to the illustration, the bubble of thought rising from level A grows in size. By the time it reaches the surface level B, it has developed sufficiently to be appreciated as a thought. This is the level of conscious mind. The subtle states of the thought-bubble below this conscious level are not appreciated.

If the thought-bubble could be consciously appreciated at the level below B, and at all levels of subtlety from B to A, it would then be possible to bring the level A within the range of the conscious mind. In this way the depth of the conscious mind (represented by W_1) would become greater (as represented by W_2), and the power of the conscious mind would be increased enormously. This expansion of the conscious capacity of the mind happens automatically on the march towards Being. It is as if the waves on the surface of the ocean have communicated with the deeper levels of water so that each wave is mightier than the wave before. The full mental potential is thus unfolded and the conscious capacity of the mind is increased to the maximum extent.

THE TECHNIQUE

Bubbles of thought are produced in a stream, one after another, and the mind is trained to experience the oncoming bubble at an earlier and earlier stage of its development (see illustration). When the attention reaches level A, it has traversed the whole depth of the mind and reached the source of creative intelligence in man.

This source of thought thus comes within the scope of the conscious mind. When the conscious mind transcends the subtlest level of thought, it transcends the subtlest state of relative experience and arrives at the transcendental Being, the state of pure consciousness or self-awareness.

This is how, in a systematic manner, the conscious mind is led, step by step, to the direct experience of transcendental, absolute Being.

INCREASING CHARM ON THE PATH OF TRANSCENDING

To go to a field of greater happiness is the natural tendency of the mind. Because in the practice of transcendental meditation the conscious mind is set on the way to experiencing transcendental, absolute Being, whose nature is bliss-consciousness, the mind finds the way increasingly attractive as it advances in the direction of bliss. A light becomes faint and dim as we move away from its source, and its intensity increases as we proceed towards its source. Similarly, when the mind goes in the direction of the absolute bliss of transcendental Being, it finds increasing charm at each step of its march. The mind is charmed and so is led to experience transcendental Being.

This practice is pleasant for every mind. Whatever the state of evolution of the aspirant, whether he is emotionally developed or intellectually advanced, his mind, by its very tendency to go to a field of greater happiness, finds a way to transcend the subtlest state of thinking and arrive at the bliss of absolute Being. This practice is, therefore, not only simple but also automatic.

IMPORTANCE OF RIGHT THOUGHT

A right thought is one which, in its nature, is harmonious and useful to the thinker and his surroundings. Every thought, like every spoken word, has some influence on the thinker and his surroundings. Just as a stone thrown into a pond produces waves reaching all the pond's extremities, any thought, word or action produces waves in the atmosphere, and these waves travel in every direction and strike against everything in the atmosphere. They influence every level of creation. The whole universe is influenced by every thought, word and action of each individual.

Since the influence of a thought is so wide, it is necessary to consider carefully the quality of any thought arising in the mind. There may be a thought whose influence is detrimental to the thinker and to the rest of the universe. Likewise, there may be a thought whose influence is favourable and useful to the thinker and to the world at large. Because each personality has its own quality, it is extremely important for each man that a special quality of thought be selected whose physical influence will be beneficial and useful to himself and to the whole world. The influence of a spoken word carried by waves of vibration in the atmosphere does not depend upon the meaning of the word. It lies in the quality of the vibrations set forth. Where it is necessary to produce vibrations of good quality for an influence of harmony and happiness, it is also necessary for the quality of vibration to correspond to that of the individual.

Individuals differ in the quality of the vibrations which constitute their individual personalities. That is why the right selection of a thought for a particular individual is of vital importance for the practice of transcendental meditation.

Since the quality of each man differs, it is all the more difficult to select the right type of vibration or the proper quality of thought. The problem of selecting a right thought, the physical quality of which corresponds to the physical quality of the thinker, becomes increasingly important when we consider that the power of thought increases when the thought is appreciated in its initial stages of development.

We know that power is greater in the subtle strata of creation than in the gross. If we throw a stone at someone it will hurt him, but if we could enter its subtle strata and excite an atom of the stone, tremendous energy would be released and the effect would be far greater. Similarly, when we enter the subtler states of a thought, we appreciate its finer levels where the power becomes greater than on the ordinary conscious level of the mind. With this in view, it is essential that, before starting this practice, the right quality of sound should be selected.

The question of selecting the right thought for a particular individual presents an enormous problem when we consider the far-reaching influence of an action on the entire universe.

An action performed by a particular individual in a particular place at a particular time may produce results favourable for the doer and his surroundings. The same action may produce a different influence under different circumstances.

The consideration of action and its influence is highly complicated. It is beyond the capacity of the human mind to fathom the influence of an action at any level of creation. Therefore the problem of selecting a right thought for this practice of meditation is something which cannot be successfully decided by any individual for himself.

In order to facilitate the finding of a right word for each individual, teachers have been trained in the art of selecting a sound or word to correspond to the special quality of the individual. These trained teachers of meditation are found in almost every country of the world in the centres of the Spiritual Regeneration Movement.

THE NECESSITY OF PERSONAL GUIDANCE

The practice of transcendental meditation has to be imparted by personal instruction. It cannot be imparted through a book, because the teacher must not only show the aspirant how to experience the subtle states of thinking but should also be responsible for checking his experiences as he proceeds on that path.

Experiences vary from man to man. Therefore it is not practical to record all the possible experiences. Nor is it to the advantage of the beginner to know in advance all that it is possible for him to experience. Firstly, because he might anticipate a particular experience and in so doing will be dividing his attention, thereby eliminating the possibility of any significant and deep experience. Secondly, because in anticipating an experience he might fall a victim to auto-suggestion and only imagine that experience. In both cases he is deprived of success. In this meditation the mind actually experiences the subtle states of thought without having to imagine, anticipate or aim at any particular experience. It is an entirely innocent process which succeeds under the personal guidance of a teacher.

A thought itself is a very abstract experience for an ordinary man. If he is asked to experience the subtle states of a thought, he is being asked to experience the subtle states of that abstract experience. This seems an impossibility, since the mind has always been accustomed to experience only gross objects or gross states of thought on the conscious thinking level.

The moment one begins to experience the subtle states of thought, one finds oneself drifting towards increasingly abstract states of experience. It takes a while for the beginner to be able to pinpoint his experience of subtle states of thought, even with the help of a personal teacher. For this reason it is of no practical value to describe in writing the details of the practice. The practice of transcendental meditation must always be taught by expert masters of meditation, who have been trained to impart it accurately as well as to check experiences.

The checking of experiences is a vital point in this practice. Again, it cannot be done through books. The practice must result in all good in life, and this depends upon the personal guidance of the teacher together with the obedience and co-operation of the aspirant. It is a highly specialised and delicate practice. It is important that it should only be learned from an authorised teacher of the Spiritual Regeneration Movement.

National Consciousness

Introduction

"Bharat Mata ki Jai!" ("Victory to Mother India!")

During the struggle for independence, this cry was heard from the Himalayas to Cape Comorin. Some obscure person would raise the slogan, and a million throats would take it up. And then, "Mahatma Gandhi ki Jai!" ("Victory to Mahatma Gandhi!") That was natural enough. Gandhi was hailed not merely because he was a great soul, a mahatma, but also because in the popular imagination he *was* India.

What was it that inspired these millions? Whom were they glorifying? What did they *mean* by Mother India? Many wondered. But no one searched the meaning as deeply or fervently as Jawaharlal Nehru did. Whether he was alone, enjoying the hospitality of British jailers, or whether he was traveling—by train, bus, bullock cart, even horse or elephant— Nehru always tried to understand the concept of India, until it almost became an obsession with him. It became for him an exciting voyage of discovery. "India with her infinite charm and variety began to grow upon me more and more. . . . The more I saw of her, the more I realised how very difficult it was . . . to grasp the ideas she had embodied. It was not her wide spaces that eluded me, or even her diversity, but some depth of soul which I could not fathom, though I had occasional and tantalizing glimpses of it."

What facets of India's soul did these "tantalizing glimpses" reveal to Nehru's sensitive mind? The diversity, of course, is obvious. It lies on the surface. Anyone can see it. In landscape and climate, race and language, artistic and literary traditions, belief and ritual, food and dress, even gesture and accent, the differences are as numerous as they are deep. But these differences lie within the framework of a wider unity. "Some kind of a dream of unity has occupied the mind of India since the dawn of civilization. The unity was not conceived as something imposed from outside. . . . It was something deeper, and within its fold the widest tolerance of belief and custom was practiced, and every variety acknowledged and even encouraged."

Nehru discovered the unity of India not through a mass of historical facts—important as they were to him—but through actual, living experience. The continuity of life in India can be *felt*, even though it may be difficult to describe or explain. To Nehru, India was "like some ancient palimpsest on which layer upon layer of thought and revery had been inscribed, and yet no succeeding layer had completely hidden or erased what had been written previously." These "layer upon layer of thought and revery," consciously and unconsciously kept alive in the mind of India, had gone to build up the complex and mysterious personality of the subcontinent. Nehru's search brought him face to face with this mysterious image. "That sphinxlike face with its elusive and sometimes mocking smile was to be seen throughout the length and breadth of the land. . . . The unity of India was no longer an intellectual conception for me: it was an emotional experience which overpowered me."

Nehru's love for India did not prevent him from noticing

the dark and ugly side of his country. It saddened him to see that India, once so full of mental alertness and technical skill, had for centuries taken a back place on the stage of world history. "One senses a progressive deterioration. The urge to life and endeavour becomes less, the creative spirit fades away and gives place to the imitative. . . . Indian life becomes a sluggish stream, living in the past, moving slowly through the accumulations of dead centuries. The heavy burden of the past crushes it, and a kind of coma seizes it." Yet this awareness of India's failure did not lead him to a wholly negative conclusion. "From time to time vivid flashes of renascence have occurred, and some of them have been long and brilliant. Always there is visible an attempt to understand and adapt the new and harmonize it with the old. . . . Something vital and living continued, some urge driving the people in a direction not wholly realized, always a desire for synthesis between the old and the new." And so the total picture which Nehru conjured up for himself, and which he presented so lucidly and colorfully in his *Discovery of India*, is a balanced and satisfying picture. Without ignoring his country's weaknesses, he was able to say: "Anything that had the power to mold hundreds of generations, without a break, must have drawn its enduring vitality from some deep well of strength, and must have had the capacity to renew that vitality from age to age."

On the fifteenth of August, 1947, the tricolor flag of independent India was raised aloft the ramparts of the historic Red Fort at Delhi. It was a turning point in the life of India. The people and leaders of this ancient land now had the opportunity of imparting a new movement and a new direction to the "sluggish stream" with which Jawaharlal Nehru had become so impatient. In a memorable speech to the Constituent Assembly, delivered on the eve of independence,

Nehru reminded his people of the tryst that they had made with destiny: "At the stroke of the midnight hour, when the world sleeps, India will awaken to life and freedom." He called for dedication to the service of India and her people "and to the still larger cause of humanity." He spoke of the "trackless centuries" through which India had carried on her unending quest, and of the great ideals that had given her strength—ideals which India had cherished "through good and ill fortune alike."

It is a measure of the maturity of India's nationalism that even at that hour, when she was shaking off two centuries of oppressive foreign rule, her leaders were not thinking merely of India but of the whole world. The "larger cause of humanity," of which Nehru spoke at Delhi, was also very much the concern of Sri Aurobindo as he hailed the freedom of India at his ashram in Pondicherry. Nehru was at the very center of events, Sri Aurobindo was in self-chosen seclusion. Both were aware of India's important role in world history. Sri Aurobindo had been among the earliest to make great sacrifices for India's freedom. On the fifteenth of August, which was also his birthday, he spoke of the dreams that awaited fulfillment—the dream of a united India, of a resurgent and liberated Asia, and of a "world-union forming the outer basis of a fairer, brighter and nobler life for all mankind." The dream of a united India was shattered, at least for the time being. But the liberation of Asian peoples, and the movement toward a universal human community, did not appear impracticable.

Sri Aurobindo also referred to another highly significant development: the spiritual gift of India to the world. "India's spirituality is entering Europe and America in an ever increasing measure. That movement will grow; amid the disasters of the time more and more eyes are turning towards her with hope and there is even an increasing resort not only to her teachings, but to her psychic and spiritual practice." These were prophetic words. During the quarter of a century that has passed since Sri Aurobindo wrote them, the movement has grown on a scale that few others could have foreseen.

India's philosopher-statesman, S. Radhakrishnan, was equally conscious of the momentous significance of India's independence: "We may make mistakes . . . but . . . these are nothing in comparison with the stimulus that comes from freedom. The existing conditions are a challenge to our competence and wisdom. The greatest calamity will be when power outstrips ability." Radhakrishnan reminded his country-men that civilization is not something external: "It is the people's dream, their imaginative interpretation of human existence, their perception of the mystery of human life." Radhakrishnan concluded his message with a call for humility in the service of "the ageless spirit of India."

These comments by Nehru, Sri Aurobindo, and Radha-krishnan, each with his own emphasis, show once again the basic unity of the Indian standpoint which runs through differences of interpretation. It is this feeling for India's unity that has inspired Bankim Chatterji's "Bande Mataram" and Rabindranath Tagore's "Jana Gana Mana." "Bande Ma-taram," presented here in Sri Aurobindo's beautiful poetic rendering, has symbolized Mother India for millions of Indians as has no other poem, and "Jana Gana Mana" has been adopted as India's national anthem.

Jawaharlal Nehru

The Quest

During these years of thought and activity my mind has been full of India, trying to understand her and to analyze my own reactions toward her. I went back to my childhood days and tried to remember what I felt like then, what vague shape this conception took in my growing mind and how it was molded by fresh experience. Sometimes it receded into the background, but it was always there, slowly changing, a queer mixture derived from old story and legend and modern fact. It produced a sensation of pride in me as well as that of shame, for I was ashamed of much that I saw around me, of superstitious practices, of outworn ideas, and above all, our subject and poverty-stricken state.

As I grew up and became engaged in activities which promised to lead to India's freedom, I became obsessed with the thought of India. What was this India that possessed me and beckoned to me continually, urging me to action so that we might realize some vague but deeply felt desire of our hearts? The initial urge came to me, I suppose, through pride, both individual and national, and the desire, common to all men, to resist another's domination and have freedom to live the life of our choice. It seemed monstrous to me that a great country like India, with a rich and immemorial past, should be bound hand and foot to a faraway island which imposed its will upon her. It was still more monstrous that this forcible union had resulted in poverty and degradation beyond measure. That was reason enough for me and for others to act.

But it was not enough to satisfy the questioning that arose within me. What is this India, apart from her physical and geographical aspects? What did she represent in the past; what gave strength to her then? How did she lose that old strength, and has she lost it completely? Does she represent anything vital now, apart from being the home of a vast number of human beings? How does she fit in to the modern world?

INDIA'S STRENGTH AND WEAKNESS

The search for the sources of India's strength and for her deterioration and decay is long and intricate. Yet the recent causes of that decay are obvious enough. She fell behind in the march of technique, and Europe, which had long been backward in many matters, took the lead in technical progress. Behind this technical progress was the spirit of science and a bubbling life and spirit which displayed itself in many activities and in adventurous voyages of discovery. New techniques gave military strength to the countries of western Europe and it was easy for them to spread out and dominate the East. That is the story not of India only but of almost the whole of Asia.

Why this should have happened so is more difficult to unravel, for India was not lacking in mental alertness and technical skill in earlier times. One senses a progressive deterioration during centuries. The urge to life and endeavor becomes less, the creative spirit fades away and gives place to the imitative. Where triumphant and rebellious thought had tried to pierce the mysteries of nature and the universe, the wordy commentator comes with his glosses and long explanations. Magnificent art and sculpture give way to a meticulous carving of intricate detail without nobility of conception or design. The vigor and richness of language, powerful yet simple, are followed by highly ornate and complex literary forms. The urge to adventure and the overflowing life which led to vast schemes of distant colonization and the transplantation of Indian culture in far lands, all these fade away and a narrow orthodoxy taboos even the crossing of the high seas. A rational spirit of inquiry, so evident in earlier times, which might well have led to the further growth of science, is replaced by irrationalism and a blind idolatry of the past. Indian life becomes a sluggish stream, living in the past, moving slowly through the accumulations of dead centuries. The heavy burden of the past crushes it and a kind of coma seizes it. It is not surprising that in this condition of mental stupor and physical weariness India should have deteriorated and remained rigid and immobile while other parts of the world marched ahead.

Yet this is not a complete or wholly correct survey. If there had only been a long and unrelieved period of rigidity and stagnation, this might well have resulted in a complete break with the past, the death of an era, and the erection of something new on its ruins. There has not been such a break and there is a definite continuity. Also from time to time vivid flashes of renascence have occurred, and some of them have been long and brilliant. Always there is visible an attempt to understand and adapt the new and harmonize it with the old, or at any rate with parts of the old which were considered worth preserving. Often that old retains an external form only, as a kind of symbol, and changes its inner content. But something vital and living continued, some urge driving the people in a direction not wholly realized, always a desire for synthesis between the old and the new. It was this urge and desire that kept them going and enabled them to absorb new ideas while retaining much of the old. Whether there was such a thing as an Indian dream through the ages, vivid and full of life or sometimes reduced to the murmurings of troubled sleep, I do not know. Every people and every nation has some such belief or myth of national destiny, and perhaps it is partly true in each case. Being an Indian, I am myself influenced by this reality or myth about India, and I feel that anything that had the power to mold hundreds of generations, without a break, must have drawn its enduring vitality from some deep well of strength, and have had the capacity to renew that vitality from age to age.

Was there some such well of strength? And if so, did it dry up, or did it have hidden springs to replenish it? What of today? Are there any springs still functioning from which we can refresh and strengthen ourselves? We see an old race, or rather an odd mixture of many races, and our racial memories go back to the dawn of history. Have we had our day and are we now living in the later afternoon or evening of our existence, just carrying on after the manner of the aged, quiescent, devitalized, uncreative, desiring peace and sleep above all else?

No people, no race continues unchanged. Continually it is mixing with others and slowly changing; it may appear to die almost and then rise again as a new people or just a variation of the old. There may be a definite break between the old people and the new, or vital links of thought and ideals may join them.

Behind the past quarter of a century's struggle for India's independence, and all our conflicts with British authority, lay in my mind and that of many others the desire to revitalize India. We felt that through action and self-imposed suffering and sacrifice, through voluntarily facing risk and danger, through refusal to submit to what we considered evil and wrong, we would recharge the battery of India's spirit and waken her from her long slumber. Though we came into conflict continually with the British government in India, our eyes were always turned toward our own people. Political advantage had value only in so far as it helped in that fundamental purpose of ours. Because of this governing motive, frequently we acted as no politician moving in the narrow sphere of politics, only, would have done, and foreign and Indian critics expressed surprise at the folly and intransigence of our ways. Whether we were foolish or not, the historians of the future will judge. We aimed high and looked far. Probably we were often foolish, from the point of view of opportunist politics, but at no time did we forget that our main purpose was to raise the whole level of the Indian people, psychologically and spiritually and also, of course, politically and economically. It was the building up of that real inner strength of the people that we were after, knowing that the rest would inevitably follow. We had to wipe out the evil aftermath from some generations of shameful subservience and timid submission to an arrogant alien authority.

THE SEARCH FOR INDIA

Though books and old monuments and past cultural achievements helped to produce some understanding of India, they did not satisfy me or give me the answer I was looking for. Nor could they, for they dealt with a past age, and I wanted to know if there was any real connection between that past and the present. The present for me, and for many others like me, was an odd mixture of medievalism, appalling poverty and misery, and a somewhat superficial modernism of the middle classes. I was not an admirer of my own class or kind, and yet inevitably I looked to it for leadership in the struggle for India's salvation. That middle class felt caged and circumscribed and wanted to grow and develop itself. Unable to do so within the framework of British rule, a spirit of revolt grew against this rule, and yet this spirit was not directed against the structure that crushed us. It sought to retain it and control it by displacing the British. These middle classes were too much the product of that structure to challenge it and seek to uproot it.

New forces arose that drove us to the masses in the villages, and for the first time, a new and different India rose up before the young intellectuals who had almost forgotten its existence, or attached little importance to it. It was a disturbing sight, not only because of its stark misery and the magnitude of its problems, but because it began to upset some of our values and conclusions. So began for us the discovery of India as it was, and it produced both understanding and conflict within us. Our reactions varied and depended on our previous environment and experience. Some were already sufficiently acquainted with these village masses not to experience any new sensation; they took them for granted. But for me it was a real voyage of discovery, and while I was always painfully conscious of the failings and weaknesses of my people, I found in India's countryfolk something, difficult to define, which attracted me. That something I had missed in our middle classes.

I do not idealize the conception of the masses, and as far as possible I try to avoid thinking of them as a theoretical abstraction. The people of India are very real to me in their great variety, and in spite of their vast numbers I try to think of them as individuals rather than as vague groups. Perhaps it was because I did not expect much from them that I was not disappointed; I found more than I had expected. It struck me that perhaps the reason for this, and for a certain stability and potential strength that they possessed, was the old Indian cultural tradition which was still retained by them in a small measure. Much had gone in the battering they had received during the past two hundred years. Yet something remained that was worth while, and with it so much that was worthless and evil.

During the twenties my work was largely confined to my own provinces and I traveled extensively and intensively through the towns and villages of the forty-eight districts of the United Provinces of Agra and Oudh, that heart of Hindustan as it has so long been considered, the seat and center of both ancient and medieval civilization, the melting pot of so many races and cultures, the area where the great revolt of 1857 blazed up and was later ruthlessly crushed. I grew to know the sturdy Jat of the northern and western districts, that typical son of the soil, brave and independent-looking, relatively more prosperous; the Rajput peasant and petty landholder, still proud of his race and ancestry, even though he might have changed his faith and adopted Islam; the deft and skillful artisans and cottage workers, both Hindu and Moslem; the poorer peasantry and tenants in their vast numbers, especially in Oudh and the eastern districts, crushed and ground down by generations of oppression and poverty, hardly daring to hope that a change would come to better their lot, and yet hoping and full of faith.

During the thirties, in the intervals of my life out of prison, and especially during the election campaign of 1936–37, I traveled more extensively throughout India, in towns and cities and villages alike. Except for rural Bengal, which unhappily I have only rarely visited, I toured in every province and went deep into villages. I spoke of political and economic issues, and judging from my speech I was full of politics and elections. But all this while, in a corner of my mind, lay something deeper and more vivid, and elections meant little to it, or the other excitements of the passing day. Another and a major excitement had seized me, and I was again on a great voyage of discovery and the land of India and the people of India lay spread out before me. India with all her infinite charm and variety began to grow upon me more and more, and yet the more I saw of her, the more I realized how very difficult it was for me or for anyone else to grasp the ideas she had embodied. It was not her wide spaces that eluded me, or even her diversity, but some depth of soul which I could not fathom, though I had occasional and tantalizing glimpses of it. She was like some ancient palimpsest on which layer upon layer of thought and revery had been inscribed, and yet no succeeding layer had completely hidden or erased what had been written previously. All of these existed together in our conscious or subconscious selves, though we might not be aware of them, and they had gone to build up the complex and mysterious personality of India. That sphinxlike face with its elusive and sometimes mocking smile was to be seen throughout the length and breadth of the land. Though outwardly there was diversity and infinite variety among our people, everywhere there was that tremendous impress of oneness, which had held all of us together for ages past, whatever political fate or misfortune had befallen us. The unity of India was no longer merely an intellectual conception for me: it was an emotional experience which overpowered me. That essential unity had been so powerful that no political division, no disaster or catastrophe had been able to overcome it.

It was absurd, of course, to think of India or any country as a kind of anthropomorphic entity. I did not do so. I was also fully aware of the diversities and divisions of Indian life, of classes, castes, religions, races, different degrees of cultural development. Yet I think that a country with a long cultural background and a common outlook on life develops a spirit that is peculiar to it and that is impressed on all its children, however much they may differ among themselves. Can anyone fail to see this in China, whether he meets an old-fashioned mandarin or a Communist who has apparently broken with the past? It was this spirit of India that I was after, not through idle curiosity, though I was curious enough, but because I felt that it might give me some key to the understanding of my country and people, some guidance to thought and action. Politics and elections were day-to-day affairs when we grew excited over trumpery matters. But if we were going to build the house of India's future, strong and secure and beautiful, we would have to dig deep for the foundations.

BHARAT MATA

Often as I wandered from meeting to meeting I spoke to my audience of this India of ours, of Hindustan and of Bharata, the old Sanskrit name derived from the mythical founder of the race. I seldom did so in the cities, for there the audiences were more sophisticated and wanted stronger fare. But to the peasant, with his limited outlook, I spoke of this great country for whose freedom we were struggling, of how each part differed from the other and yet was India, of common problems of the peasants from north to south and east to west, of the Swaraj, the self-rule that could only be for all and every part and not for some. I told them of my journeying from the Khyber Pass in the far northwest to Kanya Kumari or Cape

Comorin in the distant south, and how everywhere the peasants put me identical questions, for their troubles were the same—poverty, debt, vested interests, landlord, moneylender, heavy rents and taxes, police harassment, and all these wrapped up in the structure that the foreign government had imposed upon us—and relief must also come for all. I tried to make them think of India as a whole, and even to some little extent of this wide world of which we were a part. I brought in the struggle in China, in Spain, in Abyssinia, in central Europe, in Egypt and the countries of western Asia. I told them of the wonderful changes in the Soviet Union and of the great progress made in America. The task was not easy; yet it was not so difficult as I had imagined, for our ancient epics and myth and legend, which they knew so well, had made them familiar with the conception of their country, and some there were always who had traveled far and wide to the great places of pilgrimage situated at the four corners of India. Or there were old soldiers who had served in foreign parts in World War I or other expeditions. Even my references to foreign countries were brought home to them by the consequences of the great depression of the thirties.

Sometimes as I reached a gathering, a great roar of welcome would greet me: Bharat Mata ki Jai—Victory to Mother India! I would ask them unexpectedly what they meant by that cry, who was this Bharat Mata, Mother India, whose victory they wanted? My question would amuse them and surprise them, and then, not knowing exactly what to answer, they would look at each other and at me. I persisted in my questioning. At last a vigorous Jat, wedded to the soil from immemorial generations, would say that it was the dharti, the good earth of India, that they meant. What earth? Their particular village patch, or all the patches in the district or province, or in the whole of India? And so question and answer went on, till they would ask me impatiently to tell them all about it. I would endeavor to do so and explain that India was all this that they had thought, but it was much more. The mountains and the rivers of India, and the forests and the broad fields, which gave us food, were all dear to us, but what counted ultimately were the people of India, people like them and me, who were spread out all over this vast land. Bharat Mata, Mother India, was essentially these millions of people, and victory to her meant victory to these people. You are parts of this Bharat Mata, I told them, you are in a manner yourselves Bharat Mata, and as this idea slowly soaked into their brains, their eyes would light up as if they had made a great discovery.

THE VARIETY AND UNITY OF INDIA

The diversity of India is tremendous; it is obvious; it lies on the surface and anybody can see it. It concerns itself with physical appearances as well as with certain mental habits and traits. There is little in common, to outward seeming, between the Pathan of the northwest and the Tamil in the far south. Their racial stocks are not the same, though there may be common strands running through them; they differ in face and figure, food and clothing, and, of course, language. In the North-Western Frontier Province there is already the breath of central Asia, and many a custom there, as in Kashmir, reminds one of the countries on the other side of the Himalayas. Pathan popular dances are singularly like Russian Cossack dancing. Yet with all these differences, there is no mistaking the impress of India on the Pathan, as this is obvious on the Tamil. It is not surprising, for these border lands, and indeed Afghanistan also, were united with India for thousands of years. The old Turkish and other races who inhabited Afghanistan and parts of central Asia before the advent of

Islam were largely Buddhists, and earlier still, during the period of the Epics, Hindus. The frontier area was one of the principal centers of old Indian culture, and it abounds still with ruins of monuments and monasteries and especially of the great university of Taxila, which was at the height of its fame two thousand years ago, attracting students from all over India as well as different parts of Asia. Changes of religion made a difference but could not change entirely the mental backgrounds which the people of those areas had developed.

The Pathan and the Tamil are two extreme examples; the others lie somewhere in between. All of them have their distinctive features, all of them have still more the distinguishing mark of India. It is fascinating to find how the Bengalese, the Marathas, the Gujratis, the Tamils, the Andhras, the Oriyas, the Assamese, the Canarese, the Malayalis, the Sindhis, the Punjabis, the Pathans, the Kashmiris, the Rajputs, and the great central bloc comprising the Hindustani-speaking people, have retained their peculiar characteristics for hundreds of years, have still more or less the same virtues and failings of which old tradition or record tells us, and yet have been throughout these ages distinctively Indian, with the same national heritage and the same set of moral and mental qualities. There was something living and dynamic about this heritage which showed itself in ways of living and a philosophical attitude to life and its problems. Ancient India, like ancient China, was a world in itself, a culture and a civilization which gave shape to all things. Foreign influences poured in and often influenced that culture and were absorbed. Disruptive tendencies gave rise immediately to an attempt to find a synthesis. Some kind of a dream of unity has occupied the mind of India since the dawn of civilization. That unity was not conceived as something imposed from outside, a standardization of externals or even of beliefs. It was something deeper, and within its fold the widest tolerance of belief and custom was practiced and every variety acknowledged and even encouraged.

Differences, big or small, can always be noticed even within a national group, however closely bound together it may be. The essential unity of that group becomes apparent when it is compared to another national group, though often the differences between two adjoining groups fade out or intermingle near the frontiers, and modern developments are tending to produce a certain uniformity everywhere. In ancient and medieval times the idea of the modern nation was nonexistent, and feudal, religious, racial or cultural bonds had more importance. Yet I think that at almost any time in recorded history an Indian would have felt more or less at home in any part of India, and would have felt as a stranger and alien in any other country. He would certainly have felt less of a stranger in countries which had partly adopted his culture or religion. Those who professed a religion of non-Indian origin and coming to India settled down there, became distinctively Indian in the course of a few generations, such as Christians, Jews, Parsees, Moslems. Indian converts to some of these religions never ceased to be Indians in spite of a change of faith. All these were looked upon in other countries as Indians and foreigners, even though there might have been a community of faith between them.

Today, when the conception of nationalism has developed much more, Indians in foreign countries inevitably form a national group and hang together for various purposes, in spite of their internal differences. An Indian Christian is looked upon as an Indian wherever he may go. An Indian Moslem is considered an Indian in Turkey or Arabia or Iran or any other country where Islam is the dominant religion.

All of us, I suppose, have varying pictures of our native land and no two persons will think exactly alike. When I think of

India, I think of many things: of broad fields dotted with innumerable small villages; of towns and cities I have visited; of the magic of the rainy season which pours life into the dry, parched-up land and converts it suddenly into a glistening expanse of beauty and greenery, of great rivers and flowing water; of the Khyber Pass in all its bleak surroundings; of the southern tip of India; of people, individually and in the mass; and above all, of the Himalayas, snow-capped, or some mountain valley in Kashmir in the spring, covered with new flowers, and with a brook bubbling and gurgling through it. We make and preserve the pictures of our choice, and so I have chosen this mountain background rather than the more normal picture of a hot, subtropical country. Both pictures would be correct, for India stretches from the tropics right up to the temperate regions, from near the equator to the cold heart of Asia.

Jawaharlal Nehru

On Tagore and Gandhi

District Jail
Dehra Dun
August 27, 1941.

To
Krishna Kripalani,
Santiniketan, Bengal

My dear Krishna,

Just a month ago you wrote to me and soon after I received the Tagore Birthday Number of the Visva-Bharati Quarterly. I liked this Birthday Number very much and some of the pictures and articles were good.

How long ago it all seems! People must die some time or other and Gurudeva could not have lived much longer. And yet his death came as a grievous shock to me and the thought that I would never see his beautiful face and hear his gentle voice again oppressed me terribly. Ever since I came to prison

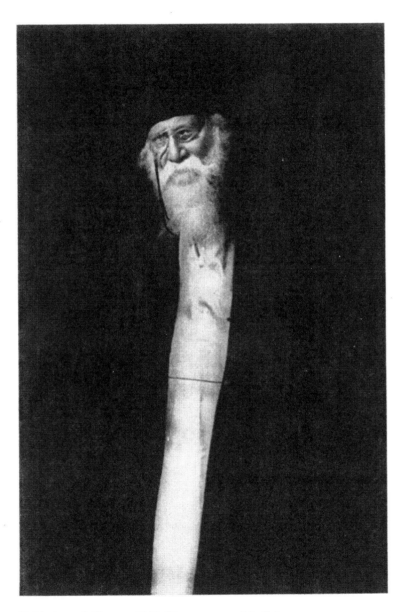

Rabindranath Tagore, 1934 (*Government of India*)

Nehru and Gandhi, 1946 *(Wide World Photos)*

this thought had haunted me. I wanted to see him once again so much. Not that I had anything special to say to him, and certainly I had no desire to trouble him in any way. Perhaps the premonition that I was not fated to see him again itself added to this yearning.

However, all that is over and, instead of sorrow, let us rather congratulate ourselves that we were privileged to come in contact with this great and magnificent person. Perhaps it is as well that he died when he was still pouring out song and poem and poetry—what amazing creative vitality he had! I would have hated to see him fade away gradually. He died, as he should, in the fullness of his glory.

I have met many big people in various parts of the world. But I have no doubt in my mind that the two biggest I have had the privilege of meeting have been Gandhi and Tagore. I think they have been the two outstanding personalities in the world during the last quarter of a century. As time goes by, I am sure this will be recognized when all the generals and field marshals and dictators and shouting politicians are long dead and largely forgotten.

It amazes me that India in spite of her present condition (or is it because of it?) should produce these two mighty men in the course of one generation. And that also convinces me of the deep vitality of India and I am filled with hope, and the petty troubles and conflicts of the day seem very trivial and unimportant before this astonishing fact—the continuity of the idea that is India from long ages past to the present day. China affects me in the same way. India and China; how can they perish?

There is another aspect which continually surprises me. Both Gurudeva and Gandhiji took much from the West and from other countries, especially Gurudeva. Neither was narrowly national. Their message was for the world. And yet both were one hundred per cent India's children, and the inheritors, representatives and expositors of her age-long culture. How intensely Indian both have been, in spite of all their wide knowledge and culture! The surprising thing is that both of these men with so much in common and drawing inspiration from the same wells of wisdom and thought and culture, should differ from each other so greatly! No two persons could probably differ so much as Gandhi and Tagore!

Again I think of the richness of India's age-long cultural genius which can throw up in the same generation two such master-types, typical of her in every way, yet representing different aspects of her many-sided personality.

My love to you and Nandita,

Yours affectionately,

Jawaharlal Nehru.

Independence Day: 15 August 1947

Jawaharlal Nehru

A Tryst with Destiny

Long years ago we made a tryst with destiny, and now the time comes when we shall redeem our pledge, not wholly or in full measure, but very substantially. At the stroke of the midnight hour, when the world sleeps, India will awake to life and freedom. A moment comes, which comes but rarely in history, when we step out from the old to the new, when an age ends, and when the soul of a nation, long suppressed, finds utterance. It is fitting that at this solemn moment we take the pledge of dedication to the service of India and her people and to the still larger cause of humanity.

At the dawn of history India started on her unending quest, and trackless centuries are filled with her striving and the grandeur of her success and her failures. Through good and ill fortune alike she has never lost sight of that quest or forgotten the ideals which gave her strength. We end today a period of ill fortune and India discovers herself again. The achievement we celebrate today is but a step, an opening of opportunity, to the greater triumphs and achievements that await us. Are we brave enough and wise enough to grasp this opportunity and accept the challenge of the future?

Freedom and power bring responsibility. That responsibility rests upon this Assembly, a sovereign body representing the sovereign people of India. Before the birth of freedom we have endured all the pains of labour and our hearts are heavy with the memory of this sorrow. Some of those pains continue even now. Nevertheless, the past is over and it is the future that beckons to us now.

That future is not one of ease or resting but of incessant striving so that we may fulfil the pledges we have so often taken and the one we shall take today. The service of India means the service of millions who suffer. It means the ending of poverty and ignorance and disease and inequality of opportunity. The ambition of the greatest man of our generation has been to wipe every tear from every eye. That may be beyond us, but as long as there are tears and suffering, so long our work will not be over.

And so we have to labour and to work hard, to give reality to our dreams. Those dreams are for India, but they are also for the world, for all the nations and peoples are too closely knit together today for any one of them to imagine that it can live apart. Peace has been said to be indivisible; so is freedom, so is prosperity now, and so also is disaster in this One World that can no longer be split into isolated fragments.

To the people of India, whose representatives we are, we make an appeal to join us with faith and confidence in this great adventure. This is no time for petty and destructive criticism, no time for ill-will or blaming others. We have to build the noble mansion of free India where all her children may dwell.

Sarvepalli Radhakrishnan

Indian Independence

History and legend will grow round the 15th of August, 1947 as that date marks a milestone in the world's march towards democracy. In the drama of a people rebuilding and transforming themselves, it is a significant date. The night of India's subjection has been long full of fateful portents and silent prayers of men and women for the dawn of freedom. For this day sacrifices have been made and there have been weepings and sorrows, haunting spectres of hunger and death. Steadily through the night the sentinels have kept watch; the lights have been burning bright and now the dawn which breaks the night of ages has come.

That this transition from subjection to freedom should have been effected by democratic procedure is an occasion as happy as it is unique. The rule of the British is ending in an orderly way.

In the House of Commons Mr. Attlee spoke with obvious pride of this courageous act of abnegation. It is the first instance, he said, when an Imperial Power voluntarily transferred this authority to a subject people whom it had ruled with force and firmness for nearly two centuries. In the past, empires were liquidated either by pressure near the centre as in Rome, or by exhaustion as in Spain, or by military defeat as in the case of the Axis powers. For deliberate surrender of authority there is no parallel except in the American withdrawal from the Philippines or perhaps the British withdrawal from South Africa, though all these are very different in scale and circumstances. To a strong people nothing can ever be harder than to do something which is likely to be attributed to motives of weakness or cowardice. If the British decided to quit India we may agree that it is due not so much to a sense of weakness as to an unwillingness to use the methods of blood and steel. They listened to the demand of the Indian people and by an act of courageous statesmanship blotted out the memory of past illwill and friction.

There is, however, a shadow over our rejoicings, a sadness in our hearts, for the independence we dreamed of and fought for has not come to us. Such is the perversity of things that Swaraj [home rule] of our dreams at the moment of its attainment has slipped through our fingers.

At a time when the States of the world are moving towards large groups, we are throwing away the one advantage of political and economic unity which British rule brought to this country. When the new conditions demand economic planning on a continental scale, we are reverting to a divided India. Whether India will be safer with two armies than with one remains to be seen.

If our leaders graciously took up the responsibility for the decision to divide the country, it is because they found no alternative acceptable to the different parties. By a succession of acts of surrender we found ourselves in a position from which division was the only way out.

Though our hearts be laden with sorrow, we must put our country on its way to progress.

There must be a sense of exhilaration when we feel that we are our own masters, that we can decide our own future. We may make mistakes—grave, perhaps avoidable—but all these are nothing in comparison with the stimulus that comes from freedom. The existing conditions are a challenge to our competence and wisdom. The greatest calamity will be when power outstrips ability. Let it not be said that when the test came we were found unequal. We have not gained the promised land. We have to work to clear the way for it. The path is long and arduous. It may be through blood and tears, toil and suffering. The people will conquer in the end. Some of us may not live to see it.

A civilisation is not something solid and external. It is the people's dream, their imaginative interpretation of human existence, their perception of the mystery of human life. Our distracted human nerves call for a purpose, larger than that which castes and communities provide, a purpose which will release us from our pettiness. Bearing ourselves humbly before God, conscious that we serve an unfolding purpose, let us brace ourselves to the task and so bear ourselves in this great hour of our history as worthy servants of the ageless spirit of India.

Sri Aurobindo

The Fifteenth of August, 1947

August 15th, 1947 is the birthday of free India. It marks for her the end of an old era, the beginning of a new age. But we can also make it by our life and acts as a free nation an important date in a new age opening for the whole world, for the political, social, cultural and spiritual future of humanity.

August 15th is my own birthday and it is naturally gratifying to me that it should have assumed this vast significance. I take this coincidence, not as a fortuitous accident, but as the sanction and seal of the Divine Force that guides my steps on the work with which I began life, the beginning of its full fruition. Indeed, on this day I can watch almost all the world-movements which I hoped to see fulfilled in my lifetime, though then they looked like impracticable dreams, arriving at fruition or on their way to achievement. In all these movements free India may well play a large part and take a leading position.

The first of these dreams was a revolutionary movement which would create a free and united India. India today is free but she has not achieved unity. At one moment it almost seemed as if in the very act of liberation she would fall back into the chaos of separate States which preceded the British conquest. But fortunately it now seems probable that this danger will be averted and a large and powerful though not yet a complete union will be established. Also the wisely drastic policy of the Constituent Assembly has made it probable that the problem of the depressed classes will be solved without schism or fissure. But the old communal division into Hindus and Muslims seems now to have hardened. . . . This must not be; the partition must go. Let us hope that that may come about naturally, by an increasing recognition of the necessity not only of peace and concord but by common action, by the practice of common action and the creation of means for that purpose. In this way unity may finally come about under whatever form—the exact form may have a pragmatic but not a fundamental importance. But by whatever means, in whatever way, the division must go; unity must and will be achieved, for it is necessary for the greatness of India's future.

Another dream was for the resurgence and liberation of the peoples of Asia and her return to her great role in the progress of human civilisation. Asia has arisen; large parts are now quite free or are at this moment being liberated: its other still subject or partly subject parts are moving through whatever struggles towards freedom. Only a little has to be done and that will be done today or tomorrow. There India has her part to play and has begun to play it with an energy and ability which already indicate the measure of her possibilities and the place she can take in the council of the nations.

The third dream was a world-union forming the outer basis of a fairer, brighter and nobler life for all mankind. That unification of the human world is under way; there is an imperfect initiation organized but struggling against tremendous difficulties. But the momentum is there and it must inevitably increase and conquer. Here too India has begun to play a prominent part and, if she can develop that larger statesmanship which is not limited by the present facts and immediate possibilities but looks into the future and brings it nearer, her presence may make all the difference between a slow and timid and a bold and swift development. A catastrophe may intervene and interrupt or destroy what is being done, but even then the final result is sure. For unification is a necessity of Nature, an inevitable movement. Its necessity for the nations is also clear, for without it the freedom of the small nations may be at any moment in peril and the life even of the large and powerful nations insecure. The unification is therefore to the interests of all, and only human imbecility and stupid selfishness can pervert it; but these cannot stand forever against the necessity of Nature and the Divine Will. But an outward basis is not enough; there must grow up an international spirit and outlook, international forms and institutions must appear, perhaps such developments as dual or multilateral citizenship, willed interchange or voluntary fusion of cultures. Nationalism will have fulfilled itself and lost its militancy and would no longer find these things incompatible with self-preservation and the integrality of its outlook. A new spirit of oneness will take hold of the human race.

Another dream, the spiritual gift of India to the world has already begun. India's spirituality is entering Europe and America in an ever increasing measure. That movement will grow; amid the disasters of the time more and more eyes are turning towards her with hope and there is even an increasing resort not only to her teachings, but to her psychic and spiritual practice.

The final dream was a step in evolution which would raise

man to a higher and larger consciousness and begin the solution of the problems which have perplexed and vexed him since he first began to think and to dream of individual perfection and a perfect society. This is still a personal hope and an idea, an ideal which has begun to take hold both in India and in the West on forward-looking minds. The difficulties in the way are more formidable than in any other field of endeavour, but difficulties were made to be overcome and if the Supreme Will is there, they will be overcome. Here too, if this evolution is to take place, since it must proceed through a growth of the spirit and the inner consciousness, the initiative can come from India and, although the scope must be universal, the central movement may be hers.

Such is the content which I put into this date of India's liberation; whether or how far this hope will be justified depends upon the new and free India.

Nationalism in Song

"Bande Mataram"

("Hymn To The Mother")

Sri Aurobindo (*translator*)

Mother, I bow to thee!
Rich with thy hurrying streams,
Bright with thy orchard gleams,
Cool with thy winds of delight,
Dark fields waving, Mother of might,
Mother free.

Glory of moonlight dreams
Over thy branches and lordly streams,—
Clad in thy blossoming trees,
Mother, giver of ease,
Laughing low and sweet!
Mother, I kiss thy feet,
Speaker sweet and low!
Mother, to thee I bow.

Who hath said thou art weak in they lands,
When the swords flash out in seventy million hands
And seventy million voices roar
Thy dreadful name from shore to shore?
With many strengths who art mighty and stored,
To thee I call, Mother and Lord!

Thou who savest, arise and save!
To her I cry who ever her foemen drave
Back from plain and sea
And shook herself free.

Thou art wisdom, thou art law,
Thou our heart, our soul, our breath,
Thou the love divine, the awe
In our hearts that conquers death.
Thine the strength that nerves the arm,
Thine the beauty, thine the charm.
Every image made divine
In our temples is but thine.

Thou art Durga, Lady and Queen,
With her hands that strike and her swords of sheen,
Thou art Lakshmi lotus-throned,
And the Muse a hundred-toned.
Pure and perfect without peer,
Mother, lend thine ear.
Rich with thy hurrying streams,
Bright with thy orchard gleams,
Dark of hue, O candid-fair
In thy soul, with jewelled hair
And thy glorious smile divine,
Loveliest of all earthly lands,

Showering wealth from well-stored hands!
Mother, mother mine!
Mother sweet, I bow to thee
Mother great and free!

"*Jana Gana Mana*"

Rabindranath Tagore (translator)

Thou art the ruler of the minds of all people,
Thou Dispenser of India's destiny.
Thy name rouses the hearts
of the Punjab, Sind, Gujrat and Maratha,
of Dravid, Orissa and Bengal.
It echoes in the hills of the Vindhyas and Himalayas,
mingles in the music of Jumna and Ganges,
and is chanted by the waves of the Indian Sea.
They pray for thy blessing and sing thy praise,
Thou Dispenser of India's destiny,
Victory, Victory, Victory to thee.

Day and night, thy voice goes out from land to land,
calling Hindus, Buddhists, Sikhs and Jains round thy throne
and Parsees, Mussalmans and Christians.
Offerings are brought to thy shrine by the East and the West
to be woven in a garland of love.
Thou bringest the hearts of all peoples into the harmony of
    one life,
Thou Dispenser of India's destiny,
Victory, Victory, Victory to thee.

Eternal Charioteer, thou drivest man's history
along the road rugged with rises and falls of Nations.
Amidst all tribulations and terror
thy trumpet sounds to hearten those that despair and droop,
and guide all people in their paths of peril and pilgrimage.
Thou Dispenser of India's destiny,
Victory, Victory, Victory to thee.

When the long dreary night was dense with gloom
and the country lay still in a stupor,
thy Mother's arms held her,
thy wakeful eyes bent upon her face,
till she was rescued from the dark evil dreams
that oppressed her spirit,
Thou Dispenser of India's destiny,
Victory, Victory, Victory to thee.

Chronology

JN Jawaharlal Nehru

MG M. K. Gandhi

SR S. Radhakrishnan

RT Rabindranath Tagore

SA Sri Aurobindo

BIOGRAPHICAL	BIBLIOGRAPHICAL	INDIAN CULTURE	WESTERN CULTURE
1815– Prominence of Ram Mohan Roy 33		1828 Ram Mohan Roy founds Brahma Samāj.	1831 (d.) G. W. F. Hegel 1833 Ralph Waldo Emerson, *Nature*
1834 (b.) Sri Ramakrishna; (d.) 1886		1835 Macaulay's Minute on Education: ". . . a single shelf of a good European library was worth the whole native literature of India and Arabia."	
			1845 Frederick Douglass, *Narrative of the Life of Frederick Douglass*
			1845– Henry David Thoreau at 47 Walden Pond
			1846 Soren Kierkegaard, *Concluding Unscientific Postscript*
			1851 Herman Melville, *Moby Dick*
		1857 Rebellion of 1857: now referred to as "The First Battle for Indian Independence."	1855 Walt Whitman, *Leaves of Grass*

BIOGRAPHICAL	BIBLIOGRAPHICAL	INDIAN CULTURE	WESTERN CULTURE
1861 (b.) Rabindranath Tagore; (d.) 1941			1859 Karl Marx, *Communist Manifesto*; Charles Darwin, *Origin of Species*; (b.) John Dewey, Henri Bergson; Richard Wagner, *Tristan and Isolde*
1862 (b.) Swami Vivekananda; (d.) 1902			1861–65 American Civil War
			1863 John Stuart Mill, *Utilitarianism*
			1864 F. Dostoyevsky, *Notes from the Underground*
1869 (b.) Mohandas K. Gandhi			1873 John Henry Newman, *The Idea of a University*
1872 (b.) Sri Aurobindo; (d.) 1950		1876 Queen Victoria proclaimed Empress of India.	
			1879 Mary Baker Eddy founds The Church of Christ, Scientist

WESTERN CULTURE	INDIAN CULTURE	BIBLIOGRAPHICAL	BIOGRAPHICAL
1880 F. Dostoyevsky, *Brothers Karamazov*			
		1881 Keshub Chunder Sen, *New Dispensation*	
			1883 MG (age 14) marries Kasturba (age 13)
1884 Friedrich Nietzsche, *Thus Spake Zarathustra*		1884 Max Müller, *Rammohan to Ramakrishna*	
	1885 Inauguration of the Indian National Congress.		
1893 F. H. Bradley, *Appearance and Reality*			1893– MG (age 24–45) in South 1914 Africa
			1893 SA returns from schooling in India (from 1879, age 7)
	1897 Swami Vivekananda returns from America; founds the Ramakrishna Mission.		
1900 Sigmund Freud, *Interpretation of Dreams* Josiah Royce, *The World and the Individual*			
1902 William James, *Varieties of Religious Experience*			

WESTERN CULTURE	INDIAN CULTURE	BIBLIOGRAPHICAL	BIOGRAPHICAL
1903 First airplane flight by the Wright Brothers Beginning of the automobile industry in Detroit W. E. B. Du Bois, *Souls of Black Folks*			1904 SA begins yoga
	1905 Partition of Bengal by Lord Curzon.		1906 SA editor, *Bande Mataram* (nationalist weekly) and leader, Nationalist Party in Bengal; principal, Bengal National College
	1906 Opening of Bengal National College.		
	1906 Publication of *Bande Mataram*.		
	1906 Founding of the Muslim League.		1906 MG leads first Satyagraha campaign, in Johannesburg
1907 Henri Bergson, *Creative Evolution* (Eng. trans. 1911) Pablo Picasso, *Les Demoiselles d'Avignon*		1908 SR, master's thesis, "Ethics of the Vedanta"	1908–09 SA in Alipore Jail, waiting trial for sedition; meditates on the Gītā
		1909 SA, editor, *Karmayogin*	

BIOGRAPHICAL	BIBLIOGRAPHICAL	INDIAN CULTURE	WESTERN CULTURE
and enjoys advanced mystical experiences.	(Nationalist weekly in English), and *Dharma* (Nationalist weekly in Bengali)		
1910 SA leaves Calcutta for Pondicherry		1911 Partition of Bengal revoked.	1912 Maria Montessori, *The Montessori Method*
1913 RT, Nobel Prize for *Gitanjali*			1913 Albert Schweitzer establishes a hospital at Lambaréné, Gabon, West Africa
1914 MG returns from South Africa after 20 years	1914– SA, writes *Arya*, philo- 21 sophical monthly, containing most of SA's major works: *The Life Divine, The Human Cycle, The Ideal of Human Unity, Essays on the Gitâ, On the Veda,* and *Synthesis of Yoga.*		1913– Marcel Proust, *Remem- 27 brance of Things Past*
1914 SA meets Mira Richard (Mother of the Sri Aurobindo Ashram, 1926–1973)			1914 Bertrand Russell, *Our Knowledge of the External World*
1914 (d.) G. K. Gokhale	1914 *The Autobiography of*		1914– First World War 18

BIOGRAPHICAL	BIBLIOGRAPHICAL	INDIAN CULTURE	WESTERN CULTURE
1916 JN marries Kamala and meets Gandhi	1915 *Maharshi Debendra-nath Tagore*; Bal Gangadhar Tilak, *Gītā Rahashya*	1916 Founding of Benares Hindu University (originally Central Hindu College, founded in 1898 by Annie Besant, president of the Theosophical Society, 1907–33).	1917 Russian Revolution
	1917 RT, *My Reminiscences*	1919 Massacre of Indians by British troops in the Jalianwala Bagh at Amritsar.	1918 Oswald Spengler, *The Decline of the West* (Rev., E.T. 1926–1928)
	1918 SR, *Philosophy of Rabin-dranath Tagore*	1920 Mahatma Gandhi leads first nationwide civil disobedience. Mahatma Gandhi elected President of All-India Home Rule League.	1920 Max Weber, *The Protestant Ethic and the Spirit of Capitalism* (Eng. trans. 1930) Paramahansa Yogananda arrives in the U.S.A. and founds the Self-Realization Fellowship based on Patanjali's Yoga-sutras and Kriya-yoga.
1920 (d.) Bal Gangadhar (Lokamanya) Tilak	1920 SR, *The Reign of Religion in Contemporary Philosophy*		1921 James Joyce, *Ulysses*

	WESTERN CULTURE	INDIAN CULTURE	BIBLIOGRAPHICAL	BIOGRAPHICAL
1922	T. S. Eliot, *The Waste Land*; Hermann Hesse, *Steppenwolf* (Eng. trans. 1963)		RT, *Creative Unity*	
1923	Martin Buber, *I and Thou* (Eng. trans. 1937; 1958)		SR, *Indian Philosophy*, Vol. I	
1924	Thomas Mann, *The Magic Mountain*; E. M. Forster, *Passage to India*		S. Dasgupta, *Yoga as Philosophy and Religion*	
1925	John Dewey, *Experience and Nature*	Founding of Indian Philosophical Congress (S. Radhakrishnan, first president).		
1926, Nov. 24				SA's "Day of Siddhi: descent of overmental consciousness into the physical"
1927	Martin Heidegger, *Being and Time* (Eng. trans. 1962)		SR, *Indian Philosophy*, Vol. II; MG, *My Experiments with Truth*, Vol. I	
1927–33	D. T. Suzuki, *Essays in Zen Buddhism* (3 vols.)			
1928			*Brahmo Dharma of Maharshi Debendranath Tagore*	

BIOGRAPHICAL		BIBLIOGRAPHICAL		INDIAN CULTURE		WESTERN CULTURE	
1930	MG leads Salt March	1930	JN, *Letters from a Father to His Daughter*. Being a brief account of the early days of the world written for children.	1930	Round Table Conference	1929	Alfred North Whitehead, *Process and Reality*; *Aims of Education*
		1931	RT, *Religion of Man*	1930	Iqbal proposes a separate state for Indian Muslims.	1929–33	Great Depression
1932	MG "fast unto death" for voting rights of Untouchables	1932	M. Hiriyanna, *Outlines of Indian Philosophy*				
		1932–55	S. Dasgupta, *History of Indian Philosophy*				
		1932	SR, *Idealist View of Life*			1934–39	Arnold Toynbee, *Study of History*
		1933	SR, *East and West in Religion*			1934	John Dewey, *Art as Experience*
		1934	JN, *Recent Essays and Writings*				
		1934	JN, *Glimpses of World History*: Being further letters to his daughter, written in prison, and containing a rambling account of history for young people				

BIOGRAPHICAL	BIBLIOGRAPHICAL	INDIAN CULTURE	WESTERN CULTURE
1936–39 SR, Professor of Eastern Religion and Ethics at Oxford University	1935 Mulk Raj Anand, "The Untouchable"		
	1936 JN, *An Autobiography*		
	1936 Karl Marx, *Letters on India*		
	1936 JN, *India and the World*		
			1938 Nikos Kazantzakis, *The Odyssey: A Modern Sequel*
	1939 SR, *Eastern Religion and Western Thought*		
	1939 SA, *The Life Divine*		
1941 (d.) RT	1941 JN, *Toward Freedom* (Rev., enl. ed., *Autobiography*, 1936)		1941 Erich Fromm, *Escape from Freedom*
	1941 JN, *Nehru on Gandi*		
		1942 India rejects Cripps offer (partial independence in return for help to the Allied cause against Nazi Germany).	
			1943 Jean-Paul Sartre, *Being and Nothingness* (Eng. trans. 1956)
			1945 Commercial television First atomic explosion

WESTERN CULTURE	INDIAN CULTURE	BIBLIOGRAPHICAL	BIOGRAPHICAL
1946 Founding of the United Nations		1946 JN, *The Discovery of India*	1946– SR leader Indian Delegation, UNESCO 51
	1947 August 15, Independence Day; partition of India and Pakistan.	1947 SR, *Religion and Society*	1947, Sri Aurobindo's seventy-fifth birthday (coincidental with Independence Day) Aug. 15
	1947– Jawaharlal Nehru becomes Prime Minister. 64		
	1947, Kashmir admitted into Oct. the Indian Union.		
1948 Norman Mailer, *The Naked and the Dead*	1948 Hindu-Muslim rioting in Bengal and Kashmir.	1948 Coomaraswamy, *The Dance of Shiva*	1948, MG assassinated by Jan. Hindu fanatic
	1948– Process of integration of 49 Indian states.	1948 SR, *The Bhagavad-Gītā*	
	1948 (d.) Muhammed Ali Jinnah, founder of Pakistan.		
	1950, Inauguration of India as a Jan. republic; Rajendra Prasad, first President.	1950 JN, *Inside America, A Voyage of Discovery*	1949– SR Ambassador to 52 U.S.S.R.
			1950, (d.) SA Dec. 5
1951– Paul Tillich, *Systematic 63 Theology*		1951 SA, *Savitri*	1951– SR, Vice-President of 61 India

BIOGRAPHICAL	BIBLIOGRAPHICAL	INDIAN CULTURE	WESTERN CULTURE
1952– SR, President of General 54 Council, UNESCO	1952 Paul Arthur Schilpp, ed., *The Philosophy of Sarvepalli Radhakrishnan*	1952 First national elections; Nehru overwhelmingly elected Prime Minister.	
	1952 SR, ed., *History of Philosophy: East and West*, 2 vols.		1953 Ludwig Wittgenstein, *Philosophical Investigations* (Eng. trans. 1953)
	1953 SR, *Principle Upanishads*		1954 Samuel Beckett, *Waiting for Godot*
	1955 SR, *Recovery of Faith*		1955 Pierre Teilhard de Chardin, *Phenomenon of Man* (Eng. trans. 1959) Jackson Pollock, "The Scent"
			1956 B. F. Skinner, *Walden Two*
	1959 Arthur Osborne, ed., *The Collected Works of Ramana Maharshi*		1959 Maharishi Mahesh Yogi founds Spiritual Regeneration Movement and tours the West.
	1960 SR, *The Brahma Sutra*		
	1961 Rabindranath Tagore, *A Centenary Volume*		
1962– SR, President of India 67			

WESTERN CULTURE	INDIAN CULTURE	BIBLIOGRAPHICAL	BIOGRAPHICAL
1963 Assassination of John F. Kennedy	1963, Oct.–Nov. Chinese incursion into northeast India.		1964 (d.) JN
1964 Herbert Marcuse, *One-Dimensional Man* Martin Luther King, Nobel Peace Prize Marshall McLuhan, *Understanding Media: The Extensions of Man*	1964–65 Lal Bahadur Shastri, Prime Minister.		
1965–73 United States military involved in Southeast Asia	1966, Jan. Indira Gandhi elected Prime Minister 1967 Zakir Husain elected President of India.	1967 SR, *Religion in a Changing World*	
1968 Assassination of Martin Luther King and Robert F. Kennedy			
1969 Buckminster Fuller, *Utopia or Oblivion*	1971–72 Bengalis brutally repressed by East Pakistanis; nine million refugees emigrate to West Bengal (India), and re-		

BIOGRAPHICAL		BIBLIOGRAPHICAL		INDIAN CULTURE		WESTERN CULTURE
		1972	SA, *Sri Aurobindo Birth Centenary Library* (30 vols.)		turn after independence of Bangla Desh.	
						1973 United States enters détente with U.S.S.R. and The People's Republic of China

Glossary of Important Names and Terms

The intent of this glossary is to provide pertinent information on the selected authors and important figures cited in the selections. Dates, events, key ideas and books are randomly listed when appropriate. The major works of most of the authors are listed in the Bibliography, but additional works which are important for an understanding of a particular author are listed here.

I. NAMES

BHAVE, ACHARYA VINOBA (1895–   ). Disciple and co-worker of Mahatma Gandhi. Founder and leader of Bhoodan ("land gift") Movement (i.e., collection of gifts of land from the wealthy—more than four million acres collected); leader of *Shanti Sena* ("peace volunteers") for resolution of conflicts. *The Essence of the Qu'ran* (1962), *Democratic Values* (1963), *Steadfast Wisdom* (1966), *The Essence of Christian Teachings* (1966).

COOMARASWAMY, ANANDA (1877–1947). Son of a Sinhalese father and British mother. Educated in England. Directed acquisition of Far

Eastern collection of the Museum of Fine Arts, Boston. *The Buddha and the Gospel of Buddhism*, 1964* (1928), *The Dance of Shiva* (1918; rev. ed., 1957); *History of Indian and Indonesian Art* (1935).

DASGUPTA, SURENDRANATH (1888–1952). Professor of Philosophy, Benares Hindu University; Lecturer, Cambridge University, 1920–22; Calcutta University, 1924–45; lectured in U.S.A., 1926. *Yoga as Philosophy and Religion*, 1924.

GANDHI, INDIRA NEHRU (1917–   ). Daughter of Jawaharlal and Kamala Nehru. In 1942 married Feroz Gandhi (d. 1960; no relation to M. K. Gandhi). Prime Minister of India (1966–   ).

GANDHI, MOHANDAS KARAMCHAND (1869–1948). Known as Mahātmā ("great soul"). Leader of Indian Nationalist movement; frequently fasted during six and a half years in prison; exponent and exemplar of satyāgraha and ahimsā; crusader for India's Untouchables and traditional Hindu values.

GHOSE, AUROBINDO: See Sri Aurobindo

IQBAL, MUHAMMAD (1873–1938). Poet, philosopher, Islamicist. President, Muslim League, 1926. Advocated Hindu-Muslim unity. *The Reconstruction of Religious Thought in Islam*, 1962 (1944).

KRIPALANI, KRISHNA. Author, *Tagore: a Biography* (1962).

KRISHNAMURTI, JIDDU. (1897–   ). Disclaimed the avatar status attributed to him by Mrs. Annie Besant, but remained close to the Theosophists. See Bibliography, sect. 7.

LAO-TZU (6th century). Probably a contemporary of Confucius. Traditionally author of *Tao-te-ching*, the classic of Taoism.

MAHARISHI, MAHESH YOGI. Founder of Transcendental Meditation technique, taught by the Students Internation Meditation Society (SIMS). See Bibliography, sect. 7.

NEHRU, JAWAHARLAL (1889–1964). Prime Minister of India, 1947–64. With Gandhi, leader of the Nationalist movement; spent nine years in jails for political "crimes"; erudite interpreter of Indian and world history; developed Indian central government and neutralist foreign policy. See Bibliography, sect. 8.

PLOTINUS (3rd century). Neoplatonic mystical philosopher.

RADHAKRISHNAN, SARVEPALLI (1888–   ). Philosopher, statesman, educator. Professor of Philosophy, Calcutta University (1921–31), Spalding Professor of Eastern Religion and Ethics at Oxford (1936–39),

* Paperback.

Ambassador of India to U.S.S.R., (1949–52), President of India (1962–67). See Bibliography, sects. 2, 3, 7.

ROY, RAM MOHAN (1772–1833). Bengali religious reformer; 1815, founded Atmiya Sabha ("Association of Friends"), and 1828, founded Brahmā Samaj (Society of God); social reformer and advocated a synthesis of Western humanism and Vedanta.

SEN, KESHUB CHUNDER (1838–84). In 1869, reconstructed the Brahmā Samaj; worked for a synthesis of Hindu and Christian beliefs; his *New Dispensation* (1881) showed the interplay of Christian piety and Vaishnava bhakti.

SHANKARA (SAMKARA). Ninth-century philosopher and saint, greatest exponent of the Advaita Vedanta system.

SHANTINIKETAN ("Abode of Peace"). University and cultural center founded by Rabindranath Tagore.

SRI RAMAKRISHNA (1836–1886). Hindu mystic; devotee of the goddess Kali; experienced the spirit of Islam and Christianity, and emphasized the unity of religions; considered by many to be an avatar; see also Swami Vivekananda. See Bibliography, sects. 1 and 7.

SRI RAMANA MAHARSHI. Twentieth-century south Indian mystic; achieved spiritual realization at seventeen years of age; settled at Tiruvannamalai, where an ashram grew up around him for more than fifty years; explained spiritual realization in terms of Advaita Vedanta. See Bibliography, sect. 7.

SRI AUROBINDO (1872–1950). Radical political leader of the Nationalist movement until 1910; with Mira Richard (Mother of the Sri Aurobindo Ashram), developed a system of integral yoga and a host of programs for spiritual and historical transformation. See Bibliography, sects. 2, 3, 4, 5, 6, 7.

TAGORE, DEBENDRANATH (1817–1905). Close collaborator of Ram Mohan Roy; emphasized the theistic rather than monistic interpretation of the Vedas and Upanishads. *Autobiography* (1914).

TAGORE, RABINDRANATH (1861–1941). Member of distinguished Bengali family; greatest poet, musician and artist of modern India; religious thinker, internationalist and educator.

TILAK, BAL GANGADHAR (LOKAMANYA) (1856–1920). Maharashtrian nationalist; leader of the extremist wing; advocated complete independence; sought a Hindu revival, and wrote *Gītā Rahasya*, a commentary on the Gītā, during his six-year imprisonment, 1907–1913.

VIVEKANANDA, SWAMI (1863–1902). Disciple of Sri Ramakrishna; represented Hinduism at the World Parliament of Religion in Chicago in 1893; helped spur a religious and cultural renaissance; founded the Ramakrishna Order in 1897.

II. TERMS

ABHYĀSA. Practice

ABHYUDAYA. Emergence, rise

ADVAITA VEDANTA. Non-dualist philosophy; expounded by Shankara; based on the Upanishads, Bhagavad-Gītā, and Brahma-Sūtra

AHIMSĀ. Non-injury, non-violence

ĀNANDA. Perfect happiness or bliss; one of the three attributes of Brahman or Sat-Chit-Ānanda

ARJUNA. Warrior in the Bhagavad-Gītā

ARTHA. Wealth; livelihood

ARYANS. Noble or ancient. Indo-Aryans migrated from central Asia; settled in India in 3rd millennium B.C.; composed the Vedas

ĀSANA. Bodily posture in yoga

ĀSHRAM. Religious community built around a guru

ĀTMAN. Spirit or Self

ĀTMĪYA SABHĀ. Society of Friends

AVATĀRA. Incarnation of the Divine in human form (e.g., Krishna)

AVIDYĀ. Ignorance

"BANDE MĀTARAM." "I bow to the Mother (Country)"; one of the national songs of India since 1906, composed by Bankim Chandra Chatterji

BENGAL NATIONAL COLLEGE. Founded in 1906 for national education, with Sri Aurobindo as Principal

BHAGAVAD-GĪTĀ. "Song of the Lord"; teaching of Krishna (reincarnation of Vishnu) to the warrior Arjuna; the most popular Indian scripture, originally part of the Indian epic, Mahābhārata

BHAGAVATA PURĀNA. One of the ancient devotional texts

BHAJAN. Devotion song

BHAKTI. Devotion

BHAKTI-YOGA. Discipline of devotion leading to liberation

BHĀRĀT MĀTĀ. Mother India

BRAHMĀ. The Creator God, the first of the three personifications of the Hindu triad (of which Vishnu and Shiva are the other two)

BRAHMA SAMĀJ (Bengali spelling: Brahmo Samaj). Society of God, founded by Ram Mohan Roy, 1828

BRAHMA-SŪTRA. A treatise by Badarayana, regarded as one of the sources of Vedanta

BRAHMACHARYA. Celibacy; first of the four stages of life

BRAHMADHARMA GRANTHA. "Source book of the Brahmo Religion"

BRAHMAN. Non-dual or absolute divine reality; in Vedanta, distinguished from the Divine in its personal aspect

BRAHMIN. Member of the highest caste (priestly or learned caste) in Hindu society

BRIHADĀRANYAKA UPANISHAD. One of the Upanishads emphasizing absolute monism

BUDDHA. Founder of Buddhism, 6th Century B.C. Originally Prince Siddhartha of the Gautama family of the Sakya clan. Achieved *Bodhi* ("enlightenment"), and thereafter taught the Four Noble Truths and the Eightfold Path leading to salvation

CHĀTURĀSHRAM. Four stages of life

CHATURVARNA. The fourfold division of Hindu society

DARSHANA. A philosophical perspective

DHARMA. Religious, moral and social obligations; one of the four ends of man according to the Hindu tradition

DHYĀNA. Discipline of meditation or contemplation

ECKHART. Fourteenth-century Christian mystic

GUNA. Quality; the three primary qualities that form the nature of the created world: sattva (knowledge; illumination); rajas (action; energy); tamas (darkness; lethargy)

GURU. Teacher; spiritual guide

HATHAYOGA. Physical yoga: postures and rhythmic breathing

HIMSĀ. Violence

IDEALISM. "Belief in the existence of an ideal state of perfection either as timelessly existent or as the ultimate goal of the universal process"

INDRIYA. Sense organ

ĪSHVARA. The absolute in its personal aspect; also God, or Brahman, from the perspective of māyā

ĪSHA UPANISHAD. An Upanishad with a theistic emphasis

JAINISM. An Indian religious system founded in 6th century B.C. by Mahavira

JĪVANMUKTI. Liberated soul

-JI. Suffix indicating respect (e.g., Gandhiji)

JNĀNA. Knowledge, especially spiritual knowledge

KĀMA. Pleasure, one of the four ends of life

KARMA. The law concerning the value of action as the determining of one's destiny

KHĀDI. Hand-made cloth

KRISHNA. Dark. One of the most popular deities of the Hindu pantheon; believed to be the eighth incarnation of Vishnu

LAKSHMĪ. Goddess of prosperity

LĪLĀ. Sport; existence regarded as the play of the Divine

MAHĀBHĀRATA. One of the two great epics of India (the other being the Rāmāyana); a compilation of history, folklore, ethics, and some philosophical sections, one of which constitutes the Bhagavad-Gītā

MAHĀVĪRA. Founder of the Jain faith

MANTRA. A sacred formula, chant, or incantation addressed to a deity, or used as an aid to concentration

MĀYĀ. Phenomenal existence; world of appearance

MĀRA. Embodiment of the principal of evil in Buddhist legend

MOKSHA. Liberation

NATARĀJA. Shiva as the Cosmic Dancer

OM. The mystic syllable in Vedic literature taken as the basis of all sound

PARAMPARĀ. Religious and philosophical tradition

PRAKRITI. Formless potentiality; formed by Purusha (Spirit)

PRĀNA. Life-breath

PRANĀYAMA. Control of breathing; one of the important steps in yoga

PŪJĀ. Ritual action

PURUSHĀRTHAS. Four ends of life: artha, kama, dharma and moksha

PŪRVA MĪMĀMSA. Earlier Mīmāmsa, distinguished from Vedanta (Uttaramimānsa or a later Mimamsa)

RĀJA-YOGA. Discipline of quieting the mind

RAMĀYĀNA. One of the two great Indian epics (the other being the Mahābhārata)

RASA. Juice, essence or taste. Asthetic delight

RIG VEDA. Earliest and most important of the four Vedas

RISHI. Sage, singer of the Vedas

RITA (Ṛta). Right order; cosmic law or truth

SĀDHANĀ. Spiritual or yogic practice and self-realization

SAMĀDHI. In yoga, the union of the individual mind with the Supreme Consciousness

SĀNKHYA-YOGA. One of the six orthodox systems of philosophy

SANGHA. Buddhist order of monks

SAMSĀRA. The world as a perpetual flow of events; endless rebirth

SANNYĀSIN. An ascetic who renounces earthly concerns and devotes himself to the study of sacred texts and meditation

SATCHIDĀNANDA. Absolute Brahman, including three characteristics: sat, Being; chit, Consciousness; ānanda, Bliss

SATYĀGRAHA. According to Gandhi, "truth-force" and by extension, "non-violent resistance"

SHAIVITE. Devotee of Shiva

SHAKTI. Power, energy; World-Mother

SHĀSTRA. An authoritative, systematic treatise

SIDDHI. Attainment of psychic or spiritual power

SRI (Shri). A prefix indicating spiritual eminence or respect

SMRITI. "Remembered," as distinguished from shruti ("heard"; "revealed")

SWADHARMA. One's personal duty

SWARĀJ(YA). Home rule; slogan of Nationalist movement

SWĀMI. Priest, monk

TANTRA. Mystical discipline of physical energy (based on shakti)

TAO. The Way. Key concept in Chinese philosophy

TRI-VARGA. Three goals of man: artha, kama and dharma

UPANISHADS. Sacred text; collection of philosophical and religious texts, believed to number between one and two hundred, but most interpreters deal with slightly more than the ten on which Shankara commented.

VEDANTA. Philosophical systems based on the Veda

VEDA. Sacred text; knowledge identical with or derived from the Vedic Hymns (including the Upanishads), which form the basis of most Hindu philosophical and religious systems

VIDYA. Knowledge, wisdom

VISHNU. Second person of the Hindu triad (with Brahma and Shiva); his avatars include Rama and Krishna

YANTRA. Design used in meditation

YOGA. As formulated by Patanjali and based on the Sānkya system, a physical, mental, and spiritual discipline leading to samadhi; more generally, any one of several disciplines such as karma-yoga, jnāna-yoga, bhakti-yoga, and dhyāna-yoga

Guide to Further Reading

NEW AWAKENING

PRIMARY SOURCES

Ramakrishna, Sri. *The Gospel of Sri Ramakrishna*. New York: Rama-krishna-Vivekananda Center, 1942.

Roy, Raja Ram Mohan. *The English Works of Raja Rammohun Roy*. Edited by K. Nag and D. Burman. 3 vols. Calcutta: Sadharan Brahmo Samaj, 1945–51.

Sen, Keshub Chunder. *Lectures in India*. Calcutta: Navavidhan Publication Committee, 1954.

Tagore, Debendranath. *The Autobiography of Maharshi Debendranath Tagore*. Introd. Evelyn Underhill. London: Macmillan & Co., 1914.

Vivekananda, Swami. *The Complete Works of Swami Vivekananda*. 8 vols. Calcutta: Advaita Ashram, 1962.

ANTHOLOGIES

De Bary, Wm. Theodore, *et al.,* eds. *Sources of Indian Tradition*. New York: Columbia University Press, 1964, Vol. II, pp. 1–107.

Nikhilananda, Swami. *Ramakrishna: Prophet of New India* (Abridged from *The Gospel of Sri Ramakrishna*). New York: Harper & Row, 1942.

Selections from Swami Vivekananda. Calcutta: Advaita Ashram, 1963.

STUDIES

Cousin, James. *The Renaissance in India.* Madras: Ganesh & Co., 1918.

Farquhar, John N. *Modern Religious Movements in India.* New York: Macmillan, 1915.

Isherwood, Christopher. *Ramakrishna and His Disciples.* New York: Simon and Schuster, 1959.

Kopf, David. *British Orientalism and the Bengal Renaissance.* Berkeley: University of California Press, 1969.

Lemaitre, Solange. *Ramakrishna and the Vitality of Hinduism.* Translated by Charles Lam Markham, New York: Funk & Wagnalls, 1969.

PHILOSOPHY

MAJOR WORKS

Radhakrishnan, S. *An Idealist View of Life.* London: George Allen and Unwin, 1956* (1932).

———, ed. and tr. *The Principal Upanishads.* London: George Allen and Unwin, 1953.

———, ed. and tr. *The Bhagavad-Gītā.* New York: Harper & Row, 1972* (1947).

———, ed. and tr. *The Brahma-Sūtra.* New York: Harper and Brothers, 1959.

Sri Aurobindo. *The Sri Aurobindo Birth Centenary Library* (SABCL). 30 vols. Pondicherry: Sri Aurobindo Ashram, 1970–1972.

———. *The Life Divine.* In SABCL, Vols. 18, 19 (1914–21; 1939).

———. *Essays on the Gītā.* In SABCL, Vol. 13 (1914–21).

HISTORIES AND SURVEYS

Dasgupta, S. *The History of Indian Philosophy.* 5 vols. Cambridge: Cambridge University Press, 1922–55.

Hiriyanna, M. *Outlines of Indian Philosophy.* London: George Allen and Unwin, 1964* (1932).

Naravane, V. S. *Modern Indian Thought.* New York: Asian Publishing House, 1964.

Radhakrishnan, S. *Indian Philosophy.* 2 vols. New York: Macmillan Company, 1962 (1923, 1927).

* Paperback.

Zimmer, Heinrich. *Philosophies of India.* Edited by Joseph Campbell. Princeton: Princeton University Press, 1971.*

ANTHOLOGIES

McDermott, Robert A., ed. *Radhakrishnan: Selected Writings on Philosophy, Religion, and Culture.* New York: E. P. Dutton, 1970.*

————, ed. *The Essential Aurobindo.* New York: Schocken Books, 1973.*

Murty, K. Satchidananda, and Rao, K. R., eds. *Current Trends in Indian Philosophy.* New York: Asia Publishing House, 1973.

Radhakrishnan, S. and Moore, Charles A., eds. *Source Book in Indian Philosophy.* Princeton: Princeton University Press, 1957.*

Radhakrishnan, S. and Muirhead, J. H., eds. *Contemporary Indian Philosophy.* (2nd ed.). London: George Allen and Unwin, 1958.

DHARMA

MAJOR WORKS

Gandhi, M. K. *Hindu Dharma.* Ahmedabad: Navajivan Press, 1950.*

Radhakrishnan, S. *Eastern Religions and Western Thought.* New York: Oxford University Press, 1959* (1939).

————. *Religion and Society.* London: George Allen and Unwin, 1959* (1947).

————. *Recovery of Faith.* New York: Harper and Brothers, 1955.

Sri Aurobindo. *The Human Cycle.* In SABCL, Vol. 16: *Social and Political Thought.*

Tagore, Rabindranath. *The Religion of Man.* Boston: Beacon Press, 1961* (1931).

————. *Sādhanā: The Realization of Life.* New York: The Macmillan Company, 1972* (1916).

STUDIES

Bhattacharya, Haridas, ed. *The Cultural Heritage of India.* Vol. II: Itihāsas, Purānas, Dharma and other shāstras. Calcutta: The Ramakrishna Mission Institute of Culture, 1962.

Sharma, I. C. *Ethical Philosophies of India.* Revised by Stanley M. Daugert. New York: Harper & Row, 1970* (1965).

"Special Symposium on *Dharma* and Li," *Philosophy East and West*, 22 (April 1972).

KARMA-YOGA

MAJOR WORKS

Bhave, Vinoba. *Talks on the Gītā*. New York: Macmillan Company, 1960.

Gandhi, Mohandas K. *Autobiography: The Story of My Experiments with Truth*. Boston: Beacon Press, 1957* (1927–29).

———. *The Gospel of Selfless Action or the Gītā According to Gandhi*. Edited and translated by Mahadev Desai. Ahmedahad: Narajivan Publishing House, 1946.*

Sri Aurobindo. *Essays on the Gītā*. In SABCL, Vol. 13.

Tilak, Bal Gangadhar. *Srimad Bhagavad-Gītā Rahasya or Karma-Yoga Shastra*. Translated by B. S. Suktankar. Poona: Tilak Brothers, 1935 (1915).

Vivekananda, Swami. "Karma-yoga," *The Complete Works of Swami Vivekananda*. Calcutta: Advaita Ashram, 1962, Vol. I, pp. 25–118.

AESTHETICS

MAJOR WORKS

Coomaraswamy, Ananda K. *History of Indian and Indonesian Art*. New York: E. Weyhe, 1927.*

———. *The Dance of Shiva*. New York: Farrar, Straus and Company, 1957.*

———. *The Transformation of Nature in Art*. New York: Dover Publications, 1956* (1934).

Tagore, Rabindranath. *Tagore on Art and Aesthetics*. New Delhi: International Cultural Centre, 1961.

STUDIES

Zimmer, Heinrich. *Myths and Symbols in Indian Art and Civilization*. Edited by Joseph Campbell. New York: Harper and Brothers, 1971* (1946).

EDUCATION

MAJOR WORKS

Sri Aurobindo. "Education and Art," in *The Hour of God*. SABCL, Vol. 17.

Tagore, Rabindranath. *Towards Universal Man*. Bombay: Asia Publishing House, 1969.

———. *Rabindranath Tagore, Pioneer in Education*. London: John Murray, 1961.

Gandhi, Mohandas K. *Basic Education*. Ahmedabad: Narajivan Publishing House, 1951.

Krishnamurti, Jiddu. *Education and the Significance of Life*. New York: Harper & Row, 1953.

STUDIES

Cormack, Margaret L. *She Who Rides a Peacock*. New York: Praeger, 1961.

SPIRITUAL DISCIPLINE

MAJOR WORKS

Eliade, Mircea. *Yoga: Immortality and Freedom*. New York: Pantheon Books, 1958.

Maharshi, Sri Ramana. *The Collected Works of Ramana Maharshi*. Edited by Arthur Osborne. Tiruvannamali: Sri Ramanasramam, 1968.

Ramakrishna, Sri. *The Gospel of Sri Ramakrishna*. New York: Ramakrishna-Vivekananda Center, 1942.

Sri Aurobindo. SABCL: *Synthesis of Yoga*, Vols. 20–21; *Letters on Yoga*, Vols. 22–24.

COMMENTARIES ON PATANJALI'S YOGA-SŪTRAS

Mishra, Rammurti. *The Textbook of Yoga Psychology*. New York: Doubleday, 1973* (1963).

Prabhavananda, Swami, and Christopher Isherwood. *How to Know God: The Yoga Aphorisms of Patanjali*. New York: New American Library, 1969* (1953).

Taimni, l. K. *The Science of Yoga.* Wheaton, Illinois: The Theosophical Publishing House, 1961.*

COMMENTARIES ON THE BHAGAVAD-GĪTĀ

Bhaktivedanta, Swami A. C. *The Bhagavad-Gītā as It Is.* New York: Collier Books, 1968.*

Mahesh Yogi, Maharishi. *On the Bhagavad-Gītā,* chapters 1–6. Baltimore: Penguin Books, 1967.*

Radhakrishnan, S., ed. and trans. *The Bhagavad-Gītā.* New York: Harper & Row, 1972* (1948).

Shivananda, Swami. *The Bhagavad-Gītā.* Sivanandanagar: The Divine Life Society, 1969.

Chinmoy, Sri. *Commentary on the Bhagavad-Gītā.* Blauvelt, New York: Rudolph Steiner Publications, 1973.*

SPIRITUAL TEACHERS IN THE WEST

Baba Ram Das (Richard Alpert). *Be Here Now.* Albuquerque, New Mexico: Lama Foundation, 1971.*

Ellwood, Robert S., Jr. *Religious and Spiritual Groups in Modern America.* Englewood Cliffs, N.J.: Prentice-Hall, 1973.*

Isherwood, Christopher. *Vedanta for the Western World.* London: Unwin Books, 1963* (1948).

Krishnamurti, J. *The First and Last Freedom.* Wheaton, Illinois: The Theosophical Publishing House, 1968* (1954).

Mahesh Yogi, Maharishi. *Transcendental Meditation* (Original title: *Science of Being and the Art of Living*). New York: New American Library, 1963.*

Needleman, Jacob. *New Religions.* New York: Pocketbooks, 1973* (1970).

Satchidananda, Swami. *Integral Hathayoga.* New York: Holt, Rinehart and Winston, 1968.*

NATIONAL CONSCIOUSNESS

Nehru, J. *Discovery of India.* New York: Doubleday and Company, 1960* (1946).

———. *Toward Freedom: The Autobiography of Jawaharlal Nehru.* Boston: Beacon Press, 1958* (1936, 1941).

————. *Nehru on World History. Condensed from Glimpses of World History* (1942). Edited by Saul K. Padover. Bloomington, Indiana: Indiana University Press, 1962.

Norman, Dorothy, ed. *Nehru: The First Sixty Years,* 2 vols., New Delhi: Asia Publishing House, 1965.

NATIONALIST MOVEMENT
ANTHOLOGIES

De Bary, Wm. Theodore, ed. Vol. II. *Sources of Indian Tradition.* New York: Columbia University Press, 1964* (1958).

Brown, D. Mackenzie, ed. *The Nationalist Movement: Indian Political Thought.* Berkeley: University of California Press, 1961.*

Metcalf, Thomas R., ed. *Modern India: An Interpretive Anthology.* London: Macmillan Company, 1971.*

BIBLIOGRAPHIES

MAJOR AUTHORS

GANDHI. Joan Bondurant. *Conquest of Violence.* Berkeley: University of California Press, 1965, pp. 51–58.

NEHRU. Dorothy Norman, ed. *Nehru: The First Sixty Years,* pp. 583–87.

RADHAKRISHNAN. Robert A. McDermott, ed. *Radhakrishnan,* pp. 339–44.

SRI AUROBINDO. Robert A. McDermott, ed. *The Essential Aurobindo,* pp. 250–54.

TAGORE. Krishna Kripalani. *Tagore: A Biography.* New York: Grove Press, 1962, pp. 401–06.

GENERAL

Mahar, J. Michael. *India: A Critical Bibliography.* Tucson: The University of Arizona Press, 1964.

Journal of Asian Studies. Annual Bibliography (September issue).

Acknowledgments

The editors of *The Spirit of Modern India* and the Thomas Y. Crowell Company wish to thank the following authors, editors, publishers, and agents for granting permission to reprint copyright material. All possible care has been taken to trace ownership of every selection included and to make full acknowledgment for its use.

BHAVE, VINOBA
George Allen & Unwin for "The Yoga of Action," from *Talks on the Gītā* (New York: Macmillan Company, 1960), pp. 40–49.
Macmillan Publishing Co., Inc., New York, for "The Yoga of Action," from *Talks on the Gītā* (New York: Macmillan Company, 1960), pp. 40–49.

COOMARASWAMY, ANANDA K.
Harvard University Press and Rama P. Coomaraswamy, M.D., Executor of the Estate of Ananda K. Coomaraswamy, for "The Origin and Use of Images in India," from *The Transformation of Nature in Art* (New York: Dover Publications, 1956), pp. 155–169. Copyright © 1934 by the President and Fellows of Harvard College; renewed 1962 by D. Luisa Runstein Coomaraswamy.

DASGUPTA, S.
Cambridge University Press (New York), for "Indian Idealism," from *Indian Idealism* (1962), pp. 18–19, 49–50.

GANDHI, MOHANDAS K.

Navajivan Trust, for the following selections from *The Hindu Dharma* (1950): "Truth and Love," pp. 59–61; "Means and Ends," pp. 9–15; Gandhi on His Mission, p. 13. For "On Non-Violence," from *Non-Violent Resistance* (New York: Schocken Books, 1961), pp. 358–361. For Gandhi on the Gītā, from Mahadev Desai, ed., *The Gospel of Selfless Action or the Gītā According to Gandhi* (1951), p. 13.

HIRIYANNA, M.

Ramakrishna Mission Institute of Culture, for "The Philosophy of Value," from *The Cultural Heritage of India*, (1953), III, pp. 645–654. Reprinted by special permission of the Secretary, The Ramakrishna Mission Institute of Culture, Gol Park, Calcutta 700 029.

KRISHNAMURTI, J.

Harper & Row, Publishers, Inc., for "Art, Beauty and Creation," from *Education and the Significance of Life* (1972), pp. 120–128. Copyright © 1953 by Krishnamurti Writings, Inc.

MAHRISHI MAHESH YOGI

George Allen & Unwin, for "How to Contact Being," from *Transcendental Meditation* (New York: Signet Books, 1968), pp. 44–52.

NEHRU, JAWAHARLAL

John Day Company, Inc., an Intext Publisher, for "The Quest," from *The Discovery of India* (New York: Doubleday & Co., 1960), pp. 21–32. Copyright © 1946 by the John Day Company.

Asia Publishing House, for "On the Ganges and the Himalayas," from Dorothy Norman, ed., *Nehru: The First Sixty Years* (1965), pp. 574–575.

The Government of India, Publications Division, for "A Tryst with Destiny," from *Indian Freedom* (London: George Allen & Unwin, 1962), pp. 94–95.

Krishna Kripalani for On Tagore and Gandhi from

Tagore: A Biography (New York: Grove Press, 1962), pp. 398–399.

RADHAKRISHNAN, S.
Government of India, Publications Division, for "Indian Independence," from *Radhakrishnan Reader* (Bombay: Bharatiya Vidya Bhavan, 1969), pp. 518–520.
George Allen & Unwin, for the following selections: "Ultimate Reality," from *The Bhagavad-Gītā* (1947), pp. 20–28; passage on dharma, from *Religion and Society* (1959), p. 107; passage on Indian philosophy, from *Indian Philosophy* (1962), I, 41–42 passage on philosophy, *Ibid.*, II, 770–771.
Oxford University Press, for "Mysticism and Ethics in Hindu Thought," from *Eastern Religion and Western Thought* (1959), pp. 80–84. Reprinted by permission of the Clarendon Press, Oxford.

RAMANA MAHARSHI
Hutchinson Publishing Group Ltd., and Samual Weiser Inc., for "Who Am I?" from Arthur Osborne, ed., *Collected Works of Ramana Maharshi* (1968), pp. 38–48.

SRI AUROBINDO
Sri Aurobindo Ashram, for the following selections from the Sri Aurobindo Birth Centenary Library (1970–1973): "The Sevenfold Chord of Being," 18: 262–270; Sri Aurobindo on Dharma, 13: 163; Sri Aurobindo on Karma-yoga, 2: 27; Sri Aurobindo on Art, 17: 237–238; "The Brain of India," 3: 330–337; Sri Aurobindo on Education, 15: 27–28; "The Principle of Integral Yoga," 21: 583–589; "The Fifteenth of August, 1947," 26: 404–406; "Bande Mataram," 8: 309–310.

SRI RAMAKRISHNA
Ramakrishna-Vivekananda Center, New York, for Parables from *The Gospel of Sri Ramakrishna* (1962), pp. 101–103, 148–149, 165, 204, 436.

TAGORE, RABINDRANATH
Macmillan Publishing Company, Inc., New York, for "An

Eastern University," from *Creative Unity*, pp. 176–203. Copyright © 1922 by Macmillan Publishing Company, Inc.; renewed 1950 by Rathindranath Tagore.

Macmillan, London and Basingstoke and the Trustees of the Tagore Estate for "The Realization of Beauty," from *Sadhana: The Realization of Life* (1966), pp. 137–144.

Macmillan Company of India, Ltd. and the Trustees of the Tagore Estate, for "An Eastern University" (abridged), pp. 176–203, and "The Realization of Beauty," from *Sadhana: The Realization of Life* (1966), pp. 137–144.

VIVEKANANDA, SWAMI

Advaita Ashrama, Calcutta, for the following selections from *Selections from Swami Vivekananda* (1963), "Lord Buddha," pp. 334–336; "Sannyasa: Its Ideal and Practice," pp. 338–341; "The Song of the Sannyasin," pp. 613–616.

The following are reproduced from:

IQBAL, MUHAMMAD

"Your Own Heart Is Your Candle" and "A New Shrine" from *A Book of India*, pp. 364–366, Collins (1965).

SEN, KESHUB CHUNDER

"Asia's Message to Europe" and "The Future Church" from *Lectures in India*, pp. 542–543, Navavidhan Publication Committee (1954).

TAGORE, RABINDRANATH

Excerpts from "Fireflies" and from "Stray Birds" from *A Tagore Reader*, Amiya Chakravarty, ed., pp. 327–340, Beacon Press (1961). "Jana Gana Mana" (translation) from *A Tagore Reader*, Amiya Chakravarty, ed., pp. 348–349, Beacon Press (1966).

Index

About the Editors

Robert A. McDermott , Ph.D., is president emeritus and chair of the Philosophy, Cosmology, and Consciousness Program at the California Institute of Integral Studies (CIIS). His publications include *Radhakrishnan*; *The Essential Aurobindo*; *The Essential Steiner*; *The Bhagavad Gita and the West*; and *The New Essential Steiner*. He has also published on William James, Josiah Royce, M. K. Gandhi, the evolution of consciousness, and American thought. His administrative service includes president of the New York Center for Anthroposophy; president of the Rudolf Steiner [summer] Institute; chair of the board of Sunbridge College (New York) and of Rudolf Steiner College (California). He was a member of the council of the Anthroposophical Society in America (1996–2004). He is the founding chair of the board of the Sophia Project, an anthroposophic home in Oakland, California, for mothers and children at risk of homelessness. He is a Lindisfarne fellow, a Fetzer mentor, and a member of the Esalen Corporation.

Vishwanath S. Naravane, was born in Allahabad, India. He received his Ph.D. from Allahabad University and taught there for twenty years. In 1965, he was appointed professor and chair of the Department of Philosophy, Pune University. He has lectured in various countries and worked as a visiting professor at several colleges and universities in the United States. In addition to philosophy and religion, Dr. Naravane taught courses in Indian history, art, and literature. His works include *Rabindranath Tagore: A Philosophical Study*; *Stories from the Indian Classics*; *Modern Indian Thought*; and *The Elephant and the Lotus: Essays in Philosophy and Culture*.

LaVergne, TN USA
25 January 2011
213906LV00002B/68/P